THE INDIANS OF NEW JERSEY:

Dickon Among the Lenapes

THE INDIANS OF NEW JERSEY
Dickon Among the Lenapes

by

M. R. HARRINGTON

(JISKÓGO)

Curator, Southwest Museum, Los Angeles

Illustrations by

CLARENCE ELLSWORTH

RUTGERS UNIVERSITY PRESS

New Brunswick   *New Jersey*

To
The Survivors and Descendants of the Lenape
Who Unfolded to Me Their Heritage, This
Book is Affectionately Dedicated

Published by arrangement with Holt, Rinehart and Winston, Inc.

Nineteenth printing, 2012

Library of Congress Cataloging-in-Publication Data

Harrington, M. R. (Mark Raymond), 1882-1971.
    The Iroquois trail : Dickon among the Onondagas and Senecas /
by M. R. Harrington ; illustrations by Don Perceval.
        p.   cm.
    Summary: In 1616 Dickon, an English boy, journeys in search of his
kidnapped Indian brother Little-Bear and learns the ways of the five
Indian nations making up the Iroquois League.
    ISBN 0-8135-0425-2 (paper)
    1. Iroquois Indians—Juvenile fiction. [1. Iroquois Indians—Fiction.
2. Indians of North America—Fiction.] I. Perceval, Don Louis, ill. II. Title
PZ7.H2386Ir   1991
[Fic]—dc20   91-28211
                                                                    CIP
                                                                    AC

INTRODUCTION

This new edition of *Dickon Among the Lenape Indians*—now called *The Indians of New Jersey: Dickon Among the Lenapes* —is a fascinating and authentic story about the Indians who once lived in the Jerseys and eastern Pennsylvania. A picture of the way of life of a primitive Indian tribe is presented in accurate and vivid detail through the eyes of a fictional English boy who was swept overboard from a storm-tossed ship in 1612, rescued by the Lenapes, and lived with them for two years.

The author of this story, Dr. M. R. Harrington, became interested in the Lenapes when he was a boy and resolved to visit members of the tribe to learn as much as he could about them. In 1929 he became curator of the Southwest Museum in Los Angeles. He wrote this book in the nineteen thirties, hoping to make it—as he says in the Introduction—"the most complete and accurate account of this interesting people that has yet appeared, in story form or otherwise." The firm of John C. Winston published it in 1938.

Harrington's interest in Indian life started when he was a small boy, but he had no contact with it until he moved to Seattle and had an opportunity to visit the Siwash Indian camps nearby. When he was in high school, his family moved to Mt. Vernon, New York, and he spent his spare time looking for Indian relics along East Chester Creek and in Pelham Bay Park. He took his collection of arrowheads and broken pottery to Professor F. W. Putnam, head of the anthropology department at the American Museum of Natural History in New York City, who was amazed that Harrington had found so many traces of Indian life on the edge of the great metropolis.

Before he had finished high school, a financial crisis arose in the family, and young Harrington turned to Professor Putnam for advice. Under the guidance of this expert, he was sent first to Trenton, New Jersey, where an ancient Lenape site was under excavation. After learning archaeologic techniques there, he was put in charge of an excavation in New York State that once had been occupied by relatives of the Lenapes.

His initial interest continued to grow throughout his career. He has visited Lenape settlements in Canada and Oklahoma and over forty other tribes of American Indians, mainly to buy specimens of their costumes, weapons, utensils, and ceremonial objects for the Museum of the American Indian, Heye Foundation, in New York City. In an official Long-House ceremony, the Oneida Iroquois named him Jiskógo, an old name among the Turtle clan that means Robin. The Seneca Iroquois called him Hosaistuggéteh (He Carries a Snake) because he wore a snakeskin band on his hat. The Zunis knew him as Tónashi (The Badger) because of his digging activities, and the Osages, as Wákhopeh (War Bundle) because of the medicine bundles of that name which he had purchased from them.

As a captive in *The Indians of New Jersey*, the boy-hero Dickon is first compelled to do women's work—gathering wood, gardening, tending fires, making clay pots and cooking utensils— then he is gradually accepted as an equal and eventually is adopted by one of the families. The text and carefully drawn, clearly detailed illustrations make it possible to copy many of the skills Dickon learned: how to make moccasins and leggings, bows and arrows, baskets, pottery, and other authentic Lenape crafts. The book is filled with descriptions of authentic Indian rituals of birth, marriage, death, and initiation into manhood and colorful details of their festivals and an adoption ceremony.

For anyone who is interested in more about the Lenapes, there are collections at the New Jersey State Museum in Trenton and the Museum of the American Indian in New York City; there is also a large collection of books and *realia* at the Rutgers University Library in New Brunswick, donated by the late Charles Philhower who, like Dr. Harrington, was an ardent collector of Lenape relics all during his life. An impressive mural may be seen in the lobby of the library at Trenton State College, whose campus is located on an ancient Lenape camp site. The mural, painted by Blossom Farley, depicts Lenape warriors in conference with Governor Bernard, with the little "Turtle Girl" in a corner of the picture.

The New Jersey Historical Society, with headquarters in Newark, and the Archeological Society of New Jersey, which is located in the State Museum in Trenton, frequently issue leaflets and other materials that are helpful to the student. Additional publications include Alanson Skinner's *The Indians of Manhattan Island and Vicinity* (Ira J. Friedman, Inc., 215 Main St., Port Washington, Long Island, New York, 1961), a 63-page reprint of a report first issued by the American Museum of Natural History in 1909; Gladys Tantaquidgeon's *A Study of Delaware Indian Medicine Practice and Folk Beliefs* (Pennsylvania Historical Commission, Harrisburg, Pa., 1942); W. W. Newcomb's *The Culture and Acculturation of the Delaware Indians* (University of Michigan, Ann Arbor, Michigan, 1956), which is No. 10 in the Anthropological Papers of the Museum of Anthropology; and *Walam Olum; or, Red Score, The Migration Legend of the Lenni Lenape or Delaware Indians* (Indiana Historical Society, Indianapolis, 1954). All of these are technical reports, but they may be used by the intelligent adult layman, as well as high-school students.

For the upper elementary grades, the best source is Sonia Bleeker's *The Delaware Indians, Eastern Fishermen and Farmers* (Morrow, 1953); second and third grades may use Schwarz and Goldberg's *The Eastern Woodland Indians* (Richards State Atlas Co., 215 Church St., Phoenix, N. Y.), which is published in two books.

However, as Alanson Skinner states in his study, Dr. Harrington's book, which you hold in your hand, is "the *dernier mot* on the subject."

Mary V. Gaver
Rutgers, The State University

February, 1963

AUTHOR'S INTRODUCTION

Along with the adventures of Dickon this book presents a picture of the Lenape, or Delaware Indians, as they lived in New Jersey and Pennsylvania before the coming of the whites. The author has tried to make it the most complete and accurate account of this interesting people that has yet appeared, in story form or otherwise.

The author's researches among surviving Lenape Indians, without which the book could never have been written, were sponsored nearly thirty years ago, by the Museum of the American Indian, Heye Foundation in New York, his more recent work by the Southwest Museum of Los Angeles.

Three present-day Indians helped in the preparation of the book and to them the author makes grateful acknowledgment. They are Miss Ruth E. Parks, Waendanak-we'now, "Boughs-Touching-One-Another," a Lenape living in Oklahoma, who verified and corrected the Indian words; Mr. F. M. Parker, Ganundai'yonh, "Distant-Village," a Seneca, who assisted with the library research, and Mr. Jasper Hill, Wapigok'hos, "Big-White-Owl," a Lenape residing in Canada, who helped in various ways.

Most of Mr. Ellsworth's illustrations of weapons, utensils, and other Indian articles are drawn from actual Lenape specimens preserved in the Museum of the American Indian, Heye Foundation, and in the American Museum of Natural History, both institutions kindly furnishing photographs of their treasures. In a few cases it was necessary, however, for Mr. Ellsworth to make reconstructions based upon descriptions and on the methods used by other eastern tribes.

Many of the customs and beliefs mentioned in *Dickon Among the Lenape Indians* are described with fuller detail in the Lenape writings of Dr. Frank G. Speck and in previous publications of the present author. Some are referred to by earlier writers, such as Heckewelder and Zeisberger, while some have never been recorded before in print. In this connection it must be remembered that Lenape customs and ceremonies varied somewhat according to locality. For this reason a description of the Mask dance might be correct for "Turtle-Town" but not quite right for the same ceremony at "Southfish Village" only a few miles away.

The New Jersey State Museum at Trenton has a large and representative collection of Lenape Indian relics. Most of these have been secured from archaeological excavations throughout New Jersey. The largest single group comes from the Abbott Farm, an old Lenape village site south of Trenton.

M·R·Harrington

1937

CONTENTS

The Countrie of the Lenape
in the year 1612 A.D.

here I fasted
r my dream

Tool-pay-oo-ta-nai

Sha-wa-mek-
oo-ta-nai

Delaware
Bay

cale of 6 Leagues

Atlantic Ocean

Of Wreck

Graven by
Clarence Ellsworth 193-

I. The Wreck

CAN tell little of the wreck of *Ye Portsmouth Maide*—everything happened so suddenly that stormy September night in the year of our Lord 1612. One moment we were rolling merrily on our way from England toward Captain John Smith's new colony of Virginia; the next moment we were hard and fast upon a shoal with great seas breaking over us.

I had just left my father in the cabin whilst I stepped out on deck to see whether or not the storm were abating, when the ship struck. The jar hurled me to the deck, which tilted suddenly. And before I could recover, a huge wave, dimly seen in the lantern light, came boiling over the side and swept me off the ship into the black water.

The wave turned me over and over. I was choking, strangling, but I tried to swim. At last my head came up; I could breathe again; but the night was black—I could see nothing. I thought my end had come.

All of a sudden I ran into something floating and I grasped and clung to it. It was made of wood, probably something from the ship; but to this day I know not what, although it saved my life.

1

I was growing so tired and so cold that I felt I could cling no longer when my knees touched upon solid ground. At the same time a great wave struck me, snatched my raft from my hands, rolled me upon a beach, then drew back. I staggered to my feet, guiding my steps toward higher ground. The next wave broke about my legs but

did not throw me. The next failed in its best efforts to reach me for then, by the mercy of God, I was safe on land. I looked seaward for some light or sign of the ship but all was blackness.

Then in the rain and the wind and the night, I felt my way into a clump of bushes and, sinking down upon the sand, I fell asleep.

When I awoke, cold and hungry, the sun had already risen out of the ocean, the clouds and the wind had gone, but the great seas still pounded upon the beach. I looked seaward for the ship, but although I could see a shoal far out where the waves broke, there was, alas, no ship in sight nor even a wreck. My dear father and all the men aboard *Ye Portsmouth Maide* must be lost.

When I thought of this, I felt very lonely indeed and was almost sorry I had been saved, and I knelt down and prayed. After a while I felt better and got up and looked about me. The land where I stood was a low, narrow island with a few bushes. On one side lay the open ocean with its great waves; on the other a lagoon or bay with smooth water. Across the bay I could see a shore with hillocks of sand and green trees.

As I scanned the shore, my heart gave a sudden leap— I saw smoke! Yes, a column of smoke was rising, and near it lay several boats hauled up on the shore and people walking about. My first thought was that the ship's crew had escaped and made them a camp, but when one of the boats put out, I could see it was no ship's shallop, but a long, nar-row craft and that the rowers sat facing the bow and not the stern as with us. It must be a boat of the Indians!

I had heard many tales of the Indian *salvages* as they were called, some saying that they were a simple, kindly people if treated fairly, whilst

others claimed that they were more like devils of the
pit, very cruel and warlike.   I wondered then what
treatment I might find at their hands and felt very much
afraid.   Yet I had to signal them, for otherwise I must
starve upon my little island.

I took off my coat and waved it to attract their notice,
but they did not see it.   Then I thought that my shirt,
being white, might be seen better, so I waved that.

Of a sudden they stopped rowing to look and then
they turned the bow of their craft toward me and rowed
with great speed, or rather I should say *paddled*, for they
used no rowlocks or pins.

As they approached, I was frightened, for they looked
strange and wild indeed as they knelt in their queer boat
hollowed out of one great log of wood and tapered to a
point at both ends.   They were a sort of coppery or
cinnamon color; their eyes dark and their hair black,
except one boy whose hair, black near his head, was
reddish brown at the ends.

In the stern, a grown man steered with an oar or
paddle.   He was tall, strongly built, and beardless, his
head shaven except for a narrow crest, erect like a cocks-
comb, running straight back from his forehead.   The
rowers or paddlers were two boys, with long hair flying

loose, a little older than myself. At the time I was fourteen. They wore no clothing except a little apron in front.

As the boat touched the edge of the salt grass, the two boys jumped out and, grasping her gunwales, ran her higher up on the land. The man, staring strangely at me, picked up a bow that lay in the bottom of the boat, plucked an arrow from a quiver near at hand, and nocked it on the string. Again I thought my hour had come, but there was nothing I could do but stand there trembling.

Now he arose and, stepping out of the boat, still with the arrow upon the string, walked cautiously toward me as if I were some dangerous beast. Without saying a word he came up to me, looked me all over, touched me with the point of the arrow, whilst the boys stared with mouth and eyes wide open. Then the man searched among the bushes and finding nothing looked out to sea to discover, I imagine, whence I had come.

Finally turning back, he asked me a question or so it seemed, in his strange tongue, which of course I could not answer. Then the boys stepped up and felt of me; they touched my hair, then they looked in my ears; now they talked and laughed with one another. I, not understanding, said nothing but stood like a prize ox at a fair, to be gazed upon.

Finally one of the boys, a short, ugly fellow with a flat nose, a big mouth, and bulging eyes, pinched me and when I cried out, he laughed. Then he snatched away my shirt, which still hung in my hand, and, running off a little way, tried to put it on. The man spoke to him, I think to bid him return the shirt, but he only laughed again.

At this the taller boy ran out and struck the big-mouthed one; then taking the shirt, he brought it back to me.   I thanked him in English and I think he under-

stood, for he smiled and a kind look came into his clear, brown eyes.   He was a good-looking youth with a well-shaped nose and a fine mouth, and I knew at once we would some day be friends.   I took off my coat, put on the shirt to keep it safe, and then the coat again, whilst the Indians looked on in wonder.

After this I pointed to my mouth, meaning that I was hungry, and the man, in return, pointed to the boat and motioned me to get in.   As I obeyed, I had a strange feeling that I was embarking upon a new life in a new world.

There were no seats nor even thwarts in this boat, so I sat me down upon the bottom with odd baskets and strange fishing gear all about me.   I never knew what such a boat was properly called in English until years later, when I learned the name: canow or canoe.   In the meantime I knew only the Indian word *moo'hool*.

So we traveled in the *moo'hool* to the spot on the mainland where I had seen the smoke.   Here lay four other canoes drawn up on shore, whilst back on higher land I could see little buildings like low sheds, some thatched with grass, some covered with mats which I afterward learned were made of rushes.

Our steersman shouted something, and at once a lot of people came running down to the shore, men, women, and children. I was made to stand whilst they crowded around to look at me, and my rescuer talked, explaining, I suppose, where and how he found me.

For my part I looked also and saw that all the men and older boys were dressed only in the little apron. The women and girls had but a skirt reaching from the waist to a little below the knees, whilst the smaller children wore nothing at all.

Now they led me up the slope to one of the sheds. Here a low fire burned, upon which sat, propped with stones, a clay pot like an egg on end. A woman dipped into this with a large, wooden spoon and ladled out some steaming stew into a wooden bowl. This she handed me, with a smaller spoon with which to eat it, a large piece of cold, baked fish, and a cake of heavy bread.

The stew tasted very good indeed and I ate my fill. My water I drank from an earthen jar with a dipper made of gourd.

The boy with the kind eyes then took me to another shed and, pointing to a pallet made of grass and mats with a blanket of skins sewed together for a cover, made signs for me to take off my clothes and go to bed. This I was glad to do, but once I was in bed, he took the clothes away. I thought perhaps they were gone for good, but when I awoke late that afternoon, they were all back, ready to wear again. My new friend had dried them.

After I dressed, I felt curious to know more about these strange folk, so I walked out into the camp, although I felt some fear that they might not fancy a stranger wandering about. Soon I noticed that besides the sheds in which they cooked and slept they had others in which smoky fires were kept a-burning. Filled with curiosity, I ventured to approach one of these. Inside above the fire I could see racks made of poles supporting many thin sticks or willows upon which small, brown lumps were spitted.

I stood there wondering what these might be, when I heard a slight noise behind me. When I turned, there stood a woman of middle age. I thought perhaps she had come to drive me away from her shed; but no, she had divined my curiosity. Stepping inside, she took down one of the willows which she handed to me with a motherly sort of smile. Then I saw that the brown lumps were shellfish: oysters or clams being cured in smoke like English bacon. She signed to me to try one; it was not bad at all.

Thousands of oyster and clam shells lay scattered about and heaped in piles, and their smell was far from sweet. The very ground where the camp stood was made mostly of old shells, the leavings of former years. Later on, after I could speak the language, I learned that certain families came to this place every fall to gather and dry the shellfish for winter use and every spring to feast.

That night I filled my stomach again with hot stew and the queer bread, which, although heavy, was very good. Most of the Indians treated me kindly and with strange respect; some seemed afraid that I might in some way harm them. There was one, nevertheless, who did not respect me, as I found when I started for bed.

When I lifted the skin coverlet, an awful smell poured out from under it! Looking to see what made it, I found that someone had placed a large dead fish in the middle of my bed. I glanced up quickly and saw the big-mouthed boy watching on the other side of the fire that burned in front of the shed. When he saw me looking, he clapped his hand over his mouth and ran away into the night. I threw the fish after him, but I fear my aim was bad.

To my sorrow, my troubles were not yet over, for I soon found that my bed did not lie as well as it had that afternoon. I raised the mats and searched among the grass beneath and then I discovered the reason—three stones as big as my two fists and one live crab.

I would have cheerfully thrown them all at the big-mouthed boy, but he was not to be seen.

In the morning I was awakened by a great commotion; somebody was taking down the mats that covered my shed and was rolling them up. The whole camp, it seemed, was rolling mats and packing bags and baskets. My friend brought me a bowl of porridge flavored with a sweet brown powder and a slice of heavy boiled bread, and a similar breakfast for himself, which we ate together, sitting on a roll of mats. He kept pointing to himself and saying, "*Nee pee-lai'chech*" which I thought was his name, but when he pointed at me and said, "*Kee pee-lai'chech*," I suspected he was trying to teach me the word for "boy." His real name turned out to be *Mahk'wa-tut* or Little-Bear.

Soon all the camp was down and loaded into the canoes, except the few sheds that were thatched and the bare poles of the rest.

I sat in the same canoe with the same crew that had rescued me. When we paddled out past the island where I had landed, very near to the shoal where the ship must have struck, I looked all about with great care but never a sign of the wreck did I see. The very search set me thinking sadly of my father, who was even then probably lying drowned beneath that green water, of my dear mother in England whom I might never see again.

Outside the shoals and islands we turned to the right and coasted along for a while over a calm sea with only a long swell rolling in from the eastward. I should say we journeyed about southwesterly, the whole flotilla of five canoes, until we came to a long point which we rounded and struck off northwesterly into a great harbor, which has since been named for the Governor, Lord de la Ware, and called Delaware Bay.

The loaded canoes paddled hard and slowly, and I wondered why the Indians, with a fair stern wind, did not try to use some kind of sail. We made no stop for a midday meal but when hungry, we chewed upon scraps of dried meat which the helmsman took from a bag and drank water from a big gourd bottle.

When the sun dropped low, we put in to land and spread our beds near a spring of water in the open air without erecting shelters, for the sky was clear. It was then I learned that Little-Bear had no bed, for the mats and fur robe I had been using were his. I felt very badly about this and made him understand we must sleep together. In this way I slept warmer, and there were no more dead fish, stones, or crabs in my bed, for the big-mouthed boy had a wholesome fear of my friend.

Regarding this big-mouthed boy, I found out as time went on that he was called *Chah'kal-wush'king*, which is to say "Toad-Face." This was only a nickname, but I never heard his real name in all the years I lived among the Indians. He was a stepson of my rescuer, *Ta-ma'kwa-week'it*, meaning "Beaver-House."

Toad-Face delighted to torment me when Little-Bear was not watching. He tried to trip me up when I tried to get out of the canoe, and he sprinkled water upon me whenever he shifted his paddle from one side to the other. He seemed to covet my clothes, and the first night he tried to steal them while I slept. After that I wore them day and night. Little I knew what was coming and how soon I would be reduced to a ragged skin mantle for clothing.

So the days went by, and the harbor became narrower as we paddled on until it was nothing more than a great river rolling toward the sea. We passed at a distance several Indian villages where people waved and shouted to us from afar. Once a great canoe, square at the ends like an English punt and filled with keen-eyed, copper-hued men, put out to meet us. We all stopped paddling, whilst the canoes drifted slowly and the men talked and talked, mostly about me, I think, for they looked at me often, although I understood not a word.

It was late afternoon of the fourth day, if I remember rightly, when the weary paddlers seemed suddenly to find fresh strength. They talked joyfully, and the canoes slipped more rapidly through the water. I looked to see the reason, and Little-Bear pointed out a spot on the left bank quite a way ahead. At first I could see little but a sort of level terrace or bench of land, with a gully breaking through it on the upstream end, but as we went on, I discovered many canoes hauled up on the shore. I could see smoke rising and the housetops showing over the edge of the bank.

Now as we approached within earshot, the men and boys began to shout and whoop with all their might, making a fearful din. The whoops were answered from the shore and before we reached the landing, a goodly crowd of people had gathered to greet us. My rescuer, Beaver-House, led me ashore and delivered a speech concerning me, after which I had no peace until each man, woman, and child had stared his fill, many in an awe-struck fashion which puzzled me. Finally we mounted the steep path into the main village—our destination.

Before us lay a sort of public square or common, with the dwelling houses of the village on three sides and the river on the fourth; whilst a large, bark-covered building at least thirty paces in length and half as wide stood in the middle. The better class of cabins were square or oblong, with gabled or arched roofs of bark, but there were some dome-shaped and covered with thatch, and many bark sheds attached to the dwellings or separate. In time I learned that the place was called *Tool-pay-oo-ta'nai* or "Turtle-Town."

Now we made our way to a house somewhat larger than the rest, the crowd following, but when we entered, they remained outside. Somehow I felt that this must be the house of some great lord or chieftain and that my fate would soon be settled, so it is not strange that my knees trembled a little as I crossed the threshold.

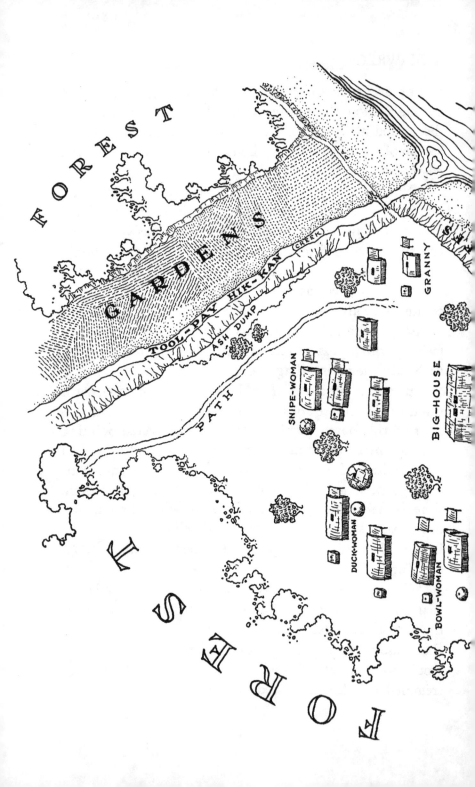

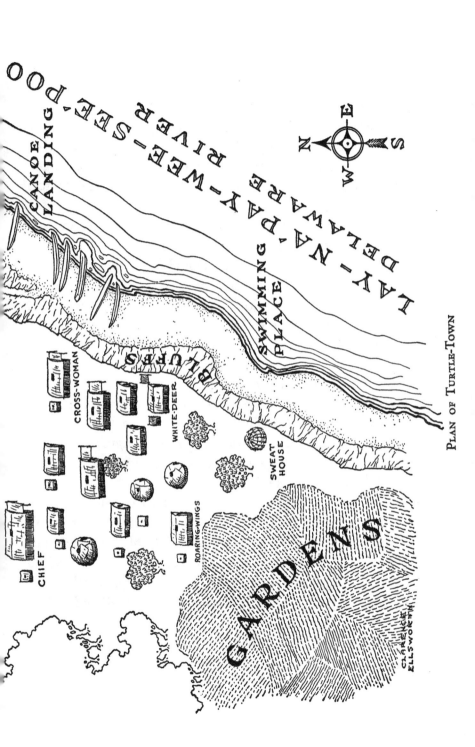

LAY-NA'PAY-WEE-SEE-POO
DELAWARE RIVER

CANOE LANDING

SWIMMING PLACE

BLUFFS

CROSS-WOMAN

WHITE-DEER

SWEAT HOUSE

ROARING-WINGS

CHIEF

GARDENS

CLARENCE ELLSWORTH

PLAN OF TURTLE-TOWN

A low fire burned in the middle of the cabin, the smoke rising to a hole in the roof. Around three sides ran a platform a little less than waist high. As my eyes grew accustomed to the dim light, I discovered that a number of elderly men were sitting upon this platform, cross-legged like tailors; and I was sure that the man in the center, because of his dignity, must be the chief.

Sure enough, Beaver-House led me before this one and explained again how he came by me. Then they all discussed me until I thought I would drop from weariness. Finally the chief dispatched one of his advisers to get another Indian, who joined in the discussion until all seemed satisfied, even relieved. I was told later that some had thought me a water spirit or goblin come out of the ocean, but that the man sent for had convinced them that I was merely a human being like themselves. He had been to Jamestown and had seen many English people.

Now everyone knew me for what I really was—just a poor boy, ignorant of their ways and language, a weak captive or slave, dependent upon my owners for every comfort, even for life itself.

From the chief's house we went to the home of my rescuer, Beaver-House, where I met with a strange welcome. It was a bark cabin like that of the chief, but smaller and very dirty, with all manner of trash scattered about the floor and baskets, bags, belongings of all kinds, thrown beneath the platforms in great disorder and covered with dust.

This I noted out of the corner of my eye. What I saw most was a huge, fat woman with a little nose and a great, coarse mouth, standing back of the fireplace

I Was Led Before a Group of Elderly Men

scowling at me. She was far from clean, and her deerskin skirt was foul with ashes and grease. Beside her stood Toad-Face, grinning, and it came over me she must be his mother.

She pointed to me and made a long-winded demand upon Beaver-House. After listening a while, he spoke the one word, "*Ma'ta*," upon which she started in again. When she stopped for breath, he repeated "*Ma'ta*" with great firmness and, taking hold of my arm, started to lead me from the house.

Later I learned that the woman had demanded me for a servant, but he had replied, "No." She was nicknamed *Ma-nunk'so-hkway*, or Cross-Woman.

Before we could get away, Toad-Face clutched me by the coat and talked to Beaver-House, and Cross-Woman joined in; finally Beaver-House grunted a reluctant assent. They must have demanded my clothes, for they stripped me with devilish glee, taking every stitch of my clothing, which Toad-Face had coveted from the first, and even my shoes.

Now Beaver-House made a demand, for something to clothe me I suppose, for Cross-Woman looked around and, seeing a yellow dog sleeping on a ragged skin robe beside the doorway, jerked it out from under him and handed it to me. It was covered with dirt and dog hairs, and, as I afterward discovered, lively and hungry fleas. Beaver-House looked disgusted but said nothing.

He led me outside the cabin, shook most of the dirt off the robe, and wrapped it about me, Indian fashion, left arm covered, right arm out. From that time on I never wore another English garment.

We crossed the public square to a still smaller cabin, and I wondered what new miseries were awaiting me there. Before we went in, I looked back and saw Toad-Face, wearing my coat and followed by his mother, going down to the river to get their camping things and their share of the dried clams from the canoe.

It was quite dark in the little cabin, because the door curtain had fallen behind us and the smoke hole above was almost covered. Suddenly a little dog jumped down from the left-hand platform and rushed at me, barking and snapping at my bare ankles. I jumped back, but before I could decide what to do, a cracked voice called to the dog from the back of the cabin and it withdrew, growling.

The voice had come from under a sort of canopy made of mats, where now I could see someone covered with a skin robe lying on the platform.

Beaver-House spoke and all at once a little old woman pushed aside the cover and rolled stiffly over to the edge of the platform and sat with her legs hanging over. She answered him, peering at me in the dim light. Then standing up, painfully she hobbled over to him and clung to his arm, whilst he put his hand around her shoulders. She was his mother.

Now I could see her plainly. She was sour-looking, wrinkled, shrunken, toothless; but her hair was brushed and her skirt clean, whilst her cabin looked clean and orderly. It was only about four yards square; but it was well built of stout poles covered with sheets of bark and lined with pretty mats with patterns in colors.

Beaver-House said some words and pointed to me, then raised the door curtain to let in more light. The old

3

woman came up and studied me with her little, watery, bleary eyes; and the corners of her mouth drew down until she looked more sour than ever. It seemed she was not favorably impressed. After a few more words with his mother, Beaver-House went out and left us together.

She jerked open my mantle and seeing that I was naked beneath she rummaged under her bed platform, finally drawing out a tanned deerskin and a flat, boardlike piece of wood. Now she took a sharp flake of flint out of a bag and laying the skin on the board she began to cut it, using the flint like a knife. When the flake dulled, she threw it away and took another. Soon she had cut a strip about four feet long and a foot wide, cut square across the ends and fringed. That was my first lesson in Indian tailoring, but I had many such thereafter.

Tying a thong of the same skin around my waist for a belt, she showed me how to pull the strip between my legs and up between the belt and my flesh so as to hang over in front and back like a little apron, such as the men wore. This was the only garment they thought necessary, wearing others or not according to their fancy.

After I had it properly arranged, she pointed to it and said, "*Sahk-koo-ta'kun*" which I knew must be the name of it. In English it is called "breechclout" or "breechcloth." I wore a *sahk-koo-ta'kun* from that time forward.

Next she pointed to herself and said, "*Nee Hoo'ma*." At first I thought the whole thing was her name, but I soon found that *Nee* meant "I" and *Hoo'ma* meant "Granny." Then she pointed to me and cupped her hand behind her ear as if listening. I said, "Dickon," but she twisted it into *Day'kay-ning* which was later accepted by everyone as my name. It meant "In-the-Forest." In time I learned to address her as *noo-hoom* or "my granny."

That was my first real language lesson. In time I learned, to my surprise, that each little tribe had its own tongue, in many cases so different that the tribes could not understand one another at all. This tribe to which Granny, Little-Bear, and the rest belonged was known as *Lay'nee Lay-na'pay* or *Lay-na'pay* for short, which is usually spelled "Lenape." The river upon which many of them lived, called in Indian *Lay-na'pay-wee-see'poo*, has since been named "Delaware," like the bay I mentioned before, after Lord de la Ware, who was governor for a while. Now I hear my Lenape tribesmen often spoken of as "Delaware Indians."

Granny taught me Lenape words every day; I tried my best to learn, and the result was that in a few months I could speak the language fairly well and could understand almost everything.

After the language lesson Granny found me a thick cornhusk mat to sleep on and helped me fix my bed. There were three platforms in the cabin: Granny slept on the back one to the west; the dog had his bed on the south platform, so I took the north one.

The dog was named *Moon-ha'kee* or "Badger," the word really means "earth digger," because his favorite amusement was digging for ground mice and moles. He had pointed ears and a bushy tail like a wolf, but he was spotted yellow and white and his face was gentle and doglike. Granny treated him like a human being, and he had not only a bed of his own but a private bowl to eat

from. He realized his own importance as Granny's
companion and was a little jealous of me at first.

Evening was now coming on, and I began to feel very
hungry, having eaten nothing since morning but a few
scraps of dried meat. So I attracted Granny's attention
and pointed to my mouth, although I had no idea where
food was coming from, there being none in sight.

Granny took one of the fur robes from her bed and,
wrapping it around her shoulders like a shawl, she
beckoned me to follow. Walking seemed so hard for her
that I took her arm to support her, which seemed to
surprise and please her very much and even caused the
corners of her sad mouth to turn up a little.

I was not at all happy when I saw we were heading
for Cross-Woman's house, and when we entered and I saw
Toad-Face dressed in my clothes, I all but lost my appetite.
Angry as I was, however, I had to laugh when I saw he
had put on my breeches hind side before.

Cross-Woman gave Granny a bowl of soup made of

hoos'kweem or Indian corn,
but me she would not notice
until Granny pointed me out.
Then the big swine picked up
from the floor a dirty, greasy,
wooden bowl which the dog
had been using and handed
it to me with a black, old,
broken spoon, pointing to
the pot as if to say, "Help
yourself." Then she watched
me to see what I would do.

I controlled myself as best I could and marched out of the house and down to the river, where I scoured bowl and spoon with sand and wisps of gritty rushes until they were clean.

Granny seemed greatly pleased when she saw what I had done, but Cross-Woman was furious and would not let me go near the soup pot. Probably I would not have had anything to eat at all if Beaver-House had not come in. He spoke very sternly to his wife, and she served me grumblingly, with a scowl black enough to poison the soup.

After I had finished, Beaver-House went home with us, and he and Granny were still talking when I curled up on my mat with my flea robe over me and went to sleep.

II. Set to Work

HEY must have decided that evening that Granny and I should eat in our own cabin thereafter, for when I awoke in the morning, the place was full of provisions: strings of Indian corn braided together were hanging from the roof poles; on the shelves were sacks of beans, dried berries, dried green corn, dried meat, a bundle of strips of dried pumpkin, a bark box of tree sugar, and a fawn skin made into a big bottle and filled with bear's grease.

Of course I did not know what all these things were when I saw them first; in fact I learned to prepare and eat most of them before I found out. The supplies had been furnished by Granny's two daughters, the sisters of Beaver-House.

Granny had cooked some beans with a little pounded dried meat and bear's grease in a clay kettle before I awoke, and this was our breakfast. After we finished, she pointed at the woodpile, then at me, then at the door, pronouncing the word *tah'han* and I knew the time had come for me to go to work. The word meant "firewood."

As I went out, Granny handed me the queerest ax I ever saw. The head was made of stone with a rather blunt edge, and the handle was fitted around a groove instead of going through a hole as our axes are made. She called it a *tay-ma'hee-kan*. The English now call such axes "tomahawks," although this word should be applied to another kind of ax which was carried by the Indian men. Granny's ax would not cut very well, but it was fine to break up dry sticks into proper length to carry.

My first wood-hunting trip was not a happy one. In the first place I was barefoot, and, having been used to shoes, every stick and stone hurt my feet. In the second place all the children in the village, or so it seemed, followed me around to see what the strange, white-skinned boy would do. Besides, the women had gathered all the loose wood for a long distance and when I tried to search the river bank for driftwood, Toad-Face saw me and pelted me with mud until I was glad to hide myself in the forest again.

Finally the idea struck me to climb up into the big trees and break off dead limbs, a thing the women had not thought of or did not dare to do. I soon had an armful of good sticks which I carried home in triumph, thinking my task was done, but I was mistaken. Granny showed me how to carry wood on my back with the *ah'pees* or "pack strap" across my chest and sent me out again. This way I was able to carry three or four times as much, and after several trips our woodpile was replenished.

Midday came, and I found myself hungry again, but Granny made no move to cook dinner. I made my hungry sign to her, but she merely pointed to the bean pot. It was still standing by the fireplace, and the beans were warm enough to be good.

Soon I learned that these people seldom had more than one regular meal a day and never more than two. They always cooked breakfast, but the rest of the day they ate leftovers when they happened to be hungry. Sometimes, especially when a hunter was expected home in

the evening, they would cook a supper or at least save food for the absent one. A good Lenape housekeeper tried always to keep a pot of food warm near the fire for hungry members of her family or for guests.

Next morning I discovered that gathering wood was only part of my duty: I was expected to keep the fire and even to cook, for Granny was not very strong. Fortunately she was able to teach me, and I was willing to learn and to do what I could for her in return for her real kindness.

It was true that men and boys were not expected, as a rule, to keep fire or to cook, except when away from home on hunting trips or at war, but I was a captive, which made a difference.

I shall never forget the first morning I got up and found that the fire had gone out because I had forgotten to bank it the night before. I had no idea how to make another, as these Indians did not know the flint and steel, so I woke Granny. She sent me with a piece of a broken clay pot to get some coals from a neighbor's fire.

Later I learned to make fire Indian-fashion by twirling between my palms a rod of hard wood about the size of an arrow, the lower tip turning in a socket made for the purpose in a piece of dry, soft wood. After a while the wood dust formed in the socket begins to smoke, then it catches fire, and from this you ignite your tinder which is made of dry, rotten wood or the fine-shredded bark of an evergreen tree called *pop-ho'kus*, cedar. The fire-making set is called *sang-hee'kan*.

As for cooking, simple dishes, such as we had the first day, were easy. I threw the beans into the old *sis-kay-wa'hos*, or clay pot, with water and set them on to boil, always with a little bear's grease and sometimes

with fresh meat or pounded dry meat.   Dried pumpkins
were cooked the same way and so was the dried, roasted
green corn that made one of my favorite dishes.

We had no butter or lard, only bear's grease, except
when there was fresh meat or fat in camp.   Bear's grease
was put up in skin bags every winter, and it grew pretty
strong in time, but I learned to like it.

Fresh meat and fish were broiled on sticks or on
clean, hot coals raked from the fire or were cut up and

boiled in the old clay pot; whilst shellfish were roasted on previously heated
stones or simply in the hot ashes.   We
always broke the larger meat bones to get
the delicious marrow.

With regard to the pot, it was egg-
shaped with a pointed bottom, and I
spilled the soup more than once before
I learned just how to prop it up on the
fire with three or four stones.   We never
washed it unless it began to smell strong
or something burned and stuck.   Then
we, or rather I, carried it down to the
river bank and cleaned it with sand
and bunches of scouring rushes, called
la-lay-nee'kan.

It spoiled the polish on a good, old,
wooden bowl or spoon to scour it, so we
never did unless it smelled—we simply
wiped it out with a wisp of grass.   In
England I used to help my mother wash
dishes with hot water and soft soap (and

did not enjoy it much) but somehow that did not seem
necessary in Lenape land. For one thing, there was
no soap.

I did not mind this work except when Toad-Face came
around to watch me and to make remarks, which I knew
were not complimentary even though I did not always
understand them. This was bad enough, but when he
tried to put gravel in my beans and sand in my bread, I
was furious. Once Granny spied him about to drop an
old stale fish head into my soup when my back was turned
and she hit him such a thwack behind with our stirring
paddle that he did not come around for several days.
When he did reappear, she slipped up behind him and
emptied our bark water bucket over his head. Toad-Face
did not like water, except to drink, and we saw little of
him after that.

Speaking of bread, that was the hardest thing I had
to make and took the most time. The Indians raised a
number of kinds of corn, both soft and hard, but they
claimed that the soft white corn called *po'hem* was best for
bread. After it is shelled from the *sa'kwem*, or ear, you boil
it in a kettle with fresh ashes and water until the grains
swell and their hard hulls begin to slip. Then you
empty it into a special basket made with holes in the
bottom like a sieve and take it down to the river. Here
you dip the basket into the water and stir the corn with a
paddle until the hulls slip off the grains and float away.
You keep on washing until the taste of the ashes is out
of it; then it is ready to grind.

Outside every Lenape house stood a *tahk-wa-ho'a-kan*,
or mortar made of wood, a two-foot section of a gum-tree

log with a bowl-shaped hollow in the top. In this you crush your corn with a pestle made of wood or stone and sift it through a flat basket sieve, *pa-wun-nee'kan*, into a large wooden or bark bowl. Mix this flour with hot water and it will form a sort of dough, which you mold into flat cakes about a span across and maybe two fingers thick. These you can bake in clean, hot ashes, watching to see they do not burn or you can boil them in water until they float up to the top, which means they are done.

Granny liked cooked beans or soaked dried berries in her bread, so I always mixed one or the other with the dough. Both baked and boiled bread were heavy, as leaven or yeast were unknown to the Indians, but they tasted good and were very satisfying. Bread in general

was called *ah-pon'*, but each kind had its own name, and there were several I have not mentioned.

Another dish I cooked every few days was *soo-tay'yo*, simply white corn hulled with ashes and washed as I have described, then boiled with meat or grease and sometimes beans to make a soup.

Sa'pan, now called "hominy" by English settlers in America was made of hard blue corn cracked in a mortar, sifted through a coarse sieve basket, and boiled with meat or grease.

I must not forget the famous *ka-ha-ma'kun*, which was not only delicious but important as the only provision carried by hunters and warriors. To make this, I raked a lot of hot coals out of the fire and set upon them a large piece of a broken clay pot, more or less like a bowl. When this became hot, I dropped a handful of white corn into it and stirred the grains with a paddle until they were nicely browned. Then I swept them into a bowl and repeated until I had enough; then I pounded the toasted grains in the mortar and sifted the meal, which I mixed with tree (maple) sugar when I had any. The result was *ka-ha-ma'kun*.

This would keep a long time in a skin sack. It was very rich and a handful mixed with hot or cold water was enough for a meal. If you had no broken pot to parch the kernels in, you could brown them in hot ashes. The coarse part left in the sieve after the meal had been shaken out, I boiled with bear's grease for mush.

All these dishes were good, but to my notion the best of all was green corn *sa'pan*. To make this, you pound dried, toasted green corn in a mortar and sift it through

a fine basket; then boil it with plain water for a little while, I should say half an hour. It is sweet enough without any sugar—the best porridge you ever tasted.

An English cook would have laughed at my utensils, or rather Granny's, for all she had was one clay kettle; the clay bowl for parching corn, made from a broken kettle; a wooden mortar and pestle; a special basket for washing corn; a coarse sifting basket, a fine one; a wooden stirring paddle; a big wooden ladle; a deer jaw for scraping green corn off the cob; a big bowl or tray made of elm bark; an elm-bark bucket for water, and a flint knife with a wooden handle. Every Lenape home had these things, but Granny had one thing more, which she called her "teeth." This was a little stone mortar and pestle for pounding meat and the like so that she could eat it, for all her real teeth were gone.

Our eating utensils were wooden bowls and spoons, nothing more. I have seen a few wooden drinking cups among the Lenapes, but we had none, for we drank our water from a gourd dipper out of a bark bucket.

Granny had a beautiful food bowl made of some hard, curly grain wood, highly polished. The rim rose in a sort of point on one side, and this as well as a border running all the way around were adorned with little white shell beads neatly set into the wood.

I have mentioned Moon-ha'kee's special bowl, which had a little carven dog's head for a handle, sticking straight up from the rim.

So that I would not feel jealous, Granny gave me a private bowl, too, a nice, old, oval one with a high point at each end, and I carved my initials on it with her flint knife—D. S.

Granny thought the "D" must represent a bow and the "S" a snake and could not understand why I used them as a private mark. My spoon was a plain wooden one (until I carved D. S. on it) with a hook to hang it on the edge of the bowl. Spoon is *em-hawn'is* in Lenape, and bowl is *lo'kas*.

I have spoken of the work I did for Granny, but my life in her cabin was not all work, for my tasks were usually finished

before midday. When the morning meal was cooked and eaten, I set the food left over on a high shelf or platform under the shed outside, for there was no need of keeping it warm all day for just us two. Then I covered the fire with ashes, took out the surplus ashes, and shook all the mats and fur robes, including the dog's, outdoors. Next I brushed off the platforms in the cabin with a turkey-wing brush, sprinkled the dirt floor with water and swept that, too, with the turkey wing, finally bringing in the robes and folding them on the platforms. Then my day's work was done, unless there was something special, like gathering wood.

It was perhaps ten days after I came to the village when one morning, while Granny was showing me how to fold the robes, I heard a step outside and I looked up expecting to see Toad-Face. It was Little-Bear, and I was certainly glad to see him. He spoke to Granny and to me, but of course I could not yet understand. Afterward he told me that he had gone with his father to another village to get his

mother who had been visiting there, and that was why I had not seen him.

After my work was finished, he asked Granny if I could go out with him for a while, and she smiled and answered, "*Kay'hay-la*," or "Yes, indeed." I think she was pleased with my work or at least my good intentions, and I was glad to see the corners of her mouth turning up and the sour look disappearing.

Little-Bear took me down to the river bank below the canoe landing to a spot where the water was deep and still. The morning was warm, and four or five boys were in swimming. Little-Bear took off his *sahk-koo-ta'kun* and signed to me to do the same; then we plunged in, and it was wonderful.

The Indian boys were amazed at the breast stroke I used in swimming. They had never seen such a thing, so they all wanted to learn it at once. For my part, I saw that they used a queer, overhand stroke, first one hand and then the other, and I tried to learn that, so between us we had a fine time.

When Little-Bear and I stepped out of the water, clean and refreshed, we were greeted with a shower of mud. Of course it was Toad-Face, hiding behind a bush, who was bombarding us.

Little-Bear took one side and I the other and, making a quick dash, we captured Toad-Face. We dragged him down to the water's edge and despite his struggles we plastered him with mud from head to foot and even rubbed mud in his hair, and whenever he opened his mouth, we filled it full of mud. When we were finished with him, he actually washed himself, something I had never seen

4

him do before. Toad-Face could swim, but he seldom went into the water except in very hot weather. The other boys were not sorry, for his favorite pleasure was ducking the smaller lads, which spoiled the fun for everyone.

We stopped by Granny's cabin to see if she wanted anything, and then we went on to Little-Bear's. I met his mother, who was very pretty for a middle-aged woman, with big, brown eyes and fine features, although short in stature; but his father was not at home. His mother was commonly called *Lo'kas-hkway*, or "Bowl-Woman"; but her real name, *Ma-sha'pee-lo'kas-hkway*, although quite a mouthful, I think was prettier, for it meant "Bowl-of-Beads-Woman," as nearly as I can figure it.

Little-Bear and I got to wrestling, as boys will, and he showed me some tricks I never knew before; but when I tried to box with him, he did not know what I was trying to do. Finally I made him understand, and as time went on, we boxed a great deal together, using as gloves the soft Indian shoes called *len-hok-sin'a* or, in English, moccasins, first stuffing them with grass. My boxing practice with Little-Bear and the strength and skill I gained by it were destined to be of great service to me later.

It was late when I got home, but there was still light enough for me to get a bucket of water and warm up the morning's left-over corn soup for supper.

I was quite happy that night, but next morning trouble came. I was bringing Granny's only pot in from the rack to cook breakfast when an awful thing happened. With my mind all on yesterday's adventures, not looking where I was going, I stepped on the dog who was lying on the ground asleep. Moon-ha'kee jumped up with a yelp and, before I knew it, I fell heavily, and the clay pot was smashed to pieces.

Granny was wakened by the noise and when she saw what had happened, she scolded me severely; that is, I suppose it was scolding although I did not understand her words. Then she began to cry and I really felt sorry for her. I felt sorry for myself, too, when I tried to cook breakfast without a pot. Finally I remembered the bowl made from a broken pot, and cooked us some *ka-ha-ma'kun*, which we had to eat with cold water and a little dried venison.

After breakfast Granny made me understand that I was to fetch Beaver-House. I went over to his cabin, but he was not to be seen outside and I did not care to go in. After yesterday's mud fight I did not want to meet Toad-Face nor his mother.

I lingered near by for a while, but Beaver-House did not appear, and I finally decided to get Little-Bear instead. Granny was surprised to see him instead of her son, but I think she understood why, because she looked at me with a sly smile. She talked a while with Little-Bear, pointing toward the hills, and finally handed me a large and very dirty tanned deerskin and a sharpened stick. Little-Bear beckoned me to follow him.

We walked up the gully that skirted the village on the north, maybe for a mile or so, following a plain path which ended finally on the bank of the little creek. I had no idea at all why we had come, until Little-Bear bent down and began to feel the earth with his fingers. Then I saw that it was clay, and there were many pits

scattered about where clay had been dug out.   Then I
understood; we had come to get material for a new pot.

He showed me how to dig up the clay with my stick,
and found me a good place; then I did the work and
carried home all I could lift, done up in the deerskin.

Granny divided out part of the clay, putting the rest
away in a basket; then she made me pound the part she

had selected with a round stone until it was almost as
fine as meal and all the lumps, pebbles, and roots were
taken out.   Then she produced a piece of rotten stone
about as big as my two fists, and this I ground up fine
between two stones and mixed with the clay, of which it
made a fourth or fifth part.   Finally I added water and
kneaded the mixture well until it was like a stiff dough.
The ground stone was to prevent cracking;   some clays
need more and some less.

Now Granny took the digging stick and dug a hole
in the ground out to one side of the house, about a span
deep and three spans round and coming to a point at the

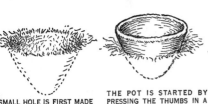

SMALL HOLE IS FIRST MADE THE GROUND AND LINED WITH GRASS.

THE POT IS STARTED BY PRESSING THE THUMBS IN A LUMP OF THE CLAY AND WORKING IT TO THE SHAPE OF A CUP INSIDE THE HOLE.

A ROPE OF CLAY IS MADE BY ROLLING A LUMP OF CLAY IN THE TWO HANDS AND THIS IS APPLIED TO THE OUTSIDE OF THE CUP IN THE FORM OF A RIBBON.

THE CLAY IS APPLIED IN SUCCESSIVE COILS IN THIS MANNER UNTIL SUFFICIENT HEIGHT HAS BEEN ATTAINED, AFTER WHICH THE COILS ARE APPLIED TO THE INSIDE TO TAPER IN THE POT TOWARD THE TOP.

A SMOOTH PEBBLE IS THEN USED WITH WATER TO SMOOTH THE POT INSIDE AND OUT.

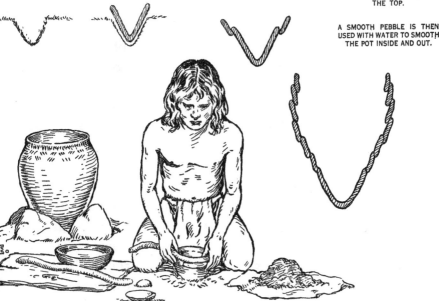

APPLYING THE COIL

, ROTTEN WOOD IS STACKED IN AND AROUND THE POT AND THEN SET AFIRE.

AFTER THE POT HAS BEEN COMPLETED, IT IS DRIED FOR A WEEK OR TEN DAYS, THEN GIVEN A PRELIMINARY HEATING THROUGH, WHICH PREPARES IT FOR THE FINAL FIRING.

FOR THE FINAL FIRING THE POT IS SET UP ON SOME PEBBLES IN AN INVERTED POSITION AND DRY, ROTTEN WOOD PLACED INSIDE AND OUTSIDE AND IGNITED. THIS BURNS WITH GREAT HEAT AND LITTLE SMOKE UNTIL IT IS ALL CONSUMED. THE ASHES ARE RAKED ASIDE AND THE POT REMOVED. IT IS NOW INSPECTED AND IS READY FOR USE.

MAKING A CLAY POT

bottom; this she lined thinly with fine grass. Then she
made a ball of clay about five fingers across and, sticking
her thumbs into the middle of it, she rapidly molded a
pointed bottom for the new pot. This she popped into
the hole and pressed it around until it fitted. When she
finished, the rim stuck up above the edge about two
fingers.

Next she took a handful of the clay and rolled it
between her palms until she made a rope of it as thick as
her thumb. This she flattened and then coiled it around
the rim until the circuit was complete, when she pinched
it off. The next task was to blend the rope or, rather,
band of clay to the rim, which she did with a smooth
pebble and a shell kept always wet in a gourd bowl of
water. Then she was ready to add another coil.

This time, though, she made me do it, and it was
great fun after I got the knack. She showed me how to
add each coil above and a little outside the previous one,
which made the pot wider and wider as its walls rose;
then when the place was reached where the walls should
begin to slope in, she made me add each new coil above
and a little *inside* the last one. As the pot grew, I kept
the walls thin and smooth by working with the same wet
shell and pebble that served for blending the coils.

When I had finished building the pot, Granny took a
little awl made of bone she used for sewing and, with the
point, she drew a pretty pattern of lines in the soft clay
just below the rim; and then she made me repeat the
same pattern over and over until I had encircled the pot.
Of course you could tell the difference between her work
and mine, but mine was not so bad.

When the top was dry enough to handle, we lifted the pot out of the hole and smoothed down the bottom, inside and out, with the wet shell and pebble. Then I set the pot upside down on the rack beneath the shed to dry slowly in the shade.

Once started at the clay work, I did not want to stop. I made another large pot all by myself and a couple of little toy ones.

For six full days after that whilst the pots were drying, we had nothing to eat but *ka-ha-ma'kun* and dried meat, except one day when Beaver-House killed a deer and the neck was given to us.

On the fifth day Granny sent me out with Little-Bear to gather punky, dry, rotten wood to fire the pots. He showed me what sort of stuff to get and where to find it on old fallen logs, but he did not offer to help me. I learned that this was supposed to be woman's work, and both men and women would find fault with him if he took a hand in it; especially the women, who regarded pottery making as their special privilege. As I said before, my standing as a captive made it permissible for me.

The seventh day we built a good fire of ordinary wood on the cabin fireplace. Then we laid the pots on their sides, mouths toward the fire, perhaps two feet away. As they

grew gradually hotter, we pushed them up until they were only about a foot from the blaze. After a while they began to change color near the rim, becoming darker; and this color gradually worked its way back until the pots had turned a uniform dark color; then they were ready to fire.

Removing all blazing pieces of wood, we turned the pots upside down with the aid of sticks upon the embers and quickly built over them a pile of rotten wood until they were thickly covered everywhere. The pile gradually caught fire until it became a glowing, white-hot mass, and the cabin was so hot we could hardly stand it.

We rested on the platforms until the fuel had burned away, leaving the pot bottoms rising out of the ashes. After they had cooled, Granny rolled the pots out with a stick, tapping each one as she did so. The two large vessels and one of my toys rang clear, showing that they were perfect; but the other toy pot gave out a sort of dull sound. It was cracked, for some unknown reason.

From that time on I never lacked pots in which to cook.

III. Winter Comes

NOW the nights were growing colder and even the days were often chilly; the leaves turned color and began to fall. I kept my body fairly warm with the old ragged robe, but my legs and feet were cold. Nobody thought of going swimming any more, except a few hardy warriors who went in every morning until the river began to freeze.

One day Granny pulled out from one of the platforms a large, square basket which contained many things made of skin and fur. After some rummaging, she extracted a cape made of deerskin, a large, square piece fringed on the edges, with a hole cut in the middle. She thrust her head through this hole, and for the first time I saw her withered, old body completely covered. She also brought out a pair of soft moccasins and the footless stockings or leggings made of deerskin, called *ka-kuh'na*.

Being now fully clothed for cold weather, she bethought herself of my naked condition, for all I wore was the *sahk-koo-ta'kun* and the robe. She found three tanned deerskins, two to make a long legging for each of my legs, the third for my moccasins. Out came the cutting board, but she found that the flint flakes in her bag were all gone, so she dug up a block of flint she kept buried just outside the doorway and showed me how to knock off some fresh, sharp-edged flakes with a round stone for a hammer.

Then she taught me how to measure my legs and with a flint flake to cut the two skins to fit. The sewing was easy; all I had to do was to bore two holes close together through both thicknesses of deerskin and then run a thong, the point stiffened a little by wetting, through the holes and tie the ends; then repeat the process every inch or so until the "seam" was finished. An awl, called *mu'koos*, made from a sliver of deer bone ground down and polished, was used for making the holes. The illustration shows how I cut and stitched the leggings under Granny's instruction. The hardest part was making the fringe, which had to be cut very even.

The *len-hok-si'na* or shoes, now called "moccasins" by our English colonists, were none too easy. First Granny measured my foot from toe to heel with a deerskin string, and then adding about an inch, tied a knot in it. Then she measured all the way around the foot at the point where the instep merges with the leg and tied another knot. With these two measurements she laid out a pattern like the one shown on the skin with a bit of charcoal as a pencil, and had me cut it out. She then turned it over on the part of the skin remaining and marked around it; then I cut the second one.

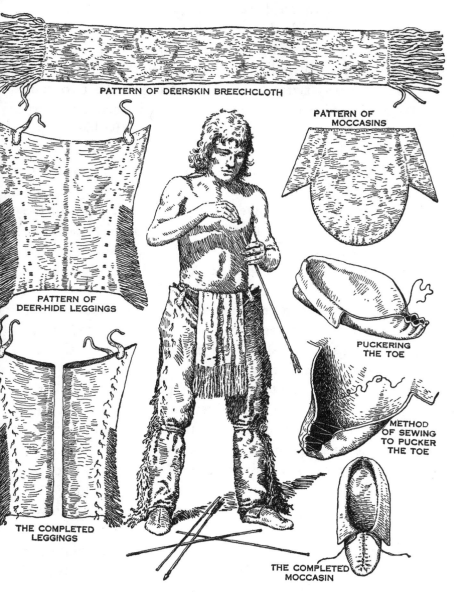

PATTERN OF DEERSKIN BREECHCLOTH

PATTERN OF
MOCCASINS

PATTERN OF
DEER-HIDE LEGGINGS

PUCKERING
THE TOE

METHOD
OF SEWING
TO PUCKER
THE TOE

THE COMPLETED
LEGGINGS

THE COMPLETED
MOCCASIN

I MADE MY NEW CLOTHES UNDER GRANNY'S INSTRUCTIONS

The next thing was to make a strong thread. Granny took a piece of dried deer sinew and split off from it a long shred, which she wet in her mouth. Then pulling up her skirt, she rolled the sinew on her thigh with her right hand, still holding to one end with her left hand. When it was twisted tight, she brought the two ends together and it twisted up on itself again, making a very strong thread, perhaps two spans long. Following her example, I made a number of these.

Each thread was thicker on one end, and on this end Granny tied a knot. Now she took her bone awl and bored a hole in the edge of the skin at the point of the toe end of each pattern and inserted a thread in each and pulled it up to the knot. No needle was needed as sinew thread is as stiff as a shoemaker's waxed end. Taking one of the patterns, she folded the sides of the toe together and made holes first in one side, then the other, drawing the thread through zigzag until she reached the top of the instep. After that she pulled the thread very tightly, and the skin puckered itself.

Making a knot to hold the puckers, she took the point of her awl and straightened them out so that they would look neat and regular; then she sewed the instep and the heel in a plain over-and-over stitch. While she worked on one moccasin, I sewed the other, and with her to watch and criticize I made a pretty good job. The illustration on page 45 shows just how the moccasin was put together.

I felt really proud when I pulled on my leggings and tied the straps to my belt and put on my first pair of moccasins. There was no shirt or coat to go with this

suit, however; I was supposed to cover the upper part of
my body with a robe or mantle when needed.

Now Granny cut two short buckskin strings and took
them over to the grease bag, where she greased them well.
I wondered what they were for, but I soon found out.

She sat down on the edge of her bed platform with the
bone awl and the strings in her hand and beckoned me to
her.   Puzzled, I obeyed; all at once she seized hold of
my right ear, raised her awl, and I felt a sharp pain.   I
jerked back, but she held on and fussed with my ear a
moment, then grabbed my left ear and did the same thing.
When she let go, I felt my ears; they were hot and
throbbing, and through the lobe of each ran a greasy
string.   She had pierced them so that I could wear earrings
as did the rest of the tribe, I suppose, for almost everybody,
young and old, wore them.   I had sore ears for many

days before the holes healed and she pulled the strings out.
A few days later she replaced them with short strings of
shell beads which bothered me quite a good deal with
their swinging to and fro until I got used to them.

I have spoken about the large, bark-covered building
that stood in the middle of the public square. I had often
wondered what it was. It could not be a town hall,
because the elders met in the chief's house. I thought it
could not be a church, because, although I had lost all
track of the days of the week, I knew many Sundays must
have passed since I came to the village, yet no services
had been held. I did not realize that these Indians knew
nothing of Sundays or even of weeks, but divided their
time only into months, seasons, and years.

One morning I saw for the first time signs of life
about the Big-House. Three men and three women were
cleaning up the building and the ground about it, and
when I came nearer, I was surprised to see that Cross-
Woman was one of the party. She looked really clean
and neat for once. They took down the heavy bark
doors at the east and west ends and let the wind blow
through. I saw them carrying dry grass out of the house
and burning it also basketfuls of ashes out through the
west door and on to the edge of the gully to be emptied.

I peeked in through the east door and saw a big,
wooden pillar standing in the middle with a great, grim
face carved upon it, painted half black and half red. I also
saw that all the posts around the sides of the house had
smaller faces carved on them. The grass had been placed
around the walls to sit upon, whilst the ashes came from
two big fireplaces, one east and one west of the pillar.

Next the women gathered fresh, dry grass to make seats; they also gathered quantities of small wood, and the men brought in some good-sized logs of firewood. They all worked several days cleaning and repairing the house, cleaning up the ground around it, and in building a new rack on which to keep food.

All this time people were gathering in the village; they came by families, some on foot from back inland, others by canoe on the river. A few of the latter brought their own mats and poles to make tents, but most of them found lodging in the cabins with the villagers.

One old couple stopped with us, and while they stayed, I had four people to cook for instead of two, and for several nights I had to give up my bed to them and sleep on the south platform with Moon-ha'kee, the dog, who did not like this arrangement very much.

I was learning the language, but at that time I did not know enough of it to understand what was about to take place. However, I heard the word *Gam'wing* on every hand. In time I learned that the *Gam'wing* was the Lenape annual meeting of worship.

One afternoon a crier went through the village making an announcement about *Gam'wing*, and that night a crowd began to gather about the Big-House. Two fires were built inside and the sparks flew out of the two smoke holes; everything was excitement—dogs barking, children shouting to one another.

In the glare of the fires shining out through the east door—the west door had been shut—I could see that everybody was dressed in his best. Until then I had never dreamed that there were so many beautiful garments embroidered with colored quills, deer hair, and shell beads, or so many rich furs in our village.

Granny dressed in a skirt and leggings that had wide borders of hair embroidery, and her moccasins were almost covered with quills of the *ka'wi-a*, the American hedgehog or porcupine, as it is now called, dyed in different colors and worked into fancy patterns. Her cape was made of thousands of soft turkey-breast feathers fastened to a fine, woven net, all lying smooth and even. She wore many strings of shell and bright copper beads about her neck, and her earrings were strings of pearls. She even painted her face with a round red spot on each cheek and tied a flat ornament on her hair behind—a curious thing made of slate and called *ah-see-pe-la'wan*.

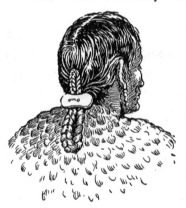

She was certainly better dressed than any other old lady in the village. All the people I knew wore embroidered garments, and even Toad-Face laid aside my English clothing to strut around in embroidered deerskin, with his face painted red and yellow and a crest made of red-dyed deer hair on his head. He seemed especially swollen with pride because his mother had been selected as one of the six attendants for the *Gam'wing*.

My new clothes, of which I had been so proud, seemed very plain compared to all this gay plumage, and the greasy strings in my ears were certainly not ornamental, but I decided to go in with the rest. Just as I approached the door, poor Moon-ha'kee came yelping out, chased by one of the men attendants armed with a long stick. When the man turned back into the building again, I followed him, but hardly had I stepped inside when Cross-Woman spied me. She spoke the words *"La'pee m'wa'ka-na,"* meaning "again a dog," and pointed me out to the man with the stick. He took after me and there was nothing to do but follow Moon-ha'kee's example.

I went back to our cabin and I am afraid I cried a little, with Moon-ha'kee whining in sympathy. Finally I went to bed, but at different times in the night I awoke to hear them drumming, singing, and preaching.

This kept up for twelve nights and ended at noon the thirteenth day. Granny and her guests were at the *Gam'wing* every night, but they always came in some time in the morning, hungry of course, so I had to keep a supply of cooked food on hand as usual. After eating, they slept until the crier called the people to the Big-House. Many others spent part of the day visiting or playing games.

One afternoon I watched a very strange game, played by two teams armed with light javelins, who stood facing each other about twenty paces apart. A wooden hoop was rolled about halfway between the two lines and each player in turn threw his javelin at it. When one of them

5

impaled the hoop and stopped it, everyone on the opposite side was required to stand in the lucky marksman's tracks and throw at the hoop as it lay.   Whoever failed to hit it, forfeited his javelin, and the team capturing all of them won the game, which was called *tat'gusk*.   There was lots

of arguing, yelling, and whooping, and I was really enjoying the fun, when I heard a queer noise behind me, a sort of rattling and a sound like a horse neighing.   I looked and nearly died from fright.   There stood a creature as big as a man, but covered with hair; it had a great moonlike face, half red and half black, and it carried a staff and something that made a rattling noise.   It saw me looking and jumped straight up in the air; then it made a dive for me.

That terrible creature chased me all over the village, making great leaps and bounds and jumping over everything that came in the way. I escaped only by pushing out into the river in a canoe. Even then I thought for a moment it would follow me there, but it finally turned back toward the Big-House, whinnying and rattling. Not until the following spring did I learn that it was a man wearing a mask and a bearskin suit. He always appears at the *Gam'wing*, representing a spirit called *Mee-sing-haw-lee'kun*, supposed to be the guardian of the deer and all other game animals.

At last the *Gam'wing* was over; I saw the very end of it on the thirteenth morning, when the people all lined up outside the Big-House facing east. They raised their hands toward heaven and all cried, "*Hoooo*" a number of times. They believed that this would attract the attention of the Creator himself.

Granny came home and put away her finery; then she went to bed. She was so tired that she never got up for three days, except for a little while in the afternoon. Her friends went home the second day.

Now came the time when the women, boys, and girls went in parties to the forest with sacks to gather nuts. There were two main kinds: one small and white, called *see'meen*, and a large black variety known as *took'kweem*. Both were more or less like our English walnuts, but the shells were harder. It took a lot of work to shell them, but they were delicious and tasted especially good in corn bread. Some women used to grind these nuts in a mortar, with a little water then strain out the shells and use the milky fluid for flavoring. Others boiled the pulp and skimmed off the oil which they kept in gourd bottles like sunflower seed oil. Granny never asked me to do this, and I did not suggest it. I thought I had plenty of

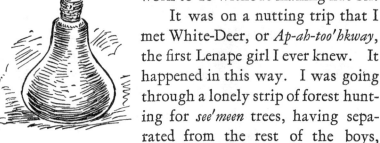

work to do without making nut oil.

It was on a nutting trip that I met White-Deer, or *Ap-ah-too'hkway*, the first Lenape girl I ever knew. It happened in this way. I was going through a lonely strip of forest hunting for *see'meen* trees, having separated from the rest of the boys, when I heard a girl's voice calling. I could not understand the words, but the tone told me she was in trouble.

Following the voice, I found the girl stuck in a fork of the tree. She had climbed a *see'meen* to shake down the nuts, but in getting down, she had caught her right foot in the crotch and could not raise herself high enough to get it out. I climbed up above her and managed to pull her up so that she could free herself. It was a good thing I had come, else she might have starved to death. When I helped her to the ground, she sank down and began to cry, whilst I stood by not knowing what to say or do.

She was very pretty in the Indian way, with fine, smooth skin, round face, large eyes a little slanted, a small, curved nose, and a very small mouth. Her hair was extra long, brushed smooth and done in one braid behind, then looped back and tied with an embroidered deerskin ribbon. I saw all this while she was crying; to tell the truth, I had not noticed before how the girls looked.

After a while she stopped crying and talked to me, but all I could understand was that she was grateful and would like to go home. I helped her to rise, and then we found that she could hardly step on her right foot. The outcome was that I carried both bags of nuts, whilst she hobbled back to the village hanging on to my arm.

She lived down near the river bank, and when I took her home and her mother heard what had happened, she asked me in and gave me a nice bowl of stewed turkey. The mother was a widow whose brother supported her by bringing in part of the game he killed and an occasional deerskin. Of course she raised her own vegetables. Her name was *Pay-ta-nay-hink'hkway*, or Fling-Her-This-Way.

I spent a pleasant hour in their cabin, but on the way back to Granny's, Toad-Face waylaid me and angrily told me, as near as I could understand, to let his girl alone. He then grabbed hold of me unexpectedly and threw me to the ground and, before I could get up, fled to his house with my bag of nuts. I managed to make Granny understand what had happened, and we got the nuts back through the help of Beaver-House.

Next day the boys teased me about White-Deer, but any one of them, in my place, would have done the same, except perhaps Toad-Face. As I thought of it, I could not believe that White-Deer was really his sweetheart, so one day after I could speak the language better, I asked her if it were true. She looked at the ground very modestly and whispered, "*Ma'ta!*"

From that time on I had a few pleasant words with her now and then, but it was not considered proper for girls and boys as old as we to associate together. Of course I became acquainted with other Lenape girls, but never one quite so pretty and quite so nice as White-Deer.

She was clever, too, for the day I brought her home her mother showed me some of the girl's embroidery work in dyed deer hair and porcupine quills, which was especially fine. The strands of hair or quills did not penetrate the deerskin at all, but were held in place with tiny stitches made with very small sinew thread. It takes a

fine-pointed bone awl to make the holes for such stitches, great skill, and very good eyes.

I might say that the only needles the Lenapes used were large, flat, curved ones made from the outer shell of a deer's rib for making the rush mats intended for tent covers and a smaller, thick kind of wood for sewing husk mats. Awls were the rule for fine sewing.

Speaking of husk mats, I learned to make one kind at Granny's: the sort used as mattresses on the bed platforms. There were two kinds, one woven on a frame something like a rush floor mat; the other, which made a more

comfortable bed
because it was
thicker, braided
and sewed to-
gether like an
English rag rug.

I spent a good many hours braiding cornhusks, the
hardest part being to add new husks to the braid and still
keep it the same thickness. The husks had to be kept
wet, which made them easier to manage. When the braid
made a very long rope, Granny showed me how to coil it
around and around and sew the coils together with the
wooden needle I mentioned and thin strips of basswood
inner bark for thread.

As the weather grew colder, it took more and more of
my time to gather firewood enough to keep the cabin
warm, for Granny was old and needed plenty of heat. We
had to keep the door curtain down all the time and the
smoke hole nearly closed, so except for the firelight the
cabin was pretty dark, which made all the work harder.

When I was not working at other
things or playing with the boys, I
braided cornhusks or played a dice
game with Granny. The dice were
different from those we know in
England, for they were flat buttons
of bone or shell, some
in the form of little
turtles. One side of
each was black, the
other white, and, if I

remember right, one kind of game called for five of the
button dice and another game needed twelve. We tossed
them in a wooden bowl.

In the five game, if all black or all white came up, the
count was ten and the player had another shot; in the
twelve game white alone counted and the player throwing
the largest number of whites took the trick and gained
one point. We kept count with beans and could make the
game long or short according to the number of beans we
put in the pile to start with, for each player took from
the pile as many beans as his dice called for. When the
main pile was gone, we took from each other's pile until
one of us had all the beans. He was the winner.

When the weather became cold enough for meat to
keep, Beaver-House brought us a plentiful supply which
we kept on a high rack under the shed outside the cabin.
Once he gave us a whole deer. The insides had been
taken out, but the skin was still on and Granny showed
me how, with her flint knife, to make the cuts necessary
to skin it. She would not let me separate the skin from
the flesh with this knife, however, for fear of cutting the
hide, for she wanted to make buckskin, but she made me
push it off with a blade made of wood.

One day Beaver-House brought us about a quarter of a
bear's carcass with all the fat still on it, although the

hide was gone, and I was called upon to try out the grease. It took both pots, boiling at once. I cut the fat parts of the bear into small pieces and boiled them until the grease rose to the surface, when I skimmed it out with a wooden ladle. An expert can take the grease off without taking anything else, but I found I was getting too much broth with it, so I ladled it into a wooden bowl and set it out on the rack to cool, when it was easy to separate. We put the grease into last year's skin bag, because there was not enough of it to start a new one.

Now a really cold spell came howling out of the north, and I nearly froze when I went out wood gathering. Granny found me a pair of large old moccasins of a different pattern from those ordinarily used, called *mahkt-chee'pak-o*, which are intended for overshoes. The English now call these "shoepacks." The leather is well greased, and when you wrap your feet in furry rabbit skins, as I did, before you put them on, you will keep warm. Another help was a sleeve made of the skin of an otter, called

kwen-a'mohk, to wear on my exposed right arm, and best of all a much warmer robe made of six large beaver skins cut to fit and sewed together.

This was the last favor poor Granny did for me, dear old soul, for although we did not know it, her long and useful life was near its end.

She set out with Moon-ha'kee one evening to attend some sort of meeting at the other end of the village and for some reason would not let me go with her. I stayed up waiting for her a long time, braiding husks and keeping up the fire. Sometime late at night I wearied of this and went to bed, thinking, of course, she would return later on.

When I awoke in the morning, the cabin was ice-cold and snow had drifted in and lay around the fireplace and near the door. I sprang up and hurriedly raked the hot coals together from their covering of ashes and soon had a good fire burning.

I called to Granny to ask her what she wanted for breakfast, but there was no response. Choking with anxiety, I hurried to her bed; it was empty, and now I saw that the dog had not come home either. Nearly sick I rushed to the door and looked out; it was snowing steadily and there seemed to be over a foot on the ground already.

I tried to console myself with the thought that she was probably spending the night with some friend, but no use. Wrapping my new robe about me and putting on my sleeve, I set out to look for her, although I did not know which cabin was to have been the scene of the meeting.

Nobody was out; the village looked deserted in the driving snow except for the smoke drifting from some of the smoke holes. I was going along not far from the river bank when I heard a sort of whine behind me. I turned quickly. There was Moon-ha'kee, and he was acting very strangely. He ran toward the river bank, then back to me, then back to the bank again. I followed him and, looking over the low bluff, I saw a long shape

covered with snow lying among the stones at its foot.
In a moment I was down there. It was Granny.

When I tried to lift her, she moaned faintly. Prob-

ably she had tried to come home in the
snowstorm, had missed her path and had
fallen over the bluff. My first thought was
to get Beaver-House, but White-Deer's cabin
was nearer, so I got her and Fling-Her-
This-Way and the three of us carried poor
Granny into the cabin. Then I ran for Beaver-House,
and finally we got her home and to bed.

Beaver-House brought a famous *may-tay'oo*, or doctor,
named *Gans-hay-woo-lon'kwan*, or Roaring-Wings, a short,
stout man with long, gray hair and a square jaw. He
walked into the cabin very straight and important, but
when he had looked at Granny, he shook his head.

"I shall try to help her," he said, "but I am afraid it
is no use. I can set the broken leg, but the real trouble is
here." He pointed to his chest. "I fear it has gone
beyond my powers. She can hardly breathe now."

He set the leg and put a splint of *len-nik'pee*, basswood
bark, upon it; then he bled Granny's chest in several
places with a little black horn, first cutting the skin with a
tiny flint chip set crosswise in a small wooden handle.
Then he tried to make her swallow
some medicine which he had brewed from
herbs in my toy ket-
tle. She could not
swallow, so he began
to sing and pray over
her, keeping time to
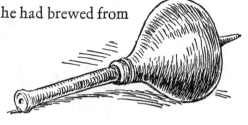

his song with a rattle made of a dry gourd, or *h'kun-ak'hakw*. He sang all night and I helped with the fire and other things, but Beaver-House's sisters arrived about daybreak and they sent me to Little-Bear's cabin to rest.

I slept until late afternoon, and when I awoke, Little-Bear told me sadly that Granny was dead. I must say I cried long and bitterly, for the kind-hearted old lady had become very dear to me. They were sitting up with her that night, and Beaver-House wanted me to come, so I felt I must, although I dreaded the ordeal. The little cabin that had been my home for months was crowded, and people were continually coming and going. Between the fireplace and Granny's bed they were playing the moccasin game, one man hiding a large shell bead under one of four moccasins whilst his opponent tried to guess which one, and they sang a peculiar song, hardly stopping for breath and they beat a drum continually. It seemed a strange thing to do at such a time, but such was the custom.

I went to look at Granny. They had her dressed in her best clothing, the same as she had worn at the *Gam'-wing*, and her face was painted the same way with a large red spot on each cheek. She was lying on her side on her mat, with her hands on her breast and her knees drawn up quite close to her body. I looked for Moon-ha'kee and found him crouched under the platform, shivering.

After a little while I returned to Little-Bear's where I lay, listening to the distant song and drumming of the moccasin game until daybreak.

The next ordeal was the funeral. Of course the frozen ground made it out of the question to dig a grave, so they cleared the snow from an abandoned storage pit on a knoll

not far from the village and buried her there, all wrapped
in mats, with her bowl, her spoon, her little mortar and
pestle, and one of the pots I had made.

While they were lowering Granny into her last bed,
the two daughters rushed forward and, grasping hold of
the mats, they cried and screamed and begged their
mother not to leave them.   Beaver-House was so dis-
traught that he ran away out into the snowy woods and
did not come back until evening.

The people brought ashes from their fireplaces to fill
the grave and stones from the river to keep away the
wolves.   Several nights thereafter I saw a fire burning
upon the grave.

Moon-ha′kee could not be consoled at first; he somehow learned where Granny was buried and lay down by
her grave, refusing the food I brought him.   Finally I
picked him up bodily and carried him to Little-Bear's
cabin, where I tied him.   After a few days he ate a little
and gradually came back to himself again.

IV. Cross-Woman's House

NOBODY ever lived again in Granny's cabin. After the funeral Beaver-House and his two sisters divided their mother's belongings; the mats were taken from the walls and from the bed-platforms; only a shell remained.

Beaver-House tried to place me with one of his sisters, I shall give him credit for that; but neither of them needed a servant, as they had half-grown daughters to help them. Besides, their houses were small and there was no room for a stranger, so I fell to Beaver-House himself, and he had no choice but to present me to Cross-Woman, his wife, as an *al-lo-ka'kan*, or servant.

I was still staying at Little-Bear's when Bowl-Woman brought the news. I was horrified, because I had expected to remain in my friend's home.

"I'll run away!" I cried. "I cannot live with Toad-Face; I hate him! And his mother is the meanest and cruelest woman I ever knew! Besides, their cabin is nasty; it smells bad!"

"You would freeze to death or starve if you tried to run away," answered Thunder-Arrow, Little-Bear's father. "Beaver-House saved your life; it is only right you should work for him. He may protect you from Toad-Face; if not, learn to protect yourself. Cross-Woman may not be so bad as she looks. Be brave!''

Shortly afterward Beaver-House came to get me. Sadly I put on my beaver robe and my otter-skin sleeve and gathered up my old flea robe, my bowl and spoon and bed mat. From the house of a friend to the house of an enemy! I gritted my teeth and squared my shoulders. Maybe I'd run away later.

I shall never forget the moment that I stepped inside that smelly cabin, carrying my scant possessions. Cross-Woman's black eyes sparkled.

"*Joo!*" she cried. "It is my happy day. At last I have found someone to fetch wood and water!"

Toad-Face glued his eyes upon me.

"See, Mother!" he shouted. "A new beaver mantle and an otter-skin sleeve! Just what I need!"

Roughly he jerked the robe from my shoulders, the sleeve from my arm; the rest of my things fell to the ground. He reached for my bowl and spoon. I stood there, wishing I could die.

"I can use these, too," he said. Then he noticed the little strings of beads which poor Granny had hung in my ears.

"*Kway!* Look at his *sah-kah-ka-hoon'a!* They are better than mine." He addressed Beaver-House. "Let me have your knife."

Beaver-House scowled angrily. "Let those beads alone, greedy one!" he commanded. "Give his things back to the poor boy!"

"In this house no servant shall wear better clothing than my son," Cross-Woman said. The outcome was that

Toad-Face kept my beaver robe and my sleeve, although he already had my English coat, but returned my bowl and spoon and did not take my ear beads.

Then something happened that astonished me. Cross-Woman of her own accord, but grumbling to herself the while, found me a mantle made of *nah'num*, raccoon, skins in very fair condition and an old beaver-skin sleeve which

was worn but still good enough for anyone to wear. These she threw to me without a word. Toad-Face did not like this a bit, for I believe the things were his. Beaver-House kept his face immovable, but his eyes twinkled.

However, Cross-Woman would not clear for me the only vacant *ha'soon*, or sleeping platform, which was piled high with all kinds of stuff, mostly trash. Instead she made me spread my mat on the dirt floor at night and roll it up every day. This hurt my feelings, but my bed was warmer than it would have been on the platform, and their dog, Wee-sao'suh, recognizing his old robe by the smell, came and slept with me, which made it warmer still, so it was not so bad after all.

For a while my only work was fetching wood and water, which Cross-Woman especially hated, whilst she did the cooking. This I would not have minded if she had let me go out with the boys once in a while, especially to Little-Bear's house, and if she had fed me better. But she made me stay in the house all the time unless I went out after wood or water, and never thought of giving me fresh food like the rest of the family ate, if she could find stale scraps and leftovers for me.

One afternoon while she was away gambling, her favorite amusement, and Toad-Face was out with Beaver-House, learning to hunt, I rebelled. I cooked up a good mess of *meehn'ah-pon*, or corn bread, with dried berries, and broiled a piece of venison I found on the rack, and had a feast.

Cross-Woman came home when I was just finishing and she was furious. "*Saaa! k'tuh-shing'huh*," she yelled at me, meaning I was disobedient. I do not know what she would have done to me if she had not noticed that the food smelled good, and she sampled a little. Then she ate up all that was left.

"*Ay-ka-yah'!* So you can cook after all!" she said at last. "They told me you could, but I would not believe it. Very well, if you like cooking so much, you shall do all the cooking of this house from now on."

She may have thought she was punishing me, but it worked out better for both of us. She had more time for gossiping and gambling, whilst I got all I wanted to eat. Trust a cook for that!

Several times Toad-Face tried his old tricks, but I told him that he was spoiling his own food when he put sand in the bread, and he saw that I was right. That did not prevent his pouring water in my moccasins and setting them outside to freeze, or cutting my pack strap so that it would break when I picked up a big load of wood. On account of my being his mother's servant, I did not retaliate at the time, but saved such things up until the time of reckoning which I hoped was coming.

One time Beaver-House took Cross-Woman and Toad-Face to another village where some relative of theirs was sick and left me to take care of the house. The first thing I did when they were out of sight was to run over to Little-Bear's to tell him my troubles. We had a boxing match and a very good time, and when I came back, I brought with me Granny's dog, Moon-ha'kee, as Bowl-Woman said he should belong to me, also his bowl and bed mat.

It was great fun to get the two dogs acquainted as both were very jealous and growled fiercely at each other, but before the day was over they were good friends.

The next day I decided to clean house because I was sick of living in so much litter and dirt. I went through everything and burned a great pile of worn-out mats, broken baskets, and useless old moccasins. I shook out all the robes and bed mats, I swept off the platforms and cleaned the floor, and when I was through, the trash was all gone and the things remaining were all in neat order and sorted out according to kind.

Among the things I found in my rummaging was a wooden doll about two spans high, dressed like a Lenape woman. It had many strings of tiny shell beads around its neck and was wrapped in a soft piece of doeskin, in a

specially made, fine, woven basket with a cover. I could
not see what use such a thing would be but I realized from
the way it had been taken care of that it must be precious

to someone.   Later on I heard a strange story of this doll,
which was called *Ow'tas*.

The rummaging and cleaning took one whole day.
The next morning I rose early and baked some extra good
corn bread and made a delicious stew with venison, hulled
corn, and beans.   I ate sparingly of these so there would be
plenty for the family, and then I waited.   When I heard
Toad-Face's voice outside, I made Moon-ha'kee lie down
under one of the platforms where he would not be seen,
then I got as far away from the door as I could, because I
did not know what might happen.

Cross-Woman was the first to raise the door curtain.
When she saw what I had done, she staggered back and
nearly fell over; for a moment she thought she was in
the wrong house.   Then her little eyes fairly bulged; she
seized a stick of firewood and started for me.

"*Ay-kay-saa'!*" she cried. "Where are my things, doglike? Let me get hold of you, *ke-kah-moot-keh'tet*, you little thief!"

I dodged around, keeping the fire between me and her.

"Your things are all here," I explained. "I have just cleaned them and put them in order."

"Where's the *Ow'tas?*"

"You mean the little wooden woman in a basket? I hung her from the roof poles over your bed."

She looked up and saw the basket there; then she found that I had put her bowls all in one place, her pots in another; the big basket that contained her best clothes was safe under the head of her bed; nothing was gone but the trash.

Toad-Face came in just then and grabbed me, but his mother had thrown the stick down, so I received no thrashing. She might not have beaten me, anyhow, because even the worst of the Lenape women think it wrong to strike a child.

"I suppose," she grumbled, "that there is nothing to eat in the house; and we shall have to go hungry."

"There isn't much," I said, "but I saved a little stew in that big pot and a few pieces of bread in the other one."

She peered into the pots and then she looked at me with almost a smile, for she loved to eat. Toad-Face caught the look and scowled darkly. It made him angry that his mother should have one kind thought of me.

Then Beaver-House came in, and after he had seen what I had done, he said he was glad I had made such good use of the days they were gone.

After they had filled their stomachs, I thought it was a good time to ask a favor, so I called Moon-ha'kee out from under the platform and asked Cross-Woman if I could keep him, quivering inside for fear she would say, "No."

Toad-Face immediately spoke up.

"*Ma-ta-ka'!* Don't let him do it; one dog is enough."

"Another dog will not do any harm," said Beaver-House.

Finally Cross-Woman spoke.

"If you do your work well, you may keep the dog," she said, "but if you are lazy or if you do not obey, I shall kill him."

I thanked her, and then Beaver-House called me over to him as he sat on the edge of the platform and asked me how I was getting along. I said, "Very well, only I should like to go out and play with the boys sometimes."

He and Cross-Woman had quite an argument about this but finally agreed that I could go out and play when my work was done. When Cross-Woman was home, she usually found enough for me to do to keep me busy all day, but sometimes she wanted to sew, which was the only kind of work she liked, and while on occasion I had to help her, as a rule she was glad to get rid of me. Of course when she went out gambling, I left as soon as my regular work was done, Moon-ha'kee at my heels.

I usually went straight to Little-Bear's and we boxed and wrestled to our hearts' content, but sometimes we borrowed one of his father's bows and practiced shooting. I was not so bad at archery, because at home in England it was customary for the boys to practice with the longbow every Saturday, and I had done this almost every week since I was about ten years old.

Sometimes we played with the other boys; they had a queer game called *cha'chees*, played with long poles. The first thing was to make a long, straight trough in the snow and pour water into it. When it was frozen, each boy in turn threw his pole down the trough, and the pole which ran farthest won the game. These poles were specially made, very smooth and polished, and a skilful thrower could cast them a long distance. Often the younger men also played this and bet on it, too, but boys my age played for fun. Moon-ha'kee enjoyed this game, running after the sliding poles and barking at them, whilst the boys laughed.

Toad-Face, who was always trying to find some way to plague me, started out along a new line. Because I was chiefly engaged with housework and gathering wood, which are regarded as work for women and girls, he began to address me as *Nahk-ay'sim-mus*. At first I thought the word was *Nahk-ee'sim-mus*, which means, "My younger brother," and sounds almost the same, but after a while it dawned on me that he was calling me his "younger sister." I angrily called him to account for it, but he just laughed and said:

"You must be a girl; you do girl's work all the time."

The next thing, he got a new idea. I have already explained how poor Granny named me *Day'kay-ning* or "In the Forest"; now Toad-Face added *hkway* to the end, which made it into a girl's name—*Day-kay-ning'hkway* or "In-the-Forest-Woman." The nearest thing we can come to this in English would be "Miss In-the-Forest," and that is what he called me on all occasions. The boy saw that it plagued me and laughed, and some of them took up the same custom, especially some older youths. Those of my own size or less did not dare, especially after I had whipped a few of them. For the rest of the winter and spring I kept away from the older boys, except of course Little-Bear and now our boxing practice had a purpose; I wanted to make myself strong enough and quick enough to thrash Toad-Face.

When I told Little-Bear, he offered to whip him for me, but I insisted I should do it myself when the time was ripe.

So the winter passed with its hard work, its pleasures, and its grief. The days grew longer and warmer; the snow melted except in shady places and the river was full of

floating ice. I got along fairly well with Cross-Woman
for all of her bad temper because she would not abuse me
as long as I did my work, but Toad-Face I hated worse and
worse.   More than once I was minded to run away from
the village and try to find my way to Jamestown. Then I
remembered my determination to thrash him, and I gritted
my teeth and stayed on.

A thing that almost caused me to run away took place
one day early in spring. I was enjoying the warm air
and sunshine whilst looking for wood at least a mile from
the village, when Toad-Face and one of his friends suddenly
appeared and caught hold of me. I fought hard, but they
overpowered me, and the other boy held me face down
whilst Toad-Face braided my hair, which was now quite
long, down my back, and looped it up and tied it like a
girl's; then they turned me loose and laughed at me.

When they had gone, I tried for a long time to untie it
but they had used wet deerskin strings and tied so many
hard knots that I could not, and I had to go back to the
village with my hair in that shape.   All the boys laughed
at me and called me "Miss In-the-Forest," and even White-
Deer saw me and laughed, and that hurt worst of all.

When I reached home, I begged Cross-Woman to take
it down, but she only laughed, and I had to wear it that
way until Beaver-House came home that night.   He
laughed, too, but he cut the thongs with his flint knife, and
I unbraided my hair and felt more like myself again.

It must have been about March when the *sha-wa-na-
mek'uk* or "southfish," shad, came up the river, and the
canoes which had been hauled up for the winter, turned
over and covered with rushes and poles, were launched

again, and the long nets or seines, called *ya-hel'la-ap*, were brought out and mended. They had wooden floats and notched, flat stones for sinkers.

Only a few people in our village had these nets, for they were very hard to make. The cords were twisted from fiber of a weed called *hal'lah-pees*, all done by hand on the thigh, much the same way as sinew threads were twisted.

Beaver-House was one of the lucky net owners, and so it happened that he and Toad-Face and I with Moon-ha'kee set out in his canoe net fishing. We paddled along until we found a smooth piece of river bank without brush or rocks, a sort of beach, and here we landed. Beaver-House got hold of one end of the net and then Toad-Face and I set out again in the canoe. I paid out the net from the stern, as he paddled out into the stream until the net was almost all out, then circled around upstream a way, then back to the beach, whilst I hung on to the end of the net.

With both ends of the net, which was about thirty yards long, on the shore, we began to pull it in. We soon could tell by the flopping that there was something in it, and we got excited and pulled faster. Soon we could see the fish dashing about trying to get away, and when we

pulled the final loop of it ashore, we could hardly drag it
in for the fish—twenty or thirty big *sha-wa-na-mek'uk.*

We killed these by hitting them on the head with a
stick, and threw them up on the shore, then made another
haul.

This time we caught about fifteen, which we killed and
added to the pile. We were having a wonderful time, and
Toad-Face even forgot to call me "Little Sister," whilst I
had almost friendly feelings toward him, in spite of what
had passed.

The third haul, something happened which spoiled
everything. Toad-Face was paying out the net and I was
paddling, when Moon-ha'kee happened to get in his way.
Before I knew what had happened, he had angrily kicked
the poor dog out of the canoe into the cold water. This
so enraged me that I swung my paddle and hit Toad-Face a
blow over the head that knocked him into the river; the
canoe nearly upset, and the end of the net went overboard.

Beaver-House yelled at me from the bank, and I came
to my senses in time to grab Toad-Face when he rose to the
surface. It was good for him that I did, because my blow
had stunned him and he would have drowned. By the
time he came to and I had helped him back into the canoe,
we had drifted away down the river; then we had to paddle
all the way back to the beach. When we arrived, Moon-
ha'kee was waiting for us; he had swum directly ashore
and was none the worse.

Beaver-House was waiting for us, too, and he gave us
both a terrible thrashing with a willow rod. I should
say rods, because he wore out several on us before he was
done. That was the first and only thrashing I ever had

from a grown person while I was among the Lenapes. As I said, they seldom strike a child.

Of course there was no more fishing. We found that the net had swung off downstream and had tangled itself in a snag, and by the time we got it loose, there were several big holes in it. The result was that Toad-Face and I had to spend about two days mending the net. The second day he had recovered himself enough to call me "Little Sister." I responded by calling him *nee-mees*, or "My Big Sister," and we let it go at that.

I forgot to tell what became of the fish. We loaded them into the canoe and brought them back to the village, and there, to my surprise, Beaver-House gave most of them away, keeping only three or four for ourselves. I saw that certain persons seemed to be specially favored, and when I inquired why, I was told that these people were "Turkeys" or *Pay-lay'ook* and that they were some kin to Beaver-House because he, too, was a *Pay-lay'* or "Turkey."

This was my first intimation that the tribe was divided into three bands: Turkey, Turtle, and Wolf, and that every person in it belonged to one of these. Membership in bands followed the mother; that is, if your mother was a Turtle, you would be a Turtle too, no matter what band your father belonged to. Cross-Woman was a Wolf, and so Toad-Face, her son, was also a Wolf. Little-Bear and his mother were both Turtles. White-Deer and her mother were both Turkeys, and I saw to it that they got a specially big southfish.

When all the Turkeys who wanted fish were satisfied, Beaver-House gave the rest away to anyone who asked for them, as long as they lasted.

When Cross-Woman asked me to cook a fish for our supper, I prepared to cut it up and boil it, but she said that was wrong. She got out a wide, flat piece of wood split from some big log and ground down smooth like a board—I had wondered what it was for—then she split and cleaned the fish and pegged it down to the board with wooden pegs that fitted into holes already made for the purpose. She then placed the board on edge in front of the fire, bracing it so that it would be secure, whilst the fish sizzled and cooked slowly. The trick was to place the board far enough away so that it would not catch fire, but  near enough so that the fish would cook. The roes of this fish were pinned on the board to cook with the rest and I found them equally good. Southfish was very bony, but delicious.

One day Cross-Woman told me to crack a big lot of hard corn for hominy, as we were going to have a feast, called *Ow'tas Kin'te-ka*. I knew *Ow'tas* was the little wooden woman in the basket and that *kin'te-ka* meant "dance," so I asked Cross-Woman whether the doll was supposed to dance by itself.

"Of course not, stupid; the dance is in honor of the *Ow'tas*."

"But why should there be a dance in honor of a wooden puppet?"

"You are very ignorant, but I suppose I must tell you.

"When my grandmother was a little girl, her father made a wooden doll for her that was very lifelike, so much so that she treated it like a real, live baby. She spent so much of her time playing with it that her parents became worried; it seemed to have life; they feared it and made her throw it away. They moved away to another place, and now the little girl became sickly; she became very thin and cried all the time. She dreamed about the doll every night: that it came to her and said, 'You must find me and keep me all the time and you will have good health in the family. Fix me up a new dress every spring and give me a dance.' Finally her father went back to the place where they lived before and looked through the bushes until he found the doll.

"Then the mother made new clothes for the doll and put shell beads on its neck and gave it back to the little girl, and she got well right away. All through her life my grandmother took care of her doll and had a feast for it every spring, and my mother carried on the custom, and now I have the doll.

"We believe that if we honor the doll in this way, that our health will be good, but if we should neglect it, sickness would follow. Now do you know why we hold the *Ow'tas Kin'te-ka?*"

I said, "*Pees'shih*" and "*wa-nee'shih*," which is to say, "Yes," and "thank you;" but it seemed to me a strange custom and different from anything I remembered in England.

I spent most of the day cracking corn in the mortar to make hominy, and that evening Beaver-House went out and found six men of the Wolf band who were willing to help Cross-Woman. Two of these were to fix a dance ground out in the forest, one was to go hunting and bring in a deer, one was to make a speech at the meeting, and two were to sing for the dancers; and Cross-Woman gave them all their instructions.

The next day I worked at cracking corn, after my regular tasks were done, until nearly dark, whilst Cross-Woman made a new dress for the *Ow'tas*. Next morning she and I went out to the dance ground early, carrying large pack baskets full of the cracked corn, she also bearing the doll basket.

The dance ground was a cleared spot under some big trees, with logs laid around to sit upon, and near by was a pile of dry wood and a deer hanging on a rack made of poles. Somebody had brought a number of big pots and bark buckets of water, and so Cross-Woman and I set to work to boil the hominy and cook the deer. Some of the venison we boiled with the hominy to give it a flavor, but most of it we cut in strips and broiled in the fire in the middle of the dance ground.

It was past midday when we finished; then we ate a little lunch and rested whilst the people were gathering for the dance.

The sun was about halfway down when the speech maker arose and began something like this:

"I am glad that so many of us are still living to take part again in this yearly Doll Dance, and that so many young people whom we have not seen before have assembled to help us."

Then he told the story of the *Ow'tas* doll, about the way I have related it, and whilst he was speaking, a young

man came up to Cross-Woman, carrying a slender pole,
and she tied the doll on the end of it. The singers knelt
down not far from the fire with a folded dry hide for a
drum, and when the speakers finished, they beat on the
hide with sticks and began to sing a lively tune.

The young man danced around the fire carrying the
doll on the pole, and other men fell in behind until a
circle was formed, whilst dancing women formed an outer
circle. When the doll-carrier tired of his task, he passed
the pole to the man behind him and so on around the
circle; then the women in the outside circle carried the
doll. I noticed with pleasure that the best dancer of this
circle was White-Deer.

The singers sang twelve songs, with intermissions,
during which the doll pole was stuck into the ground near
the fire, and after the twelfth, the speaker announced that
the doll dance was over. That was quite a while after dark.

Then Cross-Woman and I had to serve the food,
ladling the hominy out into bowls the people had brought
with them and passing out the meat, and finally the six
men who had helped were called out and Cross-Woman
gave each one a string of shell beads for pay.

The crowd danced various pleasure dances all night,
and Cross-Woman danced with them in spite of her bulk;
but I soon tired of watching; so gathering up as many of
our utensils as I could, I carried them home and went
to bed.

Some time after the Doll Dance a crier went around
through the village announcing that it was time for the
women to plant their gardens. The next day Cross-
Woman brushed her hair, put on her best dress, and took

part in some kind of ceremony to which I was not invited; also some men went out with nets and caught many little fishes like herrings, to be used in the gardens.

The next thing was to get the tools together: simply a pointed stick of hardwood to dig up the ground, and a hoe, called *kwee-pe-la'nai*, with a stone blade. I suggested to Cross-Woman that I had better have a set of tools of my own if I was going to help her, but she replied that one set was enough as I was going to do most of the work.

As we went out of the village toward her field, we passed Toad-Face playing with some boys on the edge of a gully. He called out, "There go the women to make garden," and they all laughed. I gritted my teeth, but I shouted back, "You'd better come, too, Big Sister!" Then the boys laughed at *him*.

Cross-Woman's garden lay along the creek which ran down the gully into the river just north of the village, perhaps half a mile upstream on a flat piece of rich bottom land. The big trees had all been girdled round and stood stark and dead, except one that had fallen during the past winter. The first task that faced us was freeing the land of last year's dried weeds and cornstalks. These I pulled up by main strength and laid in piles to burn, as my mistress directed.

Next day we carried baskets of fish when we came out and a lighted piece of slow match, or punk, with which

7

I set fire to the rubbish. This time Beaver-House and Toad-Face came along, and they cut the big, fallen log into short sections by building fires on it in different places, then they rolled the logs out of the way. I marked where they went, with the idea of splitting them up for firewood some day.

Cross-Woman then showed me how to dig a hole, bury a fish in it, and hoe up the ground into a low hillock over each fish. We made these hills four or five feet apart, and they covered the whole garden, which was about twenty-five yards wide and perhaps fifty yards long.

The next step was to plant the seed which Cross-Woman had carefully saved for the purpose—some extra fine ears of soft, white corn for bread and hard, blue corn for hominy. About two thirds of the field we planted in white, the rest in blue corn. Our method after the corn was shelled was for me to punch a hole in each hill with the sharpened stick, whilst Cross-Woman followed behind and dropped four or five grains in each, afterward closing the

hole with her heel. After we finished the corn, we planted a row of sunflowers on the north side of the plot.

She told me that I was to come back after the corn was up and plant some beans—four or five kinds—which would climb up on the cornstalks, and several kinds of squashes whose vines would cover the ground between the hills. As things turned out, she had to do this herself, for I never returned to that garden.

This is how it happened. I had gone out on the river bank one day—without Moon-ha'kee, for a wonder—to gather driftwood, about a mile above the village, when I saw Toad-Face coming out of the bushes with a package. He hailed me very pleasantly, for him, and I waited for him, although I was suspicious that something was afoot.

"*Ho!* *K'pet'ching-weh-hih!* Look here! I have brought a present for you," he said, "new clothes which Mother has made for you. You have done your work so well that she and I both think that you earned this gift. I have brought the clothes to you here so that you can wear them back to the village and everyone will see how fine you look."

I was taken in, because I really did need new leggings and moccasins, if nothing else.

"Oh, thank you!" I cried. "Let me see them."

"First take off your old clothes and throw them into the river! That is our custom when anyone gives a person new clothing."

Like a fool I did this, and then he opened the package.

In it were fringed garments of deerskin, new and fresh, and some I could see were embroidered a little. I was very happy until I lifted one—an oblong piece, maybe a yard wide and a yard and a half long—and it dawned on me that this was an *at'hoon*, a girl's skirt. The rest of the things, I could see now, were a cape, short leggings, moccasins—a complete costume for a girl.

"I can't wear these," I cried. "These are girl's clothes!"

"*Ay'ko-han'!* *Kee-nee'ta!* Yes, you can, Miss In-the-Forest," said Toad-Face, picking up a stick. "And you are going to wear them if I have to beat you until you do! *Ka-ta'tee!*"

Toad-Face did not expect any resistance. Why should he? He was heavier and taller and in his previous encounters with me had proved himself master. He struck me with the stick a stinging blow on the thigh. I jumped forward and hit him full in the face with all my might.

He staggered back, nearly fell, the stick dropped from his hand; I struck him several more times before he grabbed me.

"*Ah-weh'!*" he puffed, "you little brat. I'll break your back for that!" Holding my arms so that I could not hit him, he began to bend me over backward.

Realizing that I could not stand much of that, I pretended suddenly to give way. I spun myself around and wriggled out of his clutches; then, before he recovered his balance, I punched him a couple of good ones, square in the face.

He did not know how to protect his face and could not understand how I did it. Already his lip was cut and his nose bleeding, but I might as well have pounded on a log as to strike his body.

Now he tried to strike me with his fists, and several blows did graze me, but I managed to dodge most of them, at the same time landing occasional punches, most of them in the face.

I must have become careless, for suddenly he struck me a blow on my chest that knocked me away from him and nearly felled me. I staggered back quite a way, fighting for breath—he thought he had me! For a moment I thought so too.

Then an idea came to me. I dodged around trying to get my breath, really recovering; but I acted as if I were getting weaker. Finally I stopped altogether, with my hands down as if done for. Toad-Face rushed in to finish me, when I landed him one on the nose which knocked him off his feet.

With the blood spurting from his nose, he got up and rushed down the beach with me after him to a rocky spot and, before I could catch up to him, he grabbed a big stone and hurled it at my head with all his might. I dodged and it just grazed my ear. He tried to pick up another, but I was upon him.

He clutched me, and over we tumbled among the boulders, pounding and scratching. He even bit me several times, but I wriggled so hard that he could not get a good mouthful, and every time he let go of my arms I hit him in the face.

Now I found I was getting very tired, and it came over me I could not hold out much longer. Toad-Face let go of my arms with the intention of choking me I think, but before he got a good hold, I struck him in the face again. When he leaned back to avoid my blows, I raised my knee suddenly and caught him in the stomach. That was the turning point.

He staggered to his feet and tried to run, but slipped and fell in the sand. Through swollen eyes he saw me coming and he covered his face with his hands.

"Don't hit me again—don't—don't—I beg you——"

"Do you yield?"

"Yes!"

"Then *you* put on the dress!"

"*Ma-ta-ka'!* I won't!"

I yanked his hands from his face as if to hit him again.

"*Ta- Ma'ta!*" he sobbed. "Don't, *N'shin'gee!* I'll do anything you say." Then I knew that he was beaten.

I made him strip off what remained of his clothes, or rather mine that he was still wearing, and threw them away out into the river.

Then Toad-Face put on the dress complete, with me standing over him, my fists doubled up in case he wavered. When it was on him, even to short leggings and moccasins, and fastened securely, I tied his hands together behind his back with my pack strap.

Finally I braided his hair as he had done mine, looped it up, and tied it with a deerskin hair ribbon and a *ah-see-pe-la'wan* that had been in the package.

"Now, Miss Toad-Face," I said, "go back to the village and show everybody your nice new clothes!"

He hesitated, but I approached menacingly, and he started. I followed him to the edge of the village and waited behind a bush until I heard the boys shout with glee, then I slipped off into the forest.

I had a vague idea of trying to find my way to Jamestown; but before I had gone far, I realized that I was naked, very bruised and sore, and hungry.

V. The House of Bowl-Woman

AS NIGHT came on, I found a grassy place and there I slept until the chill air of the early morning hours awakened me, and then I lay and shivered until daylight. I arose very hungry, but as there was no way to get food, I limped off southeastward, where I imagined Jamestown must lie. My happy feeling of triumph and satisfaction was gone, but my bruises, scrapes, and cuts, not to mention bites, the result of the battle, were still with me.

About midday, feeling weak and tottery, I was crossing a hill where the forest was thin, when I noticed some small red berries growing on low plants near the ground. I knelt down and tasted one. It was sweet and delicious, with just enough bite to make it good. Then it dawned upon me that I had found a bed of *w'tee'heem*, or "heart berries" of which I had heard, now called "wild strawberries" by the English. I ate several handfuls of them and felt much better.

As I sat resting, it came to me that I should try to make a bow and arrow and perhaps kill a deer or at least a rabbit. The trouble was that I had no tools; how could I cut a stave to make into a bow without them? The answer was this: I must find flint and make tools. After that all I would have to do would be to make a bow and arrow, then go hunting and kill some game, then make fire sticks, find some tinder and build a fire to cook on; then perhaps I could eat. It was very discouraging, but what else could I do?

I went down into the bed of a little brook and looked for flint, but not a piece could I find. Then I thought perhaps some of the round, smooth pebbles that lay in the brook might have flint on the inside, so I picked out a tough pebble for a hammer and cracked a lot of them to see. There was no flint, but I did find a hard white stone that broke with a sharp edge.

I looked about for a bowstave and finally I found a young *see'meen* tree about two fingers thick that I thought would do. I must have spent hours cutting that sapling down; I dulled flake after flake of the white stone. Finally it was down and trimmed and rude notches scraped in for the string, but there was no way that I knew of to taper it; it was simply a slender club.

For a string I pulled a strip of bark from a basswood tree, or *len-nik'pee*, and the inner part I twisted on my thigh, as Granny had taught me, into a strong cord. For arrows, I cut two willow sprouts, trimmed and notched them with my stone chips. I did not know how to make arrow points, so I simply tied splinters of the white stone on the ends of the arrows with fibers of inner bark.

But when my bow and arrow was complete, it was a sorry weapon. The arrows were crooked, without feathers, and the points were loose. The bow was round instead of flattened, thick on one end and thin on the other. Still, it was the best I had, so I set out hunting.

As luck would have it, I had not gone more than a hundred paces when I spied two deer grazing near the little brook. I sneaked up as close as I dared, took careful aim, and let fly. The unfeathered arrow turned over several times in the air and struck a tree over their heads with a sharp sound. The deer looked up to see what it was, then calmly resumed their feeding.

The second arrow was the better of the two; I had high hopes of it. It flew straight and hit the deer just behind the left shoulder, then, alas! fell to the ground. The deer never raised its head, but reached up its left hind foot and scratched the place where the arrow had struck.

With a yell I threw the bow at them; the string fell over the head of the larger deer, and they bounded off carrying my bow with them. Not fifty yards away the bow caught on a projecting branch and I thought for the moment I had snared the animal; however it reared back to free itself; in the struggle the bow was broken and the deer was released.

I went back to the strawberry hill and sat there moping until nearly dark before I had sense enough to gather and eat some more *w'tee'heem*. I slept little, and the next morning, even after eating all the berries that remained, I found I was growing weaker.

Sitting on a log I tried to reason out what was best to do. Should I try to get back to the village? I doubted if I were strong enough to travel that far, but if I did, the least punishment I could expect would be to wear the dress. It might even be worse. I had heard that captives were sometimes killed for trying to escape. Or should I wander on, hoping to fall in with other Indians who might feed me? I realized now that the Jamestown plan was hopeless.

As I sat there, I thought I heard a dog barking. I could not believe my ears. Now the barking was plainer; there was no doubt about it, it was coming nearer. I thought I recognized it; it sounded like Moon-ha′kee's bark.

Suddenly the dog burst out of the brush. It *was* Moon-ha′kee! He rushed up, wagging his tail and fawning.

Then I heard a voice, Little-Bear's voice, calling "*Yoo′hoo!*" I answered, "*O′ho,*" as the Indians do, and in a moment he appeared.

He had a sack or pocket slung from his shoulder, full of *ka-ha-ma′kun* made with tree sugar, and he had me eating this down on the brook bank in less time than it takes to tell it. He had forgotten to bring a wood bowl or cup or even a gourd, so I moistened the parched corn with water, a handful at a time, and ate it that way until I was satisfied.

Then he told me that Toad-Face had returned wearing the girl's clothes, which of course I knew, and that every boy and girl in town had seen him before he could get home, which news delighted me almost as much as my victory. Toad-Face had told such a confused story, however, to account for his costume that Little-Bear became worried when I did not return the next day and he came out with Moon-ha′kee to look for me. My friend had feared that Toad-Face might have done away with me. They had found the place of the fight on the river bank, and Moon-ha′kee had tracked me from there back to the village and then on my wanderings.

I was thankful then that Moon-ha'kee had been out digging moles or mice when I started out that day for wood and so had remained behind.

Little-Bear suggested that we go first to his house, where he thought clothes could be found for me. But he was afraid I would have to go back to Cross-Woman because I was really her property, and she could force me to wear skirts or go naked or could even kill me if she pleased. So I returned with him in great anxiety.

I hid in the bushes outside the village whilst he went home to get a robe to cover me, because a boy my age never appeared in public without at least a *sahk-koo-ta'kun*. I pulled the robe over my head to attract as little attention as possible and slipped into Little-Bear's house. Bowl-Woman, or Bowl-of-Beads, his mother, warmed some good stew for me, and while I was eating it, she got out a deerskin and made me a *sahk-koo-ta'kun*, then she found an old pair of Little-Bear's moccasins whole enough for me to wear.

Little-Bear's father, whom I have mentioned, came in just then. His name was *Pet-hak'a-luns*, or Thunder-Arrow: a thin man with a large nose and a projecting underlip, his breast all tattooed with zigzag blue lines. The hair on the right side of his head was cut short, but on the left side it hung long and loose, a style which was still followed by some Lenape men many years later.

We told him what had happened, and he seemed quite concerned. Telling us to stay where we were, he picked up a large sheaf of new arrows and left the cabin. We wondered what he was going to do with the arrows, which had cost him many days of hard work. He could not hunt much on account of an old battle wound, so he spent most of his time making bows and arrows to trade for meat and skins.

After a long delay he came back smiling, carrying my bowl and spoon, also my bed mat, my robes, and my sleeve, also Moon-ha'kee's things. He told us that everything was settled, that he had bought me from Cross-Woman and Beaver-House for the sheaf of arrows. Cross-Woman had wanted to keep me at first, but Toad-Face objected. He did not want me back in the house, as I was a dangerous and cruel creature with magical powers. Thus it happened that I became the servant of Bowl-Woman, the mother of my best friend. Her first act was to give me three beautifully tanned buckskins to make me a new pair of leggings and moccasins, and I spent the next day with awl and cutting board as Granny had taught me.

Bowl-Woman was a good housekeeper and could make many things well, but she never had any luck with clay pots, so this was the first work she asked of her new servant. Remembering Granny's lessons, I made her three cooking vessels of different sizes and then a *hoo-paw'kun*, or smoking pipe for Thunder-Arrow, who followed the peculiar custom of drinking in the smoke from the burning dried leaves of a plant called *kw'sha'tai*, now known in English as "tobacco." His old pipe, which he always carried with him in a deerskin bag slung from his neck, had a broken stem. The new pipe, which I decorated as much as possible like the old, with fine lines and dots pressed into the clay while still wet, pleased him very greatly.

There was no special trick or art in making the pipe, except that you mold the stem around a thick stem of grass and when the pipe is fired, this burns out, leaving a hole through which to draw the smoke. You heat a pipe through and fire it just as you do a pot, and if you have enough ground stone mixed with the clay 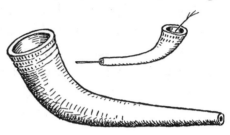 and if it is properly dried before you fire it, it will not crack. The Lenapes had a few pipes made of stone, some with long stems of wood, but the commonest kind was of clay like the one I made for Thunder-Arrow.

He let me draw a few puffs from his new pipe, but the smoke nearly choked me. I do not see how anyone could enjoy it; yet in recent years the smoking of pipes has become a fashion in England, learned from the Indians of Virginia, beginning at Jamestown, where the colonists first made pipes in Indian style.

One morning Thunder-Arrow told Little-Bear and me that he was going to teach us how to make a good bow and arrow, after we had discussed my luckless efforts and enjoyed a good laugh over the deer scratching himself with his left hind foot.

It seemed funny to us then, as we sat with full stomachs under Bowl-Woman's shed, but when it happened, I thought it anything but amusing.

Thunder-Arrow got the tools together for making a bow, and they were strange ones, not at all what I had expected. They were, first of all, two large, thick knife blades made of flint, but without handles. Then there were four wedges made of deer antler; some curious tools made of flint, called *lal-ha'kwo-kan*, or "scraper," flat on one side, round on the other, with a beveled edge all the way round; a sack of flint chips and a thick piece of deer-skin. As he collected these things, Thunder-Arrow talked, keeping such a straight face that nobody would know he was joking. I myself thought he was in earnest and believed all he said until I knew him better.

"*Hoh!* You are lucky, In-the-Forest, to have me to teach you how to make a bow and arrow. I have been making them for more than a hundred years. In truth, I made the first bow that was ever seen on this great island where we live. You might walk for months in any direction, except toward the Big Water, and everyone you met would tell you what a wonderful bow maker I am. I have heard that your people, the White-skins, are coming across the Big Water on purpose to have me teach them how to make bows. Now I believe it. Are you not the first one?

"First of all, there are two kinds of wood that are especially good for bows. One is *see-meen'shee*, hickory, and the other is *mee-ha'ka-nak*, ash; of the two, I like the first one the best, although the second is easier to work. The first also gives us the *see'meen* nuts we like so well."

Giving me the knives, wedges, and buckskin to carry, he led the way to the forest where he searched until he found a straight, young *see'meen* tree, fully three spans around and without any branches near the ground. He took some tobacco from his pouch and threw it at the foot of the tree, then he spoke to it as if the tree were a person.

"Tree, I am giving you tobacco. Give us some of your wood to make a bow. May the bow be strong and throw its arrows straight and true."

I expected to see him cut the tree down, and indeed he took one of the large flint knives and, grasping it with the buckskin so that his hand would not be cut, he began to saw into the tree about a foot from the bottom. He did not saw it all the way through, however, but stopped when he had cut a crosswise groove about an inch deep. Then he cut a like groove about five feet above the first, and then he made two lengthwise grooves about three fingers apart, connecting the two crosswise grooves. This required a long time, and Little-Bear and I took turns helping him. It was mid-afternoon when the grooves were finished to the depth of about one inch, outlining the form of a bowstave.

Now the wedges, *pahk-ha-kwo'a-kan*, came into play. He inserted one into the top groove and with a round stone for a hammer, *pah-kan-dee'kan*, drove it in so as to pry loose one end of the stave from the tree; then by driving in one wedge after the other, he split out the whole stave, leaving the tree standing. His last act was to thank the tree and give it more tobacco.

Taking the bowstave, we went back to the cabin and here he split off the edges until it was an inch and a half wide. I thought he was going right ahead to finish the bow; but no, he said that the stave must season for months before the bow could be made. He thrust it behind one of the poles that supported the shed roof, then took down another that he said had been cut the previous summer. Now he picked up a *lal-ha'kwo-kan*, or flint scraper, and drew it along the edge of the stave. A curly shaving was the result, like the shaving made by a plane, only smaller. Little-Bear and I took turns with him and by evening we had the stave fairly well shaped into a bow, flat on the back, where the bark had been, and rounded somewhat on the belly, tapering from about two fingers wide in the middle to a little more than one at the ends.

Next morning I had to pound corn for bread and then go out after wood, and when I came back, I found that

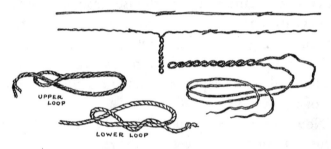

Thunder-Arrow had smoothed down the bow with flint flakes and bits of sandstone, had notched the ends for the string, sawing them into the wood with flint flakes, then had greased it well with bear's grease.

All that remained now was to make the string, which must be especially strong. Thunder-Arrow had me twist a two-strand sinew cord, rolling it on my thigh as I had made sinew thread and bark cord before, about ten yards long, twisting it very tight. Then we doubled it back and let it twist itself together and then tightened this twist; finally doubling it back a second time and twisting it. This made an eight-strand bowstring, *ha-kee-sa'pi*, that was very strong. So that it would not untwist, we wet it, then twisted it even more tightly and stretched it between two poles to dry.

The next day or two I had to chop weeds with a stone-bladed hoe in Bowl-Woman's garden and replant some beans that had failed to come up. Seeing me go out to the garden with a hoe over my shoulder, some boy was venturesome enough to shout "Miss In-the-Forest" after me, but when I turned to see who it was, he fled.

In the meantime Thunder-Arrow and Little-Bear went out and gathered some white ash sprouts as straight as they could find, a little thicker than arrow size and not quite a yard long. These they cut with a flint knife, first sawing a groove around each sprout, then breaking it off.

However, Thunder-Arrow would not use these green sprouts immediately, but tied them in a tight bundle and hung them from one of the roof poles to season. For us to make arrows for present use, he took down a bundle of seasoned sprouts and set us to scraping them down to the right size with flint scrapers and chips. We cut them off at the proper length, about thirty inches, by grooving the sprouts around and breaking them; then we filed in the nocks and the slots for the points with the edge of a flint chip. Straightening was a harder task; each sprout had crooked places which had to be heated over the fire and bent with the hands until straight.

Feathering came next. Thunder-Arrow had a bunch of hawk feathers saved for the purpose, and we split and cut these readily with fresh flint chips.

"Why don't you use goose feathers, as we do in my country?" I asked him. "Turkey feathers would be good, too."

8

"Huh! What a question!" he answered. "Geese and turkeys kill nothing bigger than frogs and bugs. Is  that all you wish your arrows to do? Hawks and eagles fly swift and strike hard. They kill real meat. That is why we use their feathers on our arrows!"

"*Wa-nee'shih*, many thanks," I said. "However, I am sure that the great hunter, Thunder-Arrow, does not need to borrow power from hawks and eagles. I know he could feather his arrows with grasshopper wings and still bring in the game."

"You know too much," Thunder-Arrow grinned.

We put three half feathers, evenly spaced, on each arrow, binding them on with fine filaments of wet sinew. In the arrow-making outfit was a *pe-sukw-pe-la-tay'kun*, a blob of dried glue, made from boiled-down sturgeon backbone, or deer hoofs, on a stick, and this we rubbed over the damp sinew bindings to make them hold. Little-Bear and I each made six arrows.

Sometimes in place of three half feathers the Lenapes used two whole feathers, but such arrows were for small game or for use as toys.

Now all that remained was to make the points, which I thought would take a long time, as flint, I knew, is a very hard stone. As a first step, Thunder-Arrow dug up a block of  flint he kept buried, with others, near one of the posts of the shed. Then I remembered that poor Granny had kept her flint buried, too, and my curiosity was aroused.

"Thunder-Arrow," I demanded. "Why do you keep your supply of flint buried?"

"*Ay-kay-sa'*, poor boy! You know too much, yet how little you know! Did you have no uncle to instruct you? We keep flint buried so that the sap will not dry up, for when that happens, it becomes much harder to chip. That is why flint you pick up on top of the ground is never so good as flint you dig from the earth."

Taking a tough, round stone for a hammer, he struck from the block a lot of flakes, an inch to an inch and a

half long. Picking these over, he selected one of the smoothest ones. Now he produced a little rod of deer antler set in a wooden handle, and holding the flake in a pad of deerskin in his left hand, he pressed the rod against the edge of the flint and gave a twisting push. At once a little scale flew off. Then he repeated the process swiftly, first on one edge, then on the other. In a few minutes he had made a beautiful little arrowhead in the form of a heart, with a stem to fasten it to the shaft. Arrowheads were called *mall-san-nuk'a*.

I took the little rod eagerly and tried to imitate Thunder-Arrow's method, but I pushed too hard in my excitement and broke several before I produced a perfect heart-shaped arrowhead; then I never stopped until I had made five more. Bowl-Woman asked me several times, so they say, to go and get her a bucket of water, but I never even heard her, and she had to go herself. Little-Bear, at the same time, was making arrowheads for himself, but his were little stemmed triangles.

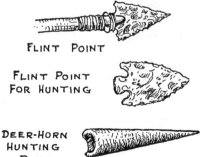

FLINT POINT

FLINT POINT
FOR HUNTING

DEER-HORN
HUNTING
POINT

POINT USED
FOR WAR

Then we proudly bound our arrowheads in the slots of the shafts with sinew shreds and glue, and our arrows were ready for use. The next thing was to make quivers, called *al-lun-sin'oo-tai*, out of two poorly dressed deerskins from Bowl-Woman's store, which were too stiff for moccasins or clothing. I strung my bow to test it, then unstrung it again. Little-Bear got out an old bow of his father's that we had used for practice, and Thunder-Arrow lent us each a flint knife. We were ready for the hunt, which, Little-Bear and I agreed, was to be the next day.

I was dreaming of hunting a bear armed only with a flint chip, when someone shook me awake; it was my friend. In the darkness of the cabin we found our bows and quivers, slung our knives around our necks, and set out as the eastern sky was just beginning to light up a little. Following well-known trails to the usual hunting grounds, we were far enough away from the village when daylight came to have some hopes of encountering deer.

We had not intended to take Moon-ha'kee, and he knew it, so he pretended to be asleep when we slipped past him. Then the rascal sneaked out after us and followed at a distance, never showing himself until we were too far from home to send him back.

We were stepping lightly along the edge of a little meadow when we saw our first deer. He spied us at the same time, wheeled and made off chased by the over-zealous Moon-ha'kee. Little-Bear and I both shot but we were so excited that the arrows went wild. It took some time to scold Moon-ha'kee and to find the arrows; mine, alas, had hit a stone and the point was broken.

Now it was getting quite late in the morning and I was becoming hungry, but Little-Bear did not want to go back empty-handed.

After walking endlessly, it seemed, we found a little valley with steep rocks on both sides and traces where deer had been feeding, although none was in sight. We made a plan then: I was to hide myself near the opening of this valley, whilst Little-Bear with Moon-ha'kee was to go up over the hill and get down into the valley farther on. He was then to come toward me, making all the noise he could so as to drive the deer ahead of him toward my hiding place.

I had waited quite a while when a slight noise in the bushes made me raise my bow. An instant later a fat young buck appeared on the trail. I let fly and hit him in the side, just back of the left shoulder. He ran, with my arrow sticking in him, a few paces and then fell. I rushed up and cut his throat with my flint knife, shouting for Little-Bear. I heard him answer, and while I was waiting,

I pulled out my arrow.   Noticing that the head was missing, I dropped the shaft in my quiver.

At that moment who should appear but Toad-Face.

"What are you doing with my deer?" he demanded.

"It's not your deer, it's my deer!" I answered hotly. "I just shot it."

"You shot it?   You did not; I shot it myself!"

"Where's your arrow then?" I asked.

"It fell out when the deer ran.   Where's yours?"

"I just pulled it out and put it in my quiver."

"A likely story," growled Toad-Face, "*k'nees'gahk-gay-loon'en!*"

He was calling me a nasty liar.

I started for him with clinched fists; he backed off, quickly nocking an arrow on the string, his eyes wild.

The fool was going to shoot me.   I nocked an arrow myself, and I do not know what might have happened if someone had not shouted, "Stop!"

It was Little-Bear.   Seeing himself outnumbered, Toad-Face disappeared.

We carried the deer in to the village as fast as we could without stopping to take out the insides as was the custom, for we feared Toad-Face would bring help and seize it.

Hardly did we get it under the shed and had called Bowl-Woman and Thunder-Arrow out to admire it, when Toad-Face appeared again, this time with his stepfather and the village chief.

"This boy says that In-the-Forest and your son took his deer away from him," said the Chief to Thunder-Arrow.

"I have come over to question the boys and to find out what really happened."

We told our story as straight as we could, then the Chief asked me:

"Where did your arrow strike?"

"*Yun!*" I replied, "right here!"

I showed him the wound; then he asked Toad-Face, who pointed out the same place, over the heart. The Chief hesitated a minute, then cut open the deer with his flint knife. The sack where the heart hangs was full of blood. He cut loose the heart and pulled it out; he washed the blood off it, disclosing a wound. Then he cut the heart open and extracted my arrowhead.

"Let me see your arrows!"

I pulled them out; the point of one was missing, its shaft bloody. The others all had heart-shaped points like the one he had just found, except that one was broken.

"Now, Toad-Face, let us see your arrows!"

He did not respond; he was sneaking away.

"*Ay-kay-sa'!* Shame on you! Come here and show your arrows!" commanded the Chief sternly.

Sullenly Toad-Face slunk up and pulled out his sheaf of arrows. Every one of them had a cone-shaped point made from deer horn, while my points were all of flint and heart shape.

"The deer belongs to In-the-Forest and Little-Bear," decided the Chief.

As they walked off, I heard Beaver-House scolding Toad-Face.

The Chief put his hand on my shoulder. "That was a good shot, my son," he said. "Some day you will be a great hunter.   Toad-Face had no right to be hunting in that district, anyhow.''

"You will not have to work so hard making arrows," said Bowl-Woman to Thunder-Arrow.   "From now on our boys will keep us supplied with meat and skins."

That was all very well, but we heard later that Toad-Face was bragging that he would get even with us for "taking his deer."

Thunder-Arrow turned to me.

"Do you know," he asked, "what a boy is supposed to do with his first deer?"

"Certainly.   He is supposed to take it home to his family and then help them eat it."

"*Ma-ta-ka'*.   Not at all.   If it is a buck, he must give it to some old man; if a doe, to some old woman."

"*Ee-kee'!*   Must we give our deer away, truly?"

"It is the custom.   Pick out some old man you like and tell him to come after it."

The only old man I knew at all well was the doctor, Roaring-Wings, who had tried to save poor Granny's life, so I sadly went with Little-Bear to his cabin.

"We give you a deer," I told him.

"Where is it?" he asked calmly.

"Over at our house."

"There? It should have been left where you killed it!"

We explained why it had been brought in, and Roaring-Wings listened attentively, puffing on his short pipe.

"I'll go and get it," he said at last.   "You wait for me here outside the cabin.   When I go in, you follow."

Soon came the old man, staggering under the weight of the deer on his back.   Just outside the door of his cabin he turned toward the east and gave a prolonged cry, "*Hooooo.*" Then he went in and threw the deer down in front of his wife, and she butchered it while we stood by.

She cut a strip of meat and broiled it, then handed it to the old man, who had seated himself very solemnly upon a mat, face to the east. He began to eat, and every few mouthfuls he would utter again the strange cry.

Finally he finished eating and began to talk to us.

"My sons," he said. "You have given me your first deer, and I have prayed in your behalf to *Kee-shay-la-muh'ka-ong*, the Creator. May you always be successful in hunting and may you live until your hair is as gray as mine. Kill what you need but never waste the gifts of the Creator. Always respect the aged and listen to their counsel. They have seen many winters and they are wise. You have given me your first deer, and Roaring-Wings will not forget. Now I have spoken."

We thanked him and quietly withdrew. We both were glad, somehow, that we had given our first deer to Roaring-Wings.

VI. Solid-Face and the New Baby

THE platform at the back of Bowl-Woman's cabin was a two-story affair; that is, the posts which carried the corners of the bunk where she and Thunder-Arrow slept continued upward and supported another platform or bunk three or four feet above. Nobody slept up there, however; the space was used only for storage.

Shortly after I joined the household, I climbed to this platform hunting for something or other, and there I saw a strange-looking mat bundle containing some kind of skins. Curiosity has always been one of my faults, so I opened the package. It held a costume made of bear skins with the hair on, and in the middle was a big, wooden mask with copper eyes, painted half red and half black, lying face downward in the package. With the mask was a hollow turtle shell with a handle, containing pebbles or something that rattled.

I recognized the mask as the face of the frightful creature which had chased me all over the village at the time of the *Gam'wing* the previous fall, and now I understood that experience a little better. However, I tied up the bundle again and said nothing to anyone.

108

It was about a month later, when one evening Thunder-Arrow said to me:

"*Hoh*, In-the-Forest! Do you remember that strange, hairy person with a big face who came around during the *Gam'wing?*"

"*Ay'ko-han'!* I should remember him!" I replied. "He nearly scared me to death!"

"Well," continued Thunder-Arrow, "he is going to visit us again soon, and Bowl-Woman and I are going to give a feast for him!"

"You mean," I said, "that someone is going to wear that wooden face in the package on the upper platform!"

Thunder-Arrow looked at me for a moment; then he spoke:

"*Huh!* Granny made a mistake when she named you 'In-the-Forest,' she should have called you 'Big-Eye'!"

"*Kwoch?* Why?"

"Because you see everything!" he chuckled.

"Cross-Woman told me all about her *Ow'tas* doll," I said. "I wish you would tell me about this mask, especially if you expect me to do a lot of cooking in honor of it! And please don't joke. I want to hear the real story."

Thunder-Arrow filled his pipe, the one I had made for him, and lighted it with a little hot coal which he raked out of the fire. After puffing for a while, he began:

"*Ku-les'ta!* Listen! One time long ago there were three boys about your age who were not treated very well; in fact, their parents did not seem to care whether they lived or died. They were out in the forest one day thinking about their troubles when they saw a strange-looking, hairy person with a big face painted half black and half red. This person said: 'I am *Mee-sing-haw-lee'kun;* I have taken pity on you and I will give you strength so that nothing can ever hurt you again. Come with me and I shall show you my country!'

"He took one boy up in the air to the place where he came from; it was a great range of mountains up in the sky reaching from north to south. While he was showing the boy his country, he promised he should become stout and strong and should gain the power to get anything he wished. Then he brought the boy back to the earth again.

"Afterwards when the boy grew up and went hunting, he used to see *Mee-sing-haw-lee'kun* riding on a buck, herding the deer together and giving his peculiar call '*Ho-ho-ho.*'

"In this way it happened that there were three men in the tribe who knew that there is a *Mee-sing-haw-lee'kun,* because they had seen him with their own eyes.

"Now the Lenape tribe had always used a Big-House, called *King'wee-ka-on,* to worship in such as we have now, but in those days it had no faces carved upon the posts inside. In this house they used to sing about their dreams and visions; but some time after the three boys had talked with *Mee-sing-haw-lee'kun* the people gave up their worship and for ten years had none."

I interrupted to ask Thunder-Arrow what the word *Mee-sing-haw-lee'kun* meant, and he replied that as nearly as he could explain it, the interpretation would be "Living Solid-Face." Then he went on:

"A great earthquake came then which lasted twelve months and gave much trouble to the Lenapes. In one of their towns a chief had a large bark house, and here the people met to worship, hoping to stop the earthquake, whilst they were building a new Big-House. When this was finished, they worshiped there, too, and sang and prayed all winter for relief.

"After spring came, they were holding a meeting one night when they heard something making a noise, *Ho-ho-ho*, out east of the Big-House. The Chief called for someone to go to see what it was. The three men recognized the call of *Mee-sing-haw-lee'kun* and offered to go because they knew who was making the noise and could find out what he wanted.

"So they went out and found *Mee-sing-haw-lee'kun* and asked him.

" 'Go back and tell the others to stop holding meetings and to attend to their crops,' he answered. 'Do not meet again until fall, when I shall come and live with you and help in the Big-House. You must carve a mask of wood to look like my face, painted half black and half red, as mine is, and I shall put my power in it, so it will do as you ask. When the man who takes my part puts the mask on, I shall be there, and in that way I shall live among you. The man must carry a turtle-shell rattle, a bag, and a staff just as I do now.'

"Then *Mee-sing-haw-lee'kun* told them to carve twelve faces on the posts of the Big-House and faces on the drumsticks to be used in the ceremony. Then he said:

" 'You must also give me hominy every year in the spring. I take care of the deer and other game animals; that is what I am for. Wherever you build a Big-House, I shall keep the deer close by so that you can get them.'

" 'Never give up the Big-House. If you do, there will be another earthquake or something just as bad.'

"The earthquake stopped, and the Lenapes have kept the Big-House and the mask ever since. The mask is left in charge of some family who will take good care of it and burn tobacco for it from time to time. At present, my family is the one so honored. That is why Bowl-Woman and I, also Little-Bear and you, In-the-Forest, are going to give a feast two days from now.

"We are glad that spring has come; we are glad that *Mee-sing-haw-lee'kun* is still with us, so we give a feast and a dance to make him happy too. In some villages the *Mee-sing'* has its dance in the fall.

"And now if you ask me to tell you any more this evening, I shall change your name to 'Big-Ear.' "

Next morning Thunder-Arrow found an experienced man to represent *Mee-sing-haw-lee'kun* and paid him a string of white shell beads in advance for his work. He was the same one who had taken the part at the *Gam'wing*, and he could not help grinning when he came after the costume and recognized me. I grinned back and told him that if he chased me again, I'd get even.

The following day he put on the outfit and went around to all the houses to let the people know that the time had come for another *Mee-sing-kin'te-ka*. He came to our house and went through his performance just as if we did not know all about it; he pointed out the direction of the dance ground, danced a few steps calling "*Ho-ho-ho*," and shaking his rattle, which excited Moon-ha'kee so that he nearly barked his head off. Then *Mee-sing'* pointed to his mouth, meaning that there would be a feast. Thunder-Arrow wanted me to give him some tobacco to put into his sack, but *Mee-sing'* looked so terrible that I could not bear to go near him, so Thunder-Arrow gave the tobacco to him, himself. The creature took it and smelled of it, then turned around and kicked back at him by way of thanks and went bounding out of the house with Moon-ha'kee barking at his heels.

It is said that they frightened disobedient children by telling them, "Be good or Mee-sing' will carry you off in a bag full of snakes!" I was frightened myself, although I knew perfectly well he was nothing but a man dressed up. However he really seemed to be possessed of some sort of power when wearing the mask; he never went around anything that came in his path; he simply jumped over it. They claimed that he even had power to find lost articles when wearing the mask.

Just as I expected, the coming feast made plenty of work for Bowl-Woman and for me; we did little except pound hard blue and white corn for two days; then we carried it out to the dance ground and cooked four big pots full of *sa'pan* with plenty of bear's grease, as well as a deer that had been provided.

Differing from the Doll Dance, the performance did not begin until the sun had set and a big fire lighted up the dark forest. Suddenly the *Mee-sing'* appeared, rattling and crying "*Ho-ho-ho*," and the people fell back. The speaker stood up and told the story which Thunder-Arrow had related to me and then, addressing himself to the moon-faced monster, said:

"O *Mee-sing'*, take care of us while we are dancing so that everything goes smoothly."

Then the two singers struck on the dry hide rolled and stuffed with grass that served as a drum, and the people danced in a circle around the fire. The *Mee-sing'* joined the group, but danced outside the circle. Later on he danced alone twelve different times, cutting up many queer capers, a weird and curious sight; and when he finished, the dawn was breaking. I was terribly sleepy and could hardly rouse myself to take the big wooden ladle and serve the hominy into the bowls that the people brought. Bowl-Woman was not to be seen.

Suddenly a loud *ho-ho-ho* right in front of me startled me wide awake and I looked up right into the huge red-and-black face of the monster. For a moment I thought I should run, but the creature held out a big wooden bowl. *Mee-sing'* had come to be fed. At last the great pots were empty, and the people sat down to eat. I had forgotten to save any hominy for myself, but I managed to scrape a little from the pots.

As I gathered our ladles and stirring paddles into the pack baskets, I heard the speaker say:

"Now we have eaten with our *Mee-sing'*. Next spring we shall enjoy this dance again." It was broad daylight now.

I was wondering how I should carry the four big pots which were borrowed, in addition to the two baskets and other things, when White-Deer appeared and told me that Bowl-Woman had not felt well and had gone home about midnight, and that she, White-Deer, would help me carry the things home. She packed two pots in each basket, one inside the other, with wisps of grass between to prevent breaking, then all the small articles went into the inside pots, wrapped in grass. In this way each had a loaded pack basket, and the weight was divided.

About halfway back to the camp we sat down to rest on a mossy bank and unslung our baskets so that we could talk in comfort.

"They tell me," began White-Deer, "that you can make good bows and arrows, that you shoot very well, and that you killed a fine deer not long ago. You are a good fighter too; the whole village knows you must have whipped Toad-Face the day you ran away, and he is a larger and stronger boy. Why do you keep on doing this kind of work?"

"Because I am asked to do it," I replied. "I would not refuse if I could, because Bowl-Woman and Thunder-Arrow have been so good to me, and Little-Bear is my best friend. I could not refuse anyhow, because I am a captive, and Thunder-Arrow bought me from Cross-Woman. I must do as my masters bid me."

White-Deer sighed and looked at the ground.

"I hope things will be different, some day," she said. "Of course you are only a boy, and our boys often help the women and girls with their work, boys who are not captives, either. But after they get their blessings, then everything is changed."

9

"What do you mean by 'blessings'?"

"It would not be right for me to tell you," she replied. "You must find out from Thunder-Arrow. May I ask you something?"

"*Kwoch at'ta*, why not?"

She looked at the ground again and stirred the grass with the toe of her moccasin.

"Do you know how to play the *ah-pee'kawn?*"

"You mean that wooden tube with holes on which they play music?"

"Yes!"

"In my language they call them 'flutes' or 'flageolets.' I was learning to play the flageolet when I left my home, but I do not know how to play this kind."

"It would be nice for you to learn," murmured White-Deer.

"Why?"

She looked up at me mischievously from beneath her long lashes. "I think we had better go now," she said, evading my question. "Somebody might see us sitting here together and then he would tease us."

We picked up our baskets again and started out, but she walked along so fast that I could hardly keep up, and when I tried to get her to answer why I should learn to play the *ah-pee'kawn*, she giggled and hurried all the faster.

Arriving at the house, she set down her basket under the shed and went in to talk with Bowl-Woman, who was still in bed, and when my back was turned, she slipped out and ran home.

I took the pots and the other things down to the river and cleaned them thoroughly with gritty rushes and sand, then setting them up on our shelf to dry, I walked over to talk with Little-Bear and Thunder-Arrow, who were lying in the shade of a tree.

I blurted out what was uppermost in my mind:

"White-Deer wants me to learn to play the *ah-pee'-kawn*. Why should she——?"

I got no further; both of them burst out laughing. Finally Thunder-Arrow addressed me.

"Do you know what the *ah-pee'kawn* is used for? No? Well, I shall tell you. It is used by young men to play pretty music for their sweethearts outside the house after dark. When the girl hears the right call, she comes out and they talk together. If White-Deer has asked you to learn to play, it looks bad for Little-Bear. He likes White-Deer, too!"

I did not know what to say, but I felt my ears getting hot. Little-Bear got up hastily and disappeared into the house. After a while he came out grinning sheepishly, with an *ah-pee'kawn* in his hand.

"I have one of the things, but I can't play it," he mumbled. "See what you can do."

I tried it, and after a while I managed to play two or three little English tunes after a fashion. I thought they sounded pretty good, but Little-Bear stuck his fingers in his ears, and Thunder-Arrow made a sour face, whilst Moon-ha'kee howled dismally.

"*A-kee'!* That sounds terrible. Let me take it," Thunder-Arrow demanded.

He took up the instrument and played a curious, quavering tune, with a sort of hum running through it, something like the drone of a bagpipe. I had never heard anything like it before, but it sounded good. He played it over five or six times.

Just then we heard a cough and, looking up, saw Bowl-Woman at the cabin door.

"I thought I heard my young man playing our call, so I came out," she said with a smile, as she joined us under the tree.

I took the *ah-pee'kawn* and struggled with it for a while; at last I managed to play something resembling the tune, whereupon Thunder-Arrow seized the instrument and played it over correctly. Then I took it again. Before we had finished, I could play the tune as well as he. Both my teacher and Bowl-Woman were delighted, and Moon-ha'kee did not howl, but Little-Bear looked glum.

"I worked three whole days trying to learn how to play that thing," he grumbled, "but it was no use. It still sounded like a crow squawking. Now you learn it in no time at all!"

It was true; I had really learned to play, and every time I heard a new call I added that to my stock. The *ah-pee'kawn* was the only true musical instrument which the Lenape tribe knew. Their other instruments, drums and rattles, were only for keeping time to their singing.

They knew hundreds of songs, for all sorts of purposes, but most of them belonged to dances and ceremonies. Almost every night you could hear several men drumming and singing for practice somewhere in the village, and sometimes a woman singing even when there were no ceremonies going on.

I even learned how to make an *ah-pee'kawn*. You cut a straight stick from a young *pop-ho'kus*, red cedar tree, a stick about three spans long and three fingers thick.

The Indians, before cutting the tree, always threw a little tobacco at the roots and told it that its wood was to be used to make sweet music. They claimed that a tree is a living thing like ourselves and should have consideration.

You remove the bark from the stick and then carefully split it from end to end; then you hollow out the middle

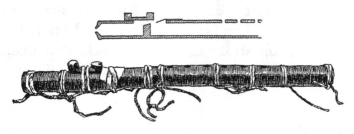

of both halves so that when you put them back together, they will make a tube with an opening in the end you blow in, a partition, a place for a reed, and a large opening the rest of the way. Then you make the finger holes with a drill made of flint. I copied Little-Bear's *ah-pee'kawn* so as to get these holes in just the right places, because if the finger holes are wrong, you can't play. You stick the tube together with pine pitch or deer-hoof glue, and then you wrap it neatly with thin deerskin thongs, placed about three fingers apart. The reed is made of a thin piece of copper or the quill of a large feather boiled and split and flattened out. The illustration shows just how it is put together.

The tools I used were a wedge made of deer antler, a flint knife, some flint flakes, and, to hollow out the inside, a little chisel made of a beaver tooth set in a wooden handle.

Of course I was kept busy with many other things whilst I was making my *ah-pee'kawn* and learning the calls. Bowl-Woman was not very well, so I did most of the garden work, which was mainly pulling weeds and hoeing up the ground around the plants, and all of the wood gathering and corn pounding.

With the coming of warm weather came the swimming season, and never a day passed that Little-Bear, Moon-ha'kee, and I did not enjoy the water. I mastered the Indian overhand stroke and found it much faster than the English breast stroke or even the side stroke. The Indian boys were very skilful in swimming under water, being able to sink without a splash and rise in some unexpected place without a sound. Under Little-Bear's instructions I practiced this until I, too, was proficient.

One day on entering the water I saw Toad-Face down at the other end of the pool ducking a small boy, his favorite sport. The child was screaming for mercy. I sank without a sound and swam under water until I saw Toad-Face's legs. I grabbed his ankles and dragged him under; he must have thought a water monster had him! When he rose, I ducked him again; then before he had time to recognize me, I slipped under, swam to the other end, and rose behind a bush where I could land unobserved. I never saw him ducking small boys again.

Bowl-Woman's sister, Duck-Woman, or *Kwee-kwin'-gum-hkway*, was a great basket maker and bag weaver, and sometimes she called upon me to help her when I was not otherwise busy. One day we cut down a straight young

pahk-gam'mak, black ash tree, about two spans around.
First she threw tobacco at the roots, explaining to the tree
that she was taking its life that needed baskets might be
made, for it was considered wrong to kill any living thing,
even a tree, wantonly.   Then I plastered wet mud on the
trunk, leaving about ten inches bare just above the roots.
Here I stripped off the bark with a flint knife and built a
small fire encircling the tree.   Between burning and
chopping out the charred portion with a stone ax, it soon
came down.   We cut off a piece about six feet long and
peeled it.

After I had fetched home the log for her, Duck-Woman
handed me a wooden club with a thick head and a long
handle.

"Give it a good beating all over!" she said.

I could not imagine why, but she would not explain.

"*Al-la'pee!*   Do as I tell you, and you'll see!"

So I beat the log until I was tired and she was satisfied.

"*Tay'pee;* that's enough; look at this."   With a
small antler wedge she loosened a splint of wood at one
end of the log and pulled upon it.   To my astonishment it
peeled away from the log all the way to the other end;
the pounding had caused the layers composing the wood
to separate.

This wide splint she split into several narrow ones of
equal width, trimmed and scraped them with a knife
made of shell ground to a keen edge, which worked very
well; but I have seen this work done with a thin flint
flake or a beaver-tooth chisel.   Once the material was
prepared, she wove her baskets in about the same manner
as an English basket maker handles his willows, taking

care to keep the splints ever wet as she worked. I made several baskets after watching her, which Bowl-Woman said were not bad at all.

Baskets for storing clothing and valuables were made square or oblong, with covers, out of very wide splints, and these were the only ones I ever saw decorated with color. Duck-Woman folded a bit of thick buckskin so that the edge formed a figure like a flower; this she dipped in red *pa'kon*, dye, and used it as a stamp on the baskets.

Duck-Woman sometimes made very fine open-work baskets from the split roots of a kind of evergreen tree, the splints running in four directions instead of the usual two; but the weave was so difficult I never mastered it.

As for bags: the ordinary coarse kind she made of strips of basswood inner bark, boiled with a little ashes to soften it. These strips were hung across a suspended horizontal stick and woven together with a pair of bark strings which she twisted together one half turn between each strip of bark, as shown in the illustration. When completed, the edge of the bag was finished by braiding together the ends of these bark strips—the hardest part of the task. Of course these bags were woven with the mouth down.

Such common bags I could weave almost as well as Duck-Woman; but her fine bags, made of Indian hemp cords, dyed black, yellow, and red, were another matter. These, too, she wove upside down, but the up-and-down strands were cords instead of bark strips, and the crosswise strands, although run in pairs, as in the common bags, were pressed close together so as to make a fabric like

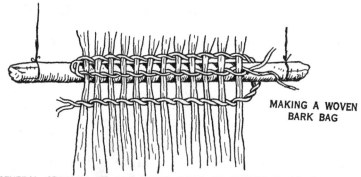

MAKING A WOVEN
BARK BAG

SEVERAL STRANDS OF THE INNER BARK OF BASSWOOD OR CEDAR ARE
DRAPED OVER A SUSPENDED STICK TO FORM THE BOTTOM OF THE BAG.
NOW TWO THIN STRANDS OF CORD MADE OF BARK OR OTHER MATERIAL
ARE TWISTED ONCE AROUND EACH STRAND OF THE BASSWOOD BARK, THEN
AT THE END TURNED AND THE WEAVING REVERSED. WHEN THE END IS
REACHED, THE WEAVING IS CONTINUED UNDER THE STICK ROUND AND ROUND
UNTIL THE BAG IS DEEP ENOUGH.

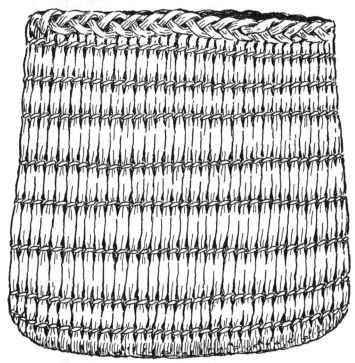

THIS SHOWS A FINISHED BAG. THE LOOSE ENDS AT THE MOUTH OF THE
BAG ARE BRAIDED TOGETHER IN MUCH THE SAME WAY AS CORNHUSKS
ARE BRAIDED INTO A LONG ROPE FOR CORNHUSK MAT MAKING.

MAKING A BARK BAG

coarse canvas. This much I could do myself, but the beautiful colored patterns Duck-Woman knew so well how to weave in were beyond me. She even wove herself a skirt with the same sort of patterns from Indian hemp, or *hal'lah-pees*, which she showed me with great pride.

As I have related, I learned how to make ordinary threads and cords by rolling them on my thigh; that is, short lengths, whilst living with poor Granny; but it took an expert like Duck-Woman to make great balls of twine without a break. Holding the ends with her left hand, she could roll two strands of fiber at the same time on her thigh with her right hand, the forward motion twisting them separately, the backward motion combining the two into one strong cord. She kept adding more fiber on the left and winding the finished cord in a ball on the right. It looked almost magical.

During the summer Little-Bear and I went hunting every once in a while and usually brought in a deer or at least a rabbit or two. The fresh venison would not keep very well, so we cut it in thin strips and hung it on a rack to dry, with a smoky fire underneath to keep away the flies and help to cure it. We were careful not to waste any meat or food of any kind. As Thunder-Arrow expressed it, the Creator intended man to use these things, but not to destroy them without reason.

Another summer duty and pleasure was berry gathering. There were two main kinds in our part of the country, one black and one red, called *muh-win'gwes* and *ay-ko'kwa-lis*, both of which I enjoyed, especially the latter. My favorite of all was a small, black, round berry called *meehn*, which could be found only in certain places.

This had no thorns, which made it easier to gather, and it was delicious mixed in bread.

Berrying was one of the few occupations that all boys shared with the girls and women, and on berry-gathering trips I became acquainted with many girls who I would never have met otherwise, but I still liked White-Deer best and picked berries with her whenever I could. I

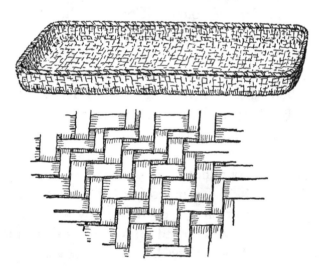

noticed that other boys liked to pick with her, too, but I never stepped aside for any of them except for Little-Bear. When I saw he wanted to talk with White-Deer, I wandered off elsewhere.

We carried our berries in small pack baskets made for the purpose. Large baskets would not do at all, as the weight of the berries above crush the bottom ones. We ate some of the berries while picking and some after we reached home, but most of them were dried in large, flat baskets made of wide splints, set up on the roofs of the sheds in the sun. They were good mixed into bread in the winter time or simply boiled up and eaten hot or cold.

One night when Little-Bear and I returned from a hunt, Bowl-Woman was not to be seen, and Thunder-Arrow was looking very serious.

"You will have to do the cooking for a while, In-the-Forest," he said.

"N'*wing'kee*, of course, if you wish," I answered. "But where is Bowl-Woman?"

"In the little house."

Behind every cabin is a smaller one, sometimes very tiny, where the women of the family retire when they wish to be alone, and I had started to go there to ask her what I should cook next morning, when Thunder-Arrow stopped me.

"Don't go out there!" he commanded.

"*Kwoch at'ta?* I want to ask her what to cook."

"Don't disturb her; you will know why soon."

Thunder-Arrow climbed up to the platform above his bed where the *Mee-sing'* mask and costume were stored and rummaged around for a while. "I know we still have Little-Bear's *am-bee'son*," he said. "Oh, here it is!"

He clambered down with a little board between two and three feet long and about ten inches wide. Near one end was fastened a thin, flat, wooden piece bent in the form of an arch and there were loops of deerskin thong running down both edges of the main board. Thunder-Arrow pulled out all the old strings and put in new ones. "This is ready," he said. "All we lack now is some cedar bark and a name."

"A name for what?" I demanded.

"For a stranger who is coming to stay with us."

He would say no more, and Little-Bear was equally silent.

As I was getting together the cooking utensils for morning, puzzled as to the meaning of all this mystery, two women came into the house, one, Duck-Woman, the sister of Bowl-Woman, bearing a large bundle done up in white-tanned fine deerskin.

"Has he come yet?" the older woman asked. "I hope we are in good time."

"You are in time," Thunder-Arrow answered. "I was just saying that all we lacked was the cedar bark and the name, and this boy did not know what I meant!"

"Here is the bark," said Duck-Woman, laying the package down, "and my aunt, here, has the name."

"I hope so," Thunder-Arrow answered. "Let us hear it."

"Last night I dreamed that a great canoe with white wings came into the river," said the aunt, "and someone said over and over, '*Pay-yay'week! Pay-yay'week!*' I think that would be a good name."

I knew that the word meant, "It-is-approaching."

"That must be the name," said Thunder-Arrow. "Maybe it will bring good luck."

I said nothing, but in my heart I thought the old woman must have seen an English ship either in reality or in a vision, and that such a ship would bring anything but good luck to the poor Lenapes, being full of strong drink, firearms, and land-greedy men.

Thunder-Arrow let the two relatives go out to talk with Bowl-Woman, and they took the package with them.

He and Little-Bear seemed restless, unwilling to go to bed. I sat up for a while, waiting for the "stranger"; then I curled up on my mat.

I was awakened in the morning by a peculiar wailing; half asleep I looked around; but Thunder-Arrow and Little-Bear were gone. Now fully awake I recognized it.

The noise was a baby crying, and it came from the little cabin in the rear. I picked up the board that Thunder-Arrow had been fixing, and now I saw that it was a Lenape cradle. I had not recognized it without its bedding and ornaments, and the word *am-bee'son* had been a new one to me.

Not knowing what else, if anything, was expected of me, I set about to get breakfast. The fire was barely lighted when a strange old woman came to the door with a wooden bowl in her hand.

"You are Bowl-Woman's servant? I am her mother, and you will be pleased to hear that the baby is a boy, and everything is all right. She wants you to cook a little *ka-ha-ma'kun* for her this morning and take it to her in this bowl. And please give me some old robe of Thunder-Arrow's. A buckskin light robe would be best; fur is too hot."

I got her an old light robe, and off she went. Fortunately I had some *ka-ha-ma'kun* in a sack, in powder form, so I did not have to parch and pound corn. I simply mixed it with hot water, and carried a bowl of it out. Thunder-Arrow and Little-Bear were squatting beside the little house, and the old lady came out to get the food. I went back and cooked breakfast, and Bowl-Woman's mother came in with the others to eat it.

Later on she let me look at the baby; its skin was quite light and its hair reddish brown.

"Many of our children are born that way," she said, "but skin and hair soon turn dark and handsome. It would be terrible if they stayed pale and sick-looking."

I noticed that the child was wrapped in Thunder-Arrow's old robe.

"Why do you wrap the baby in that dirty, big, old mantle? Why not a small, clean, fresh one?"

"*Say'hay!*" she whispered, putting a finger to her lips. "It's to fool the ghosts. You see new babies do not have a strong foothold in this world and it is easy for wandering ghosts to coax their little spirits away. We wrap the baby in a grown person's robe by way of disguise so that the ghosts will not see he is a newborn."

Then she showed me that thin strips of cornhusk had been tied around the little wrists.

"They are to fool the ghosts, too; to make them think that the child is bound to this earth. When we put the baby on his *am-bee'son*, we will give him a little pair of moccasins with a tiny hole cut in the sole of each. Then he can say when the ghosts call and beckon, 'See, I have holes in my shoes, I cannot travel.' "

"What was in the buckskin bundle Bowl-Woman's sister took to her last night?"

"Oh, that was fine, shredded cedar bark to keep the baby clean. We will make a soft pad of it, too, for him to lie on when he uses his *am-bee'son*."

Even Moon-ha'kee was allowed to inspect the baby. He sniffed the new arrival gingerly, wagging his approval.

After breakfast the old lady took charge of the household for twelve or fifteen days. When Bowl-Woman returned, the first thing she asked me to do was to get wood. I was busy breaking up sticks a long way from the village and thinking, I must admit, about White-Deer, when the ax glanced from a tough piece of wood and struck a stone. The ax head broke square in two at the groove. I knew it was the only ax that Bowl-Woman had and I felt very badly about it, so badly that I dreaded to go home.

However, I did return and I did confess what I had done, and strange to say one thing led to another until from the breaking of the ax came one of the most enjoyable adventures I ever had among the Lenape Indians.

VII. Axes and Fish

I BACKED up to the woodpile and let go the strings of my pack strap; when the sticks had fallen clear, I hung up the strap under the shed and entered the cabin. Bowl-Woman was sitting on her platform, the baby in her arms.

"*Ee-kee'! Nee-mahk-ta-lo-ka'-kan!*" I told her. "Alas, I am a bad servant. I have broken your ax." I showed her the pieces.

"*A-la'kwee!* What a pity!" she replied. "It was the only one I possessed."

"I wish I could pay you for it," I continued. "But truly, I am *das-hoo'kee*, miserably poor."

Thunder-Arrow, who was scraping arrow shafts on one of the side benches, chuckled.

"Your language is improving," he said. "However, Bowl-Woman would not want your possessions. Your bowl and spoon are old and probably smell sour, and your bedding is full of fleas. Why don't you find a good piece of stone and make her a new ax?"

"*N'wing'kee!* I'd like to. Only I don't know how."

"I wish I knew how myself," said Little-Bear, who had come in while we were talking.

"I'll teach you both," Thunder-Arrow proposed with a grin. "Every man should know how to make axes. The knowledge will very likely keep him out of trouble some day. Just suppose, In-the-Forest, that you should get married and should break your wife's ax! Think of the fix you'd be in if I had not taught you how to make her a new one!"

"I wish you'd teach me how to make pottery, if you're so smart," put in Bowl-Woman. "As it is, I have to depend on this boy here to make pots for me."

"I could do it," boasted her husband. "I made the first pot that was ever seen on this great island. If you pay me enough, I'll teach you. The price, however, will be high!"

"You can out-talk everybody," grumbled Bowl-Woman. "That much I believe!"

Thunder-Arrow, with a grimace, led us out of the house and set us cracking pebbles on the river bank, using special round stones which he kept in a sack, as hammers.

"To be good for axes," he said, "the stone must not only be hard but tough as well. Flint will not answer, although it is hard. Why? It splinters too easily."

He reached down and picked up a pebble.

"Look at this fine-grained green stone; it is both hard and tough and would make a fine ax if it were large enough. We have another kind on this river that is almost as good; it is gray in color, but spotted. Besides, there are several other kinds that will answer the purpose, but are not so good.

"Keep on cracking stones until you find one that defies you; then bring it to me. The right size will be about a span and a half long, four fingers wide, and two or three fingers thick.''

After breaking some hundreds, or so it seemed, my friend found a gray stone of the right size that wouldn't crack, and I one of the fine-grained green ones. We bore them home in triumph, and Thunder-Arrow set us to work at once.

"Yours, In-the-Forest," he said, "will be *ohk'way-wee tay-ma'hee-kan*, or a woman's ax. It will have a groove

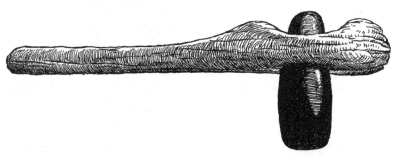

around it to hold the handle and a cutting edge. Little-Bear will make a man's ax, *lay'na-wee tay-ma'hee-kan*. This will have a cutting edge on one end and taper to a point on the other, the point fitting into a hole in the handle.''

Thunder-Arrow showed us how to strike the selected pebbles with the hammerstones, which were themselves very hard and tough, so as to crumble off a little stone with each blow and gradually batter the ax head into form. We took our work out on the river bank so that the noise would not wake the baby and we pounded away until we were tired, then carried our ax heads in for Thunder-Arrow to criticize, and worked again next day. It must have taken a "moon," or month, of such work to finish them. The last step was to grind the ax heads smooth with pieces of sandstone and polish them with ashes applied with a bit of deerskin.

By this time the corn in the gardens was large enough to use, yet of course not yet ripe. The sweet corn, especially, was delicious roasted or boiled on the cob and eaten with bear's grease or scraped off with a deer's jaw and made into cakes and baked or boiled with green beans and grease. One kind of squash was ready, too, and could be baked whole in the ashes or cut up and boiled. These were called *lay-nas-kund-ha'ka*, and were round and flat, with scalloped edges. I had never seen their like before.

Bowl-Woman, carrying the baby out to the field on his *am-bee'son*, or cradle, showed me how to dig a trench about eight feet long, a foot deep, and perhaps two feet wide. In this I built a good fire, and when it had burned down to coals, I laid two green poles the length of the trench. On these poles I leaned many ears of unripe, hard, blue corn, stripped of their husks, and when they browned on one side, I turned the other until all the grains were roasted. Later I shelled this corn and spread the kernels in a big, flat basket to dry in the sun on our shed roof. When dry, I sacked them and thus I learned how to prepare the dried, toasted green corn used for making the tasty porridge, my favorite, known as green corn *sa'pan*,

which I have described before.   We made also a lot of
green-corn bread, which we broke up and dried for winter.

Green corn time was always a happy time in Lenape
land, with much feasting; yet I never saw a public dance
to celebrate the occasion, as I hear is the custom among
many other tribes.   Of each kind of First Fruits, however,
a little was offered to the *Man-it'to-wuk*, or unseen powers.

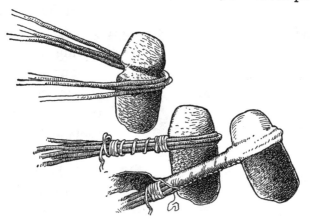

When the toasted green corn and bread were all dried
and put away, we went back to our axes, for handles had
still to be made.   For my ax I cut three limber *see'meen*
switches, peeled them, and bent them around the groove
of my ax head, then fastened the switches together directly
back of the ax head and in several other places with wet
deerskin thongs.   Then I took a piece of raw deerskin
from which I had removed the hair and covered the
handle, also the poll of the ax with it, leaving only the
blade uncovered.   Stretching the green skin as tightly as
I could, I sewed it fast with sinew thread.   When the
green skin dried, it shrank and held ax and handle together
like one piece.   Finally I presented it to Bowl-Woman.

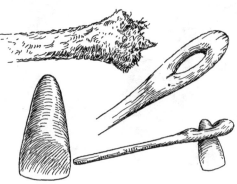

"*Ka-yah'!* Wonderful!" she cried. "Truly it is a better ax than the one broken. *Wa-nee'shih*, thanks!"

"Huh!" Thunder-Arrow grunted. "Of course it is wonderful. Did I not teach him how to make it? But if you think so much of your precious new ax, you should make a special basket for it and keep it on a soft cedar-bark bed, like the baby!"

The handle of the man's ax was more difficult. Little-Bear, after making a tobacco offering, dug up a *see'meen* sapling about three or four fingers thick at the butt. After trimming off all the roots and cutting off the trunk about two feet above, he had a sort of club. This he peeled and bored a hole through near the thick end with flint drills and hot coals to make a socket for the pointed end of his ax head, which had to fit close. Then he scraped down his handle until it was very smooth and fastened his ax head tight in the socket with little wooden wedges in such a way that every blow struck with the ax tightened the grip of the handle on the blade. How both axes were made I have shown in the illustrations.

Finally Little-Bear presented the finished ax to his father.

"Wherever I go," Thunder-Arrow said, "being a great man, people always give me wonderful presents, so

many that I cannot possibly carry them home. That is
why you never see them! However, I like this *tay-ma'hee-
kan* that you have given me, my son, better than any of
them." He thought for a moment.

"You boys have done very well," he resumed. "How
would you like to borrow my canoe for a trip on the
river—maybe stay away several days?"

"*Kay'hay-la!*" we both shouted.

It was to be a fishing trip, so our first thought was
the necessary tackle. Bowl-Woman gave us a ball of cord
made from the inner bark of a tree which the English now
call slippery elm, all hand twisted, of course, that she had
put away to sew rushes together for a mat tent cover.
This saved us a lot of work preparing fibers and twisting
cord for our fish lines, *a-ma-na'tak-a*, but hooks were
another matter. There was not a fishhook in the cabin,
although we rummaged through a lot of bags and baskets
in hopes. Finally, Thunder-Arrow agreed to teach us how
to make some.

First of all, he sent us over to the village ash dump on
the bank of the ravine to get some pieces of deer thigh
bones. All of them smelled bad, but we succeeded in
finding a few that had lain there long enough to lose some
of their aroma.

Thunder-Arrow showed us how to saw out parts of
these bones and grind them down into flat, oval pieces like
those shown on the next page. The edge of a flint blade
was used for sawing and bits of sandstone for grinding.
Then came the hardest work—to cut out the center part of
the ovals so as to leave only a narrow rim of bone. This
was done by cutting a groove with a flint point and

gradually deepening it. Each oval, when it was finished, made two hooks, very much like English fishhooks but lacking the barb. These were for small fish; for larger ones we fastened sharpened splinters of deer bone to wooden shanks as seen in the illustration; but these, too, were barbless. Sinew was not suitable for binding the parts together, as it softens in water; so we untwisted a little of our slippery elm bark fish line and used the fibers, smearing them with pine pitch to make them hold fast.

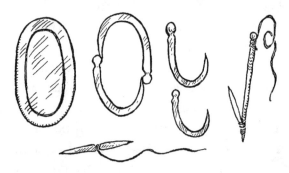

We made still a third kind, which was easiest of all— just a little splinter of bone, sharpened at both ends, with the line fastened to the center. This was run through the middle of the bait, and if a fish swallowed it, the bone would turn crosswise in its insides and the fish was caught.

The hooks were all finished before dark, so Little-Bear, Moon-ha'kee, and I started up the river at dawn the next morning, taking with us in the canoe only our bed mats, our fur robes, a fire-making outfit, a flint knife, and a bow and arrows, besides the line, the hooks, and the paddles and pole for propelling the craft. For provisions we carried only a little *ka-ha-ma'kun* and a small sack of dried venison, intending to live mainly on the fish we would catch. We even promised Bowl-Woman a good mess upon our return.

But alas for our hopes! The river was very low and very clear, and although we stopped in favorable places and used the best of worms and grasshoppers for bait, the fish did not wish to bite, and we caught only two or three small fry the first day. I soon discovered that it was necessary to pull up rapidly and smoothly when a fish took the bait, for the barbless hooks did not hold very well.

That night we set out lines with the straight "hooks" I have mentioned baited with worms, and when morning came, we each had a *wee-sa'mek*, or fat-fish, now called cat-fish by the English— 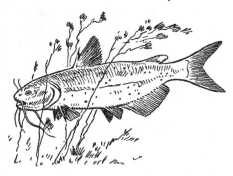 perhaps because the fish has whiskers something like a cat's. They were rather small, but they tasted good broiled on sticks in front of the fire, and with the *ka-ha-ma'kun* made a pretty fair breakfast. Our luck the second day was terrible, so about midday we abandoned fishing with hook and line, and cut a couple of long slim poles which we sharpened for fish spears, hardening the points in the fire. Such spears were called *no-ta-ma-es-hee'kan-a*.

With these we poked about beneath large stones and in holes under cut banks and just missed catching several fish, including one big *wee-sa'mek* which actually wriggled off my spear and escaped. We would have gone to bed hungry if I had not set out with the bow and arrows and

brought back a *che-mum'es*, or rabbit.   We broiled the
meat and used the entrails as bait for our night lines,
Moon-ha'kee taking care of the bones.   Next morning we
had one fair *wee-sa'mek*, but the other line was gone;
some big fish had run off with everything, even the stake
to which the line had been tied.

About midday we came to a swift rapid or small
waterfall, a little way above the bend of the river, and
could not go farther without the labor of dragging the
canoe around overland or up through the rocks and swift
water, so we turned back toward home, a pair of discouraged fishermen.

The following morning no catfish were caught, and
we ate the last of the *ka-ha-ma'kun*, the dried meat being
all gone.

It must have been sometime in the early afternoon
when we stopped to stretch our legs on a wide bar of sand
and gravel which was usually entirely under water.   The
deep channel of the river was near the right bank and,
leaving this, we walked toward the left bank, where I
noticed a pool fed by a shallow trickle of water from the
upstream end of the bar and drained by a similar one which
rejoined the main river some distance below.

As we approached, something darted from the edge
into the middle of the pool, stirring up a cloud of mud.

"Look, Little-Bear!" I cried, "a fish—a big fish!"

"It must be a big *wee-sa'mek*," he answered.   "Wish
we could catch him.   You know what we promised
Mother!"

"Come on!" I said, wading in.   "We'll catch him
with our bare hands."

"You'll never find him in that mud he's stirred up," replied my friend. "Besides the *wee-sa'mek* carries sharp spears. He's dangerous! Let's make an *ahk-wo-an-ee'kan;* maybe that will work."

"What's an *ahk-wo-an-ee'kan?*"

"It's a sort of net made of bushes tied together. You'll see!"

We pulled or cut twelve or fifteen little bushes of dense growth, each two or three feet across, and laid them in line on the gravel bar, then stripped some bark from a young basswood tree and with strips of the inner bark for string we tied the bushes all together as closely as possible, making a "net" about twenty feet long, just long enough to cross the pool from one side to the other.

Beginning at the upper end of the pool, we began to drag the bush net through it, very slowly. We had reached about the middle when there was a mighty swirl and a splash in the muddy water.

"*Ka-ya'! A-man'ga-mek!*" yelled Little-Bear. "It's a water monster! *K'nay-ha'sin!* Be careful!"

We were standing there trying to make up our minds to go ahead when I happened to look at the outlet of the pool. A gigantic fish was trying to force itself, half swimming, half crawling, through the shallow water toward the river.

I yelled and pointed and we both started for it, but I reached it first, threw myself upon it, clutched it in my arms. It thrashed, it squirmed, it struggled fiercely in the muddy water; sometimes I was underneath, but I hung on, whilst Moon-ha'kee danced about, barking. Before I knew it, the monster had dragged me to the edge of the bar and was just launching itself, and me, into the main current of the river when Little-Bear grabbed my ankles.

He pulled me, and I gripped the fish, and gradually we worked back from the brink. Suddenly it made a spurt and nearly dragged us both in, but we fought desperately and finally won out.

Then we got it out on the bar, and it took all of my strength to hold the fish whilst Little-Bear clubbed it with a stone on the head until it lay still.

The creature was enormous, larger than I, and we could see now that it was no *wee-sa'mek*.

"*Joo!* It's a *wee-sa'ho-seed*," Little-Bear panted happily. "One of the finest fish that swims. We could never have seen it if its back had not stuck out of water." Such fish are called sturgeons in English.

We made fine time going down the river with the current, and, in addition, I tied my robe on the pole to make a rude sail, but it was dusk when we reached the village. We beached the canoe at the landing, and our whoops brought a crowd, mostly boys and girls, Toad-Face and White-Deer among them.

When we lifted our prize from the canoe, there was a sort of murmur of awe and admiration, but I got a glimpse of Toad-Face, and his expression was sour and glum enough, envious, I suppose. Our progress to the cabin was a sort of triumphant procession, but he did not join in.

Thunder-Arrow and Bowl-Woman thought that our sturgeon was wonderful, but their pleasure and ours was short lived. A little boy ran up with the bad news that our canoe was adrift; some girl had seen it and sent him to tell us. We hurried down to the landing but it was gone!

That was a real disaster—the borrowed canoe! We made our way as fast as we could down the shore, fighting our way through the bushes and looking out on the river but no canoe was seen. We were about to turn back when Little-Bear's keen eyes sighted a black speck on the darkening water. I should have taken it for a rock or a snag in the river, but he could see that it was moving with the current. We both plunged in and swam; it was the canoe! Our bedding was still in it, but the paddles, the pole, and the fish lines were gone. We swam in with it to shore and then I guarded it whilst Little-Bear went back to the village to get some paddles; on his return we paddled the canoe back to the landing.

We were dead tired and nearly starved when we returned to the cabin, but Bowl-Woman had a good hot supper ready. Whilst we were eating, Thunder-Arrow spoke his mind.

"I thought you boys were just about grown up, but when you get so excited over a fish that you forget to pull up your canoe, and it drifts away, that shows you are still too young to be trusted."

"Truly, Father, we did pull the canoe high up on the beach; somebody must have pushed it off again," Little-Bear argued.

"Somebody took the paddles and fish lines out," I said. "Probably the same person cast it adrift."

"You must go down after your bedding, then," ordered Thunder-Arrow, "or the evil-disposed-one may take that."

Just then the door curtain was lifted softly and someone slipped quickly inside. It was White-Deer!

"*Ay-kay-sa'!*" Bowl-Woman cried. "What are you
doing here this time of night, child? Don't you know it's
not proper for a young girl——."

"I don't care," was the response. "I have something
important to tell. It was Toad-Face who cast your canoe
adrift!"

"How do you know?" Thunder-Arrow demanded.

"I noticed he did not come with the rest of us, so
when we got up on the top of the bank, I slipped back and
peered over the edge to see what he was going to do. He
first threw the pole and paddles up into the bushes, then
he took something out of the canoe and kept it, then he
pushed the canoe itself out."

"Why didn't you tell us sooner?" questioned Little-
Bear.

"I sent a little neighbor to tell you that the canoe was
adrift but I did not dare come myself until now. If
Toad-Face should find out that I told on him, he might
harm my mother or me. He is a very bad boy."

"You had better go home right away," Thunder-
Arrow advised. "And don't let anybody see you. We
thank you for coming!"

After White-Deer had gone, an unpleasant thought
came to my mind. Suppose Toad-Face should come back
and push the canoe out again? I mentioned this pos-
sibility, and Thunder-Arrow agreed that Little-Bear and
I should go down and sleep in the canoe.

Arriving at the landing, I suggested that we hide in
the bedding which was still in the canoe, but he thought

the space was too small for both.   So, after trying to
persuade me in vain to go back to the cabin, Little-Bear
went himself, taking Moon-ha'kee with him.   After a
while I succeeded in arranging the mats and robes so that
I would be comfortable but still concealed from sight.
The moon was just rising over the trees across the river.

I was dropping off to sleep, tired from the day's
labors and excitement, when a rattle of gravel aroused me
with a start.   However, I had presence of mind enough
not to reveal myself, but lay there with every muscle tense
as a bowstring.

After a few breathless seconds I felt the bow of the
canoe moving, grating, slipping on the beach.   Someone
was pushing it off!

I sprang up, flinging aside the robe, and confronted
Toad-Face!   He staggered back as if he had seen a ghost.

"*A-kee'! Chee'pai!*" he gasped.   Then he recognized me.

Frantically he looked about for a weapon, but I was
upon him before he could lay hand upon stick or stone.
I was confident, he the reverse, so the beating this time
did not take long.   In a few minutes he was groveling in
the sand, begging for mercy.

"Toad-Face!" I demanded.   "Where are the paddles
and the pole from this canoe, also the fish lines?"

"I threw them into the river," he muttered sullenly.

"That is too bad," I said, "because now I shall have
to begin and beat you all over again.   Stand up and take
it like a man!"

"*Ta' ma'ta!*" he begged.   "What I said was not true.
Don't hit me again."   He was shielding his face with
his hands.

"*Ta-a'ne?* Where are they, then?"

"*Tak-ta'nee.* I don't know."

I yanked his hands from his face and slapped him across the mouth, then clenched my fists as if to punch him.

Dumbly he pointed to the bushes.

"Go fetch them!" I ordered.

He staggered off, with me following closely, and located the missing articles.

"Put them back in the canoe. *Al-la'pee!*"

When I saw the things safely replaced, I said to him:

"Toad-Face, I am going to let you go home now. But if anything ever happens to this canoe or its gear again, I shall beat you to a pulp every time I see you, and Little-Bear will do the same. Now go!"

"What if somebody else shoves off your canoe?"

"That will be your misfortune, for you will get the beating. *Ay'ka-li-uh'!* Get out!"

I remained on guard for fear he would come back, perhaps with a weapon, until the moon rode high; but there was no sound except the soft whisper of the river and now and then the lonesome call of a *shwon-hil'la*, or shore bird. Finally I went back to the canoe and fell asleep.

I was wakened by something warm and damp gliding over my cheek. Rising up with a start, I discovered Moon-ha'kee was licking my face! Down the path from the village came Little-Bear, and when I told him what had happened, he looked grave.

"You have probably made the canoe safe enough," he said. "The trouble is, Toad-Face will now be more eager than ever to get revenge. He might even lie in wait for you somewhere and shoot you from ambush."

When we told Thunder-Arrow the story, he put his hand on my shoulder.

"You are very lucky," he said. "Lucky with hunting, lucky with fishing, lucky with fighting. If your luck holds out, you may be as great a man as I am, some day! In truth you are so lucky that I suspect you may have received an *an'go-oo*, or blessing, in your former home. Tell me, is that the case?"

"Not that I know of," I answered. "Just what is an *an'go-oo*, and how do you get one? White-Deer told me to ask you that some day."

"She did, eh? Well, I *could* tell you, but not so well, perhaps, as some others." He held out his bowl, and his wife refilled it with porridge. He paused a moment, thinking; then he continued:

"Roaring-Wings would be a good one—you gave him your first deer, didn't you? Well, he is the one you should ask for a pipeful of tobacco!"

"Why should I ask him for tobacco? I don't smoke."

Thunder-Arrow laughed.

"That's just a way of speaking," he explained. "You see, you ask him for the tobacco, and he hands you his *pin-das-sen-a'kun*, or tobacco pouch. You put your hand into it, but instead of taking tobacco out, you put in some *kay'kwuk*, or shell beads, as a present to the old man. Then he feels obliged to tell you all he can."

"The trouble is, I have no *kay'kwuk*," I lamented, "except these little strings poor Granny put in my ears."

"I'll give you some," said Bowl-Woman.

Thus it was that I went first to old Roaring-Wings for advice.

11

.I found him under his shed looking over his stock of herbs, each kind apparently done up in a separate deerskin package which was kept with the others in a big, square basket.

I addressed him as "father," and told him I was glad he had lived to see another day, which was the custom,

then I mustered my courage and asked him to lend me a pipeful of tobacco. He smiled faintly.

"Let me see your pipe," he said, knowing well that I had none.

"It is truly a very small one," I replied, taking my cue from the smile. "So small I never show it to anyone."

"Then you will not empty my pouch," he responded, passing over a bag made from the skin of a *ta-mask'was*, muskrat, taken off whole, except for an opening in the throat. I slipped my hand inside, depositing the string of *kay'kwuk* beads which Bowl-Woman had given me, and handed it back.

"I'll see how much tobacco you have taken," he chuckled, feeling the pouch with his fingers. "Truly it was not necessary for you to bring me beads. Have you not already given me a deer? Now how can I help you?"

"Different ones have told me that I should have a 'blessing,' but nobody would explain what it was or how I should go about it to get one. Will you tell me?"

He made me seat myself on a mat, then he threw a little tobacco into the fire and prayed in an undertone. Finally he turned to me.

"Do your people believe in a Creator?" he asked.

"Why, yes! Of course!" I responded, astonished.

"I suppose He is your chief God?"

"He is our only God; there is only one."

"Has He no helpers?"

"Why, why, I suppose so. There is Christ and the Virgin Mary, the angels, and the saints."

"Do they help people who pray to them?"

"That is what we believe."

"Then you will understand when I tell you that our Creator has many helpers whom we call *Man-it'to-wuk*, and that people pray to them for help. Sometimes a *Man-it'to* will appear in a dream or vision to a person in trouble and give him some power or blessing that will help him all through life. Probably you will be given one some day, so be sure to remember any dream you may have when in trouble. And remember, a 'blessing' is a special power that has been given to you by one of the helpers of the Creator. If you waste it or abuse it, it will be taken from you. Was there anything else you wished to ask me?"

"There is something else. Will you please tell me just what is man's work and what is woman's work? People are always talking to me about it, and I should like to know the truth."

"*Kay'hay-la,*" he replied. "That is very easy. The man furnishes the greater part of the food we eat, both meat and fish, also the skins we wear, and defends his family and his tribe against their enemies. He works in wood, in stone, in bone, in shell, and in copper. I think that is all."

"What about the woman?"

"She furnishes the lesser part of the food; that is, the corn, the beans, the squashes from her garden, the roots, the nuts, the berries that grow wild. She cooks the food; she takes care of the cabin and the children. She works in skins, in splints, cornhusks and fibers and in clay. She embroiders with deer hair, porcupine quills, and shell beads and makes garments of feathers."

"Can a woman own land?" My desire for information grew.

"She owns her garden while she is working it, but the land belongs to the tribe. I should not say that, because no man or woman or tribe can really own land. Land was given by the Creator, as air or water, for the use of all men. What I mean is this: our Lenape tribe holds the right to use this land where we live, and each little clan holds its own hunting grounds. The woman really owns her house, though, and its furnishings. She owns the crops which she raises in her garden and even the meat and the skins which the man brings in after they have been turned over to her."

"What, then, does a man own?" I demanded.

"*Hoh!* A man needs little. Just his clothes, his weapons, his fishing gear, his tools, and his medicines—maybe also a bed mat!"

This all seemed to me very strange, for in England the man owns everything, the woman usually next to nothing.

I thanked Roaring-Wings and made my way homeward. As I thought it over, I realized that while the old man had told me, more or less, what a "blessing" was, he had not instructed me how to obtain one. This I found out, however, before many moons had passed, through a very trying experience.

VIII. Outcast

E HAD eaten part of the sturgeon fresh and had given away a lot of it; there was still enough left for Bowl-Woman to cut in strips and smoke. I never ate anything that tasted quite so good as that smoked sturgeon picked into flakes and boiled in the clay kettle, or eaten just as it was.

Little-Bear and I decided that we should like to catch another, but when we asked Thunder-Arrow for his canoe again, he turned a deaf ear. We had come so near to losing it before that he was afraid to take a chance.

"A good canoe is a precious thing," he said. "Truly even I, who made the first canoe that was ever seen on this great island, find canoe making the longest and hardest task of any work I do."

"Would you teach Little-Bear and me to make one?" I asked, meekly.

"Bowls and spoons are made the same way," he said. "So are wooden mortars. You had better begin on a mortar, because that is the easiest. If you make the other things well, maybe I shall teach you to make a canoe."

"A canoe would be more fun," said Little-Bear, "but I suppose we shall have to learn how first. What is the best wood for a mortar?"

"It is called 'mortar tree,' *tahk-wa-ho'a-kan-ee-min'-shee*," he said. "I saw a good, dry log of this kind on the river bank just above the place where you and Toad-Face had your first fight. Bring back a piece about four or five spans long, then I shall tell you what to do next."

"How shall we recognize the log when we see it?" I asked.

"One end has been cut off already, by burning, of course. It is too bad, because the man who did it got the best piece, which is just above the place where the roots come out."

"I suppose we, too, shall have to burn off our piece."

"There is no other way. Sometime I shall point out to you the growing tree, so you can remember the best wood for mortars."

He did this, and the tree he showed me was the kind now called tupelo, or sour gum, by the English.

I had some firewood to gather that day, so we did not start our work on the mortar until the next. We finally found the log and carefully smeared the lower two feet of it with a layer of wet mud; then we left a gap of dry, bare wood about a foot wide; then coated the log again with mud for a foot or so. The next task was to build a fire on the bare stretch of wood between the two coated portions, using a piece of burning slow match, or punk, to light it, called *pah-sah-ay-nee'kan* in Lenape, which I had brought from home. We kept the fire burning until we saw that it had eaten deep into the log; then we pulled the brands off and chopped out the charcoal with the ax which I had made for Bowl-Woman, then built a new fire. It was nearly midday when the log was burned in two.

We took turns carrying it back to camp, and there, after refreshing ourselves with the contents of a porridge pot, we called upon Thunder-Arrow to tell us what to do next.

"You are a bold pair," he declared with mock sternness. "Here you are, demanding that I teach you something, without putting a single bead in my tobacco pouch. How can I teach you, unless you make me strong with *kay'kwuk?*"

"We have already made you strong, O Wise One," I said. "Did we not give you recently a large sturgeon?"

"Did you? Oh, yes, I remember the little minnow you brought home. Perhaps you did give it to me or to Bowl-Woman; but if I recall, you two ate the most of it. Very well, if you insist, I shall have to tell you about making that mortar. First, get the two ends cut off square by burning with hot coals and scraping; then turn your log on end and pile hot coals on the middle of the top. Blow the coals with your breath until they are burned out; then scrape out the charcoal with a clam shell or a flint scraper and put in some more coals, then scrape again, and so on until you have the mortar hole in the top of the log burned deep enough."

It is hard to believe, but the most troublesome part of making that mortar was cutting square the ends, which in a burned-off-log are likely to be rounded or even pointed.

We burned and scraped and scraped and burned until at last the ends were square enough so that the log would stand upright. Burning the hole in the top was easy by comparison, although it took quite a long time to make it a span deep and as wide as the log would stand. I was proud and happy when the mortar was finished, little realizing that trouble was coming.

The first thing I noticed was when Little-Bear, for some reason I could not imagine, lost interest in our work and left me to make the pestle alone. I searched the river banks for days before I found a long, gray, fine-grained stone to make this, and it took all my spare time for many more days to batter and grind it into a smooth, long pestle suitable to use in the new mortar, using the same methods that Thunder-Arrow had taught us for ax making.

Bowl-Woman thanked me in a sort of indifferent way when I gave it to her and stowed it beneath a sleeping bench, whilst Thunder-Arrow acted very strangely and showed no interest at all.

One time I found him sitting under the tree in front of our cabin fastening red-dyed deer hair and black turkey beards on a string which was stretched on a stick bent like a bow to keep it taut. I imagined he must be making a crest such as the men and older boys sometimes wore on their heads; but when I questioned him, he answered never a word, but jumped to his feet with a sour face and stalked into the house. Later on I learned how to do this work myself; how to fasten the hair and beards on the string and then how to coil it upon itself and sew the coils together to make the crest as shown on the next page.

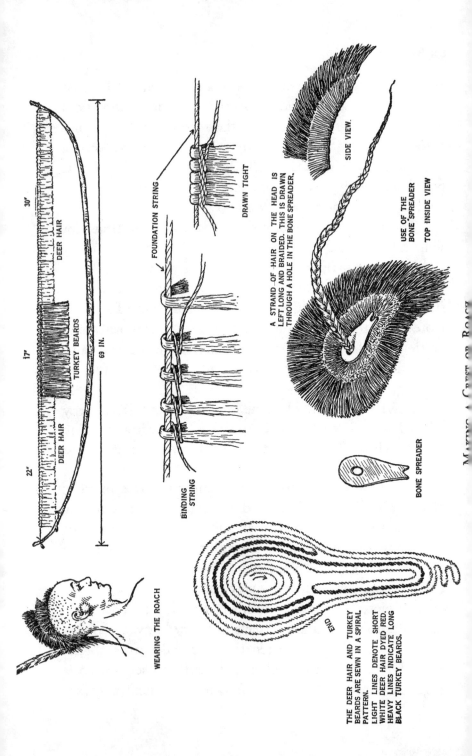

DEER HAIR

30"

17"

TURKEY BEARDS

22"

DEER HAIR

69 IN.

FOUNDATION STRING

DRAWN TIGHT

BINDING STRING

A STRAND OF HAIR ON THE HEAD IS LEFT LONG AND BRAIDED. THIS IS DRAWN THROUGH A HOLE IN THE BONE SPREADER.

SIDE VIEW.

USE OF THE BONE SPREADER

TOP INSIDE VIEW

BONE SPREADER

WEARING THE ROACH

END

THE DEER HAIR AND TURKEY BEARDS ARE SEWN IN A SPIRAL PATTERN.

LIGHT LINES DENOTE SHORT WHITE DEER HAIR DYED RED. HEAVY LINES INDICATE LONG BLACK TURKEY BEARDS.

MAKING A CREST OR ROACH

At the time, however, Thunder-Arrow's actions made me feel sick. I could not understand what I might have done to offend, but every day it was plainer that something was wrong.

I tried my best to interest Little-Bear in following up our original scheme to make some wooden bowls and spoons next, but he would not answer me one way or the other; so I abandoned the plan in discouragement.

Bowl-Woman would not even look at me in the face when I tried to find out what I had done. She who had been so kind and motherly now began to stint my food; she insisted on doing all the cooking and serving and she saw to it that I received nothing but scorched bits or stale leftovers. She even hid away my good bowl and spoon and gave me only a cracked gourd bowl to eat from.

In desperation I went to Roaring-Wings for advice, but the instant he heard my story he shut up like a *tahk-gohk'*, a box turtle, and I could not get a word out of him. Maybe, I thought, White-Deer would help me find out what the trouble was; but she was just as bad as the others when I told her. She went quickly out of the cabin whilst I waited. When half the afternoon had

passed, she had not returned and I asked news of her from her mother. I was told that she had gone to the house of one of her aunts to spend the night.

I think the worst moment was the time when I came in with a big back load of wood and found that Bowl-Woman had taken my bedding off my platform and had laid the things on the ground, piling bags and baskets where my bed had been.

Moon-ha'kee felt the trouble, whatever it was, and stuck to me pretty close. He knew I needed a friend and he even gave up his favorite amusement, digging for mice, in order to comfort me. Now that my bedding was on the ground, he slept with me every night.

If it had not been for Toad-Face, I think I would have asked Cross-Woman to buy me back. I am afraid, however, that when she heard my reasons, she would have treated me like all the rest.

The climax came just before dawn one morning when I was rudely awakened with a pail of cold water. I recognized Thunder-Arrow's voice.

"Get up, *k'ahk-peek'soo*, flea-bitten one! I am sick of seeing you around, *as-huk'tet*, miserable brat! Hurry!"

I staggered to my feet; someone scraped together a few coals in the fireplace and threw on some fat pine, which blazing up, lighted the cabin.

"You must leave this house, *k'nis'kay-wush'king*, dirty-face! But before you go I offer you food and drink."

He held out my cracked gourd, half full of water, and a scorched sliver of venison.

In a rage I knocked them out of his hands and rushed out of the house, Moon-ha'kee at my heels. The sky was just paling over the woods across the river. My first thought was to run away, but, before I had gone far, I realized that I had not brought my bow and arrows, without which I would starve. I was standing trying to plan what to do, when I saw somebody coming, following me. It was my former friend, Little-Bear.

"*Ka-kuh-ka-ta'tum?*" I demanded crossly. "What do *you* want?"

"You must come back," he said. "Don't you know that you have to eat and drink before you start and rub yourself with ashes? And do not take Moon-ha'kee; he would spoil everything."

For a moment I thought he was trying to torment me; then suddenly it came over me. "This is some sort of ceremony; if I do my part, I shall find out later what it is." So I went back with Little-Bear. Thunder-Arrow, scowling fiercely, gave me a gourd of water and a scorched shred of meat, which I accepted this time; then I smeared myself with ashes and charcoal from the fireplace and took down my bow and quiver. I was just going out of the door when Thunder-Arrow called to me. "Better leave your bow and arrows in the shed; you will not need them. I hope something will be given to you."

I did as I was told, then stopped to tie up Moon-ha'-kee. Whilst I was under the shed, Little-Bear stepped close.

"You do not know just what to do," he whispered. "I can see that. The best place to fast for power is a big pile of rocks up on Turtle Creek above the last gardens. Some of the rocks overhang so as to form a shelter in case of storm. It really is a good place; several of our boys have been given blessings there."

"Blessings," I thought. "So that is what I am supposed to get—a blessing! I need one badly enough!"

"In case you do not know the rules, I shall tell you that you must not eat anything whilst the sun is in the sky nor drink. Father or I will come to see you every morning whilst you are there, but do not stay out until you get too weak. Be sure to remember anything strange you see or dream about. And do not feel too badly if you get nothing this time; you can try again later." He went quickly into the house with a furtive glance around to see if anyone had caught him advising me.

I started out, following the creek path up past the gardens to the clay beds, where it ended. Still I followed the creek and came at last to a great pile of rocks on its south bank. Here I climbed up to the top of the highest one and looked off. To the east and southeast I could see the silvery river, but in other directions nothing but forest. After sitting up there for a while, I clambered down and pulled some long grass to make myself a nest under one of the shelving rocks, and there I lay.

I fell to thinking of my strange situation, of the curious events that had taken place. I had a kindlier feeling now toward Little-Bear, for he had taken pains to give me some notion of what was expected; but the others —well, if they wished to think ill of me, let them do so.

Anyhow, here I was, waiting to receive a blessing from some helper of the Lenape's Creator. How it would come, if it came at all, and what it might be, I had not the remotest idea. Thinking thus, I fell asleep.

I woke some time in the afternoon, very hungry indeed, and I was sorely tempted to go back to the village and beg Bowl-Woman for a dried-up scrap of bread, but something inside told me not to go. The afternoon dragged slowly away, and I amused myself by watching a colony of ants. How they worked and struggled, bearing heavy burdens, each for the benefit of others rather than himself! Sometime in the night I got to sleep again.

At daybreak I awoke to see Little-Bear standing in front of my cave; he handed me a gourd bottle of water which I drained and a strip of cold broiled venison which I devoured greedily. He asked me in a low voice whether I had been given anything, and when I said, "No," he turned and disappeared in the direction of the village without another word.

This day was a dreary one; I watched the ants until I was tired; I thought of my younger days in England which were like memories of another world. I thought of my dear mother which made me weep. I slept a little, then watched the ants again.

Once more I thought about my errand here, and a new idea came to my mind which alarmed me. I had heard in England that the Indians of America were said to be worshipers of the Devil, and now I feared that Satan himself might appear to me and offer me some power like witchcraft, demanding my soul in return. This was a frightful thought and for a while I was tempted to run away, come what might.

But again when I considered the Indians I knew, it did not seem possible that these good people, who had been so kind until recently to me, should have traffic with the Evil One. Toad-Face might, that was true; but I could not believe that even Cross-Woman, harsh and disagreeable as she might appear, could be inspired by Satan. As for the Lenape ceremonies I had seen, surely there was nothing satanic about them. *Mee-sing'* might look like a demon, but after all, *Mee-sing-haw-lee'kun* was said to be the guardian of game animals, and there is nothing devilish in that, I thought.

Still I was worried when darkness came, and between my hunger and fear of seeing the Devil, it was a long time before I fell asleep.

That night I had a very strange dream. It appeared that I was sitting on a rock in front of my little cave looking off down the creek toward the village, and I was very hungry. As I looked, a number of women came out of the forest, bearing bowls of bread, *sa'pan*, *soo-tay'yo*, and *ka-ha-ma'kun*, and men appeared also, carrying roast venison and broiled fish for me to eat. In my dream I ate until I was satisfied and thanked the bearers. Then one of the men gave me a little bundle saying, "Here it is," and I thanked him. When they turned to go, I saw that they were not men and women, but gigantic ants! I opened the bundle and found inside a flint chipper, a sewing awl, a bow, and a war club, all in miniature.

I awoke more hungry than ever, then slept and dreamed the same thing over again. When I awoke this time, it was daylight, and Thunder-Arrow was standing there with my water and meat.

After I had refreshed myself, Thunder-Arrow asked me if I had received anything. I told him of my dream, and he looked pleased and amazed.

"Truly," he said. "The *Man-it'to-wuk* have given you a vision. I do not know what it means, but we can find that out later. Come, wash yourself in the creek and we shall go back to the village."

I washed off what remained of the ashes and charcoal and then I addressed Thunder-Arrow.

"Before we start, I am going to ask you something and I want you to answer it."

"I'll answer it if I can."

"What have I done to make everybody hate me? Why did you and Little-Bear treat me the way you did? Why did Bowl-Woman put my bed on the floor and try to starve me? Why did Roaring-Wings refuse to talk to me? Why did White-Deer, when I came to talk to her, run off to her aunt's and leave me sitting in her mother's cabin?"

Thunder-Arrow laughed. "That is the way every boy is treated when he is about to take his fast. Surely in your country they do the same."

Then it was nothing that I had done after all! A great load was lifted from my mind. However, I did not wish him to think English people were ignorant, so, remembering the Church fasts, I said:

"Oh, my people know something of fasting. Yet I do not understand why a boy who is about to fast should be abused."

"It is an old custom with us," Thunder-Arrow explained. "Some say it is to deceive the *Man-it'to-wuk* so that they will take especial pity on a child who appears so unfortunate."

"That would not be right, would it?"

"No, not to my mind. I think it was done originally for its effect on the boy himself. If he really thinks he needs help, he is more likely to get it."

When we entered the village, everyone stared at me as if I were a stranger, and when we approached the cabin, Moon-ha′kee rushed out barking and wagging his tail and jumped up on me as if he had not seen me for a long time. Bowl-Woman politely spread a fresh mat for me to sit upon on my old bed platform, and I noticed that my sleeping mat and my robes were no longer on the floor, but were rolled up at the back of the *ha′soon* against the wall. She hurriedly raked up some hot coals in the fireplace and set a pot over them, whilst Thunder-Arrow got down a long skin sack that was hanging from the roof poles. I never had known what was in that sack, but now he took out a stone pipe with a long, wooden stem, filled it, lighted it, and handed it to me. I was about to refuse it when I realized that this too must be a ceremony, so I drew a few puffs and handed it back.

Now Bowl-Woman set a dish of good hot *sa′pan* before me, which I ate with a relish, and then she filled it up again. Little-Bear came in about that time, but neither he nor the others even started their breakfast until I had finished. I was now treated as a guest of honor.

However, I could not rest until I learned the meaning of my vision, so I begged another string of *kay′kwuk* beads from Bowl-Woman and went to Roaring-Wings, asking him again to "lend me a pipeful of tobacco."

When I had told him my dream, he sat for a long time in silence. Finally he said:

"Ants are very hard workers, and the fact that your gift bringers took that form means that great power to work has been given you. When they brought you plenty of food in your dream, that meant that through your work you will live in plenty. In the bundle they gave you the little flint chipper and the sewing awl mean that you are given skill in the work of both men and women; the little bow means skill in hunting and the tiny war club skill in war. You know of course that ants are not only workers but hunters and warriors as well."

"Then I really have a blessing?" I asked.

"*Keet-shee!* Certainly! When the ant man handed you the bundle and said, 'Here it is,' that meant that they were giving you a blessing. There is, however, one thing lacking. You must have a special song before you can take the lead at the *Gam'wing*. Of course you are too young to lead the worship in the main part, but if you had a song, you could sing it and dance on the last night. That is the time when women and young men sing their visions."

"How can I get a song?" I asked Roaring-Wings. I liked the idea of leading a dance at the *Gam'wing* instead of being chased out of the Big-House like a dog, as I was the previous year. Besides, I liked vision songs, having heard a number.

"Just keep thinking about your vision and wishing you had a song," Roaring-Wings replied. "It will come to you. Maybe, even, you will have another dream and your helpers will give you the song that way."

"You say, 'my helpers.' Just what do you mean by that?"

"I mean the ants, of course."

"Just ordinary ants?" I persisted. "*Lay-nee-lee-kwes' suk?*"

"*Ma-ta-ka'*. Of course not!   Your helpers are spirit ants, *Man-it'to-wuk*, who can take the form of ants."

"What relation are they to real ants?"

"I hope you are not joking," said Roaring-Wings seriously.   "If you make fun of your helpers, you are likely to lose their blessing. We believe that every kind of animal has a *man-it'to*, or spirit, that takes care of it, and that this *man-it'to* is related to the animals in some way. Ants seem to have a number of such spirits to care for them, perhaps because there are many different kinds of ants."

"I think I understand," I replied.   "And thank you. When do you think my blessing will begin to work?"

"That I cannot tell you.   Perhaps right away; perhaps not until you find yourself in special danger.   If you need help at any time, throw a little tobacco on the fire and pray to your *Man-it'to-wuk*."

This seemed a strange and perhaps an un-Christian thing to do, yet I knew a number of people in England who prayed to their patron saints.   The *Man-it'to-wuk* appeared to be the patron saints of America.

I thanked my teacher again and was about to take my leave when he stopped me.

"I have just thought of something that may help you. You should really have a little bundle like the one in your dream, with all the different things in it.   If you like, I can make you such a bundle; then if you ever get faint-hearted, you can open it and see just what powers were given you."

I returned home in great excitement and was about to tell the whole family what I had learned when Thunder-Arrow stopped me.

"In your place," he said, "I would not talk about my blessing to anyone but Roaring-Wings."

I was disappointed. "What about the *Gam'wing?*" I demanded. "I thought I was supposed to tell my vision and sing about it at the *Gam'wing!*"

"Even there you must not state exactly what your Helper is or tell just what happened when you received your blessing. You may talk or sing about them, however, so that your hearers can guess."

Next day Little-Bear and I started in on our long-delayed plan to make some wooden bowls. We searched the river banks for swellings or burls on logs and when we found one, we split it off with deer-antler wedges. By burning and scraping, we dressed these down to about the size and shape of the bowls we planned to make. There were no burls big enough for the largest size, used for mixing bread or for serving food at feasts, but we had a number suitable for ordinary food bowls and the smallest size used for medicine. Thunder-Arrow showed us how to burn out the inside, which had to be done very carefully with hot coals and a flint scraper, using first one and then the other and controlling the burning with wet clay.

I spoiled two bowls and Little-Bear one by burning holes clear through the bottom before we learned to regulate the use of the hot coals.   After the bowls were almost thin enough, we finished them by grinding with pieces of sandstone, first coarse and then fine, putting on the final finish with scraps of deerskin and fine sand.

We each made several spoons, too, from small burls or pieces of larger ones, but these really had to be cut, not

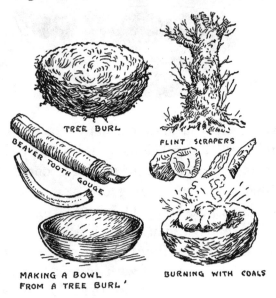

TREE BURL

BEAVER TOOTH GOUGE

FLINT SCRAPERS

MAKING A BOWL
FROM A TREE BURL

BURNING WITH COALS

burned into shape, with such tools as flint flakes, flint knives used as saws, and chisels made of beaver teeth set in wooden handles.   These last could be resharpened when they dulled, as an English iron chisel, but were not so strong.   In making a spoon, you saw grooves into the parts of the wood you wish to remove and split out the wood between the grooves with a small deer-antler wedge. On a spoon the only burning you do is when you hollow out the bowl; then you can use a few hot coals if you watch them very carefully.

Lenape spoons were very different from those we use in England, being round of bowl and short of handle, and sometimes they had a little hook in back to hang them up by.

I did this work from time to time as the chance offered, for Bowl-Woman and I were very busy these early fall days. The corn was now ripe and we gathered it in baskets, leaving the outer covering or husk on; then we stripped the husks back without detaching them and braided them together, making strings of several dozen ears each. The largest and most perfect ears of each kind we made into special strings to keep for seed.

Bowl-Woman had a long pole stretched between two trees by the side of her garden, and we tied the strings of corn together in pairs and slung them over the pole to dry. We had five different kinds of corn to keep separate; that is, *po'hem* or soft, white, flour corn; three colors of hard corn for hominy; blue, red, and white, and the fifth kind, *pee'seem*, or sweet corn, which was best eaten green as I have mentioned. The short or imperfect ears we stored in a big basket to use first.

The *ma-lahk-see'ta*, or beans, we gathered in pack baskets—I think we planted six different kinds that year—took them home, shelled them, and dried them on the shed roof in large flat baskets, the same that had served for drying berries in the summer.

Every night when we came home from the gardens, we would bring all the pumpkins and squashes we could carry and stack them in the shed. We still had a few of

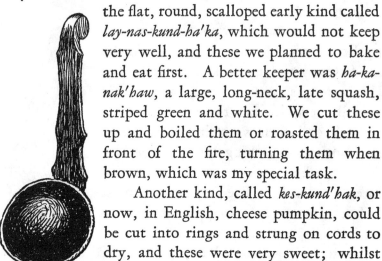

the flat, round, scalloped early kind called *lay-nas-kund-ha'ka*, which would not keep very well, and these we planned to bake and eat first. A better keeper was *ha-ka-nak'haw*, a large, long-neck, late squash, striped green and white. We cut these up and boiled them or roasted them in front of the fire, turning them when brown, which was my special task.

Another kind, called *kes-kund'hak*, or now, in English, cheese pumpkin, could be cut into rings and strung on cords to dry, and these were very sweet; whilst a fourth sort, the big, yellow pumpkins called *king-kas-kund-hak'a*, we planned to cut round and round into strips, which could be woven into the form of square mats, dried, and kept for a long time. Both rings and mats could be broken up and boiled when needed. Some Lenapes liked to bury yellow pumpkins and the large striped squashes in deep pits to keep them from freezing, then dig them up along in the winter. The sunflower heads we dried on the shed roof.

We had just reached the cabin with a load of pumpkins late one afternoon when Beaver-House came over to ask if Little-Bear wished to go again to the *kit-ta-hik'kan*, or ocean, to dry clams. I should liked to have gone, especially as Toad-Face, having had a quarrel with his stepfather, would not be a member of the party, but unfortunately I was not invited.

Little-Bear accepted, so I asked him to fetch home some shells, as I had a mind to learn the art of making beads; also I asked him to inquire among the coast Indians whether they had seen any wreckage from the ill-fated ship and to bring me a piece of her if he could.

I saw them off at the canoe landing the following morning and it gave me a strange, lonely feeling to see the little flotilla, the same that had rescued me, disappear down the river.

I returned to the cabin and Bowl-Woman, seeing the tears in my eyes, asked me what was the matter. I could not tell her but I set about shelling beans with a sad heart.

"Never mind," she said, "the *Gam'wing* will soon be here again, and then everybody will be happy."

The *Gam'wing!* That brought to my mind again something I had almost lost sight of; the fact that I still lacked a song in honor of my vision and without that I could not take part in the ceremony. I resolved to think about it all I could in the hope that, in the words of Roaring-Wings, the song would "come to me," but it certainly had not yet.

It was the second day afterwards, that returning unexpectedly to the cabin, I found Bowl-Woman busily working on some deerskin clothing. When she saw me in the doorway, she gave a little scream and hurriedly put the things away.

"*Ma'ta*," she said. "I will not tell you what I am making. But this much I can promise you. Before many moons have passed, you shall know."

The sickening suspicion came that she might be making me a girl's outfit as Cross-Woman had done. I recalled how badly she treated me before I went out to fast. I was frankly worried, because White-Deer had told me that after I had received a blessing things would "be different," yet here I was, still doing woman's work, helping Bowl-Woman with her harvest.

I decided then and there to call upon my new-found *Man-it'to-wuk* to see whether the promised help would be given me.

IX. Manittos, Witches, and Scalp Locks

STEPPED out of the cabin, feeling glum enough; there sat Thunder-Arrow under the big tree, working as usual at his trade of arrow maker and humming a lively little tune. I flopped down beside him.

"*Hey*, Big-Chief!" he said, "what are you going to do today: make canoes or catch whales?"

"Neither one," I mumbled.

"What's the matter? Did you eat too much *sa'pan?*"

"Oh, no; it's nothing. *At-ta-ka'*, nothing at all."

"If it's as bad as that, why don't you call on your *ma-nit'to?*"

"Maybe I would if I knew how," I grumbled. "Roaring-Wings said something about burning tobacco and, I think, praying. But that does not tell me just how to go about it."

Thunder-Arrow deftly twirled an arrow with one hand whilst with the other he guided the wet sinew filaments binding feathers to shaft. The bindings completed, he touched them with his glue stick.

"The best way I know," he said slowly, "is to build a fire in some wild and lonely place, burn some tobacco, twelve pinches of it, address your helper, then ask aloud or silently for what you desire.   After that, think about it, wish for it, and wait."

I heard a slight noise and looked up.   There stood Roaring-Wings, as solemn and dignified as ever, not two paces away.

"If you are in trouble," he said in his deep voice, "go up to the hilltop and let the north wind blow your trouble away; or let the south wind talk to you and give you comfort."

"That is good advice," said Thunder-Arrow.

"*Wa-nee'shih!*" Roaring-Wings replied.   "I come, however, not to give advice, but to bring a gift to this young man. *Hoo! Mah!* Take it!" He handed me a little bundle wrapped in fine deerskin. I untied it and peered in.   There lay a miniature flint chipper and a sewing awl; a tiny bow and a small war club, all beautifully made and just like those I had dreamed about; also a little bag of tobacco.

"You must take care of this bundle as long as you live," he added, as I carefully tied it up.

Of course I was pleased, but my heart was still "bad," as the Indians say.   However, I managed to thank the old man and then I struck off up the creek carrying the bundle with me.   Moon-ha'kee followed as usual.   My mind struggled with the problem of what Bowl-Woman was making.   If it wasn't another dress, why didn't she want me to see it?   And why couldn't I get a song if my vision was a real one?   I doubted everybody and everything.

In this frame of mind I reached the pile of rocks where I had fasted; there was the ant hill and there was the little cave, with my grass bed still in it.   I hung the bundle with my bow and quiver on a bush and sat down on a rock. Moon-ha'kee bustled about and found a mouse hole, the dirt began to fly! I listened; there was no sound but his panting and scratching, the ripple of water, the rustle of leaves. I took my firesticks out of my quiver, my punk from my shoulder pouch and in a few moments I had a small fire burning. I remembered the tobacco in the bundle, took the little bag in my hand. I felt very strange making my first offering.

"Now I am throwing tobacco," I whispered. "Listen, ye *Man-it'to-wuk*. Ye who have promised to help me, listen!" Twelve times I sprinkled tobacco, and the smoke rose white.

"Now I have finished," I said. "Help me. Give me a song at the *Gam'wing*. Help me. Clear my mind with regard to Bowl-Woman."

I stood a moment but no response came. Well, I would wait a while, as Thunder-Arrow advised. And while I waited, I might as well be comfortable. I stopped a moment to look at the ant hill. The ants were still as busy as ever; then over I went and settled down in my grass bed, wishing and wishing that the promised help would come.

As I lay there, a warm wind blew from the south up the little valley; it really seemed to soothe me; somehow I ceased to worry. After all what difference did it make if I didn't sing about my vision at the *Gam'wing*? I could listen to the others; then, maybe next year I might have a suitable song of my own. As for Bowl-Woman, I thought back over her treatment of me. Except for the time just before my fast, she had always been most kind.

She could not play such a scurvy trick upon me. I must trust her, in spite of appearances; I *would* trust her. At peace with the world, I fell asleep.

And then another dream came, even stranger than my original vision. I was just as small as the ants in the little ant hill; there were crowds of them sitting all around me, and the blades of grass looked as big as forest trees. Two of the ants were kneeling in front of a beetle shell which they were using as a drum, beating on it with little sticks, keeping time to my singing! I would sing a line, then they would repeat it, then I sang another, and they repeated that. I awoke, still singing. These were the words:

> Bringing food
> Men and women
> Now I live
> Live in plenty
> Thin, black legs
> Thus he said
> Bringing blessing
> *Kway-hay-yay!*

The words did not seem to mean much, but the tune was a good one, and I remember it to this day.

I staggered to my feet, only half awake. All at once I heard excited, short yelps, eager panting, then a shrill squeal. Moon-ha'kee had his mouse at last. Not until that moment did it dawn upon me that my prayers, like his, had been answered.

When we got back to the cabin, it was dusk. Thunder-Arrow was lying back against a pile of rolled mats, smoking. His day's work was over, because he could not make arrows or anything else by firelight. He saw that I was carrying the bundle.

"Better hang your bundle over your bed," he said. "Such things should never touch the ground."

Bowl-Woman laid the baby on the *ha'soon*, pulled some coals out of the fire, and propped a pot over them.

"Your food will soon be ready," she informed me. "Do you know," she added, "this place was lonely this afternoon with you two boys away."

"I cannot understand it," mourned Thunder-Arrow. "Here am I, the greatest man in the tribe, honoring her by sitting in her house and eating her *sa'pan;* yet she is lonely for a couple of fledglings!"

I had my stew about half eaten when the door curtain was lifted and a young warrior, a stranger to me, stepped inside. He was straight and slender with a hooked nose and fierce, black eyes. His head was shaven but for the stiff, short crest and dangling scalp lock; head and face were rubbed with red paint. After staring at me a moment, he beckoned to Thunder-Arrow, who, laying down his pipe, went outside with the new arrival. Then came a murmur of voices, and somehow I knew that they were talking about me, although I could not catch the words.

After a while Thunder-Arrow came in and picked up his pipe again. He scraped out the ashes, refilled it, lighted it with a burning brand from the fireplace, and lay back against the mats with a sigh. Soon he was enveloped in a cloud of white smoke, a curious habit!

I waited a while hoping he would tell me what had passed between them, but he did not, so I asked outright:

"Who was that young man?"

"Oh, nobody important. Just a messenger."

"From whom?"

"From the Turtle Band Chief, if you must know."

That did not mean much to me, so I tried another line.

"Did he say anything about me?"

"Maybe he did and perhaps he did not."

"What did he say?"

"*Hoh, tak-ta'nee.* I don't know. Some good and some bad. Maybe you can sing the last night of the *Gam'wing*, if you have a song by that time."

"I have one now."

"Good! The only trouble is, you must be a member of the tribe before they will let you sing."

My heart fell; that was indeed an obstacle, for of course I was nothing but a captive. I came pretty close to tears. Thunder-Arrow was watching me to see how I would take it.

"Don't feel too badly," he advised. "Maybe we can find someone to adopt you."

"Who would ever adopt me?"

"*Tak-ta'nee.* Maybe we can coax Bowl-Woman to do it." Thunder-Arrow grinned. "In truth she mentioned it several moons ago."

So Bowl-Woman had been planning all along to adopt me! My joy was mixed with shame that I should have misjudged her. One thought suggested another. Perhaps she was truly making me some new clothes, not a dress either! It was some time, however, before I learned what she was really making.

Next day I was going along quite happily out into the forest to gather firewood when I came suddenly face to face with two curious persons trotting rapidly along the path toward the village. They wore ugly little masks of wood with cornhusk hair and their clothes were made of cornhusks: sleeveless jackets, leggings, and shoes coarsely woven.

They pounced upon me before I knew what had happened and held me tight. They smelled bad.

"Give us a present!" demanded one in a queer, cracked voice.

"Give it quick or we shall smear you," ordered the other.

"Who are you?" I faltered.

"We are the Smearers!" said the cracked voice. "Quick!"

"The present!" said the other. "*Shai!*"

"But I have nothing," I protested.

"Give us your pack strap!"

"I can't, it belongs to Bowl-Woman."

"Your breechclout then."

"It's the only one I've got," I argued.

"*Hoh!* Smear him!"

One held me in an iron grip whilst the other took a horrible smelly mess out of a skin sack and smeared it over my body.

"*Ta'lee!*" said the cracked voice. "This will make you remember the Corn Dance, five days from today." They trotted off down the path.

Just then Toad-Face appeared and, seeing my condition, began to laugh.

"Oh, ho-ho-ho!   Look at yourself!   Smell yourself! Oh, ho-ho-ho."   He leaned up against a tree.   "Oh, ho-ho-ho!"

I was minded to punch him; then I got a better idea— perhaps the Smearers were not out of hearing.

"*Yoo'hoo!*" I yelled.   "Smearers!"

"*Oh'ho!*" came the answer.   "What is it?"

"Come back!   A present!"

Toad-Face was laughing so hard that he did not notice what I was up to.   When the Smearers appeared, I pointed to him.   They understood.   In a second they grabbed him as I had hoped.   Toad-Face had nothing to give them and he made the mistake of fighting them; as a result, he was given a bigger dose, smeared over even his face and hair.

"*Ta'lee!*   Remember!   Corn Dance!   Five days!" And away they went.

Then *I* laughed.   "Ho-ho-ho-ho!   Look at yourself! Smell yourself!   Ho-ho-ho-ho-ho!"

"*Cheet-kwe'se.*   Shut up!" said Toad-Face with a murderous look.

"Oh, ho-ho-ho-ho!   Miss Toad-Face.   Pretty little spring flower.   Smells sweet.   Oh, ho-ho-ho-ho!"

"I'll get even!" Toad-face threatened.   "You'll be sorry!"

"Skunk smells Toad-Face," I chortled.   "Skunk is jealous!   Why?   Toad-Face smells strongest!   Oh, ho-ho-ho-ho!   By and by skunk gets sick, dies.   Can't stand smell!   Oh, ho-ho-ho-ho!"

"You'll die, too, or wish you could," Toad-Face growled.   "Just wait."

"Better go now, Big Skunk," I retorted. "Wash yourself for once or they won't let you into the village."

I slipped down to the river myself and washed; but still I smelled badly. Finally I had to find some *win'gay-musk*, or sweet grass, to rub on my body before I could endure my own company. Little-Bear had shown me how sweet grass grows in old fields or natural meadows about knee-high and may be recognized by the fine fuzz or down on the leaves. The Indians braided this grass and dried it for use as perfume. Clothing laid away with sweet grass had a very pleasant odor. The smell of a good-class Lenape house was always quite agreeable: a combination of wood smoke, corn, and sweet grass.

Two days later, whilst I was out nutting with a crowd of boys and girls and a few older women, White-Deer beckoned me aside.

"You will have to look out for Toad-Face," she whispered. "My cousin saw him taking a deer to old Black-Medicine-Woman's cabin. She is a witch, you know, and he may be paying her to cast a spell over you. If you feel strangely, don't wait, but get a doctor—somebody like Roaring-Wings."

In England I had heard many tales of witches, and indeed one old woman had been burned as a witch very near our home, which had made a great impression upon me, although Mother would not permit me to see the burning. I remembered the yelling crowd and the smoke in the street only too well. I did not like a bit the idea of having an Indian witch working upon me here in America.

I promised White-Deer that I would go to Roaring-Wings immediately, should I feel anything wrong, then

I told her the good news that Bowl-Woman was planning to adopt me and that I might be allowed to sing my
vision on the twelfth night of the *Gam'wing*.   She was
delighted and promised to stay awake that night to hear it.

She laughed when I told her about the Smearers and
what they did to Toad-Face.

"This time of year everybody carries something for
a present in case they meet the Smearers, like this," she
said, showing me two or three shell beads tied on a
string around her left wrist.   "A few beads, an arrowhead, even a little package of tobacco or a braid of sweet
grass will do.   I am surprised that Toad-Face was caught
without anything.   Of course you would not know,
because the Smearers' Corn Dance was over last fall before
you came to the village, and nobody thought to tell you."

"Will you go with me to the Corn Dance?" I asked
her.

White-Deer looked at the ground.   "Among our
people," she said, "young women do not go with young
men to dances unless they are married.   I should like to
go with you, but even I would not dare to do that, and
you know I break the old rules sometimes.   The only
way we could do it would be——"   She looked up
roguishly.

"Would be what?" I pursued.

"Don't you wish you knew?" she giggled softly and,
jumping up, seized her bag of nuts and, running swiftly,
joined the older women who were about to start homeward.   I wondered what she could have meant, but I
did not find out for a long time.   White-Deer was a great
tease, but I liked her all the more for it, I think.

The Corn Dance was the biggest meeting I had attended in Lenape Land except the *Gam'wing* the preceding fall. They had a speaker as usual, a number of men and women cooks, and even waiters to pass the food around. For a wonder I did not have to work myself to death this time in honor of *Ka-hay'sa-na Kas'kweem*, or "Mother Corn," as I had for the *Ow'tas* doll and the *Mee-sing'* mask; in fact I did not do a stroke of work.

I noticed, however, with a cook's eye that the principal dish was a thin *sa'pan*, or hominy, ground very fine and cooked like gruel. It tasted good with tree sugar.

The speaker told a curious story.

"A long time ago," he began, "the Corn Spirit, whom we know as Mother Corn, left the earth. She was angry, it is said, because certain young men had stated that they did not believe she existed or that the people could ever lose their seed corn.

"The very grains of corn took flight with wings like little bugs. One man said that his wife's seed corn would never get away from him, so he put it in a deerskin bag and kept it under his head whilst he slept; but this corn flew away, too, in the form of bugs or weevils when the bag was opened.

"It was two boys who persuaded Mother Corn to return to the earth. It is claimed that they found means to fly, as the seed corn had done, from the earth to the place where Mother Corn resides. At first she refused to return, but they made her an offering of burnt mussel shells, and finally she accepted; then she instructed them how to hold this Corn Dance in a manner pleasing to her, and this has been continued ever since. The two boys were the first Smearers.

"She gave each of the boys a little, good seed corn, and this they brought back with them. From two handfuls of seed came all the corn we now have.

"Mother Corn exists today in the form of an aged woman. She is the *man-it'to* taking charge, not only of corn, but of squashes, beans, all the things the Lenapes raise."

He thanked the goddess for the bountiful harvest just gathered, prayed that we should have as good a one next year, and that all would enjoy good health. Finally he called upon everyone to behave at this ceremony and not have any disorder. Mother Corn was counted as one of the Helpers of the Creator and a special guardian of the Lenape tribe.

When the dance started, I was not surprised to see that the leaders were my sweet-scented friends, the Smearers: masks, cornhusk clothing, sleeveless jackets, leggings, shoes, and all. The men danced with these two; the next set the women danced behind two leaders of their own who, however, wore no masks; then the men again. If I recall, they danced six sets each, or twelve in all. Then the feast followed, and after dark a fire was built around which the people danced until morning, for pleasure only, or so I heard, for I did not stay. Really I was ashamed to remain, because I did not know how to dance; whilst White-Deer, who had come with her mother, was one of the best dancers. I resolved to learn.

Once the Corn Dance was over, Thunder-Arrow and Bowl-Woman told me the truth. They had been planning to adopt me for quite a while and intended to announce the adoption at the time of the *Gam'wing*.

"There is only one thing that worries me," said Thunder-Arrow, in a serious tone, unusual for him. "I have heard that your tribesmen, the White-Faces, who have landed south and east of here and built a village, are now abusing the Indians and fighting with them. I want you to tell me truly. If war comes between the White-Faces and the Lenapes, which side will you take?"

I could not answer for a long while, for my mind was in a turmoil. I was very sorry that trouble between the English at Jamestown and the Indians should raise such a problem and very doubtful what should be my reply. Finally I spoke:

"You ask me a hard question. I love the English people who gave me birth, and I love you Lenape people who have been so good to me."

Thunder-Arrow looked very grave. "I shall ask the question in a different way. Suppose I was away and a white man came into this cabin and tried to harm Bowl-Woman or the baby, what would you do?"

"I'd fight him!" I cried. "I'd fight anyone who offered to harm them!"

"That is all I wanted to know," answered Thunder-Arrow, relieved. He filled and lighted his pipe. "The *Gam'wing* will be here before many days," he continued. "We shall begin our preparations tomorrow."

Bowl-Woman, who had been listening intently, now pulled out a covered basket from beneath one of the platforms and opened it. Inside was some new deerskin clothing. Was it a dress after all?

"These are yours," she said, "to wear at the *Gam'wing.*"

Truly I feared to pick up a garment. Bowl-Woman noticed my hesitation and drew out a breechclout, or *sahk-koo-ta'kun.* Such a relief! Then out came a pair of long leggings, a pair of moccasins all embroidered, a crest made of red-dyed deer hair and black turkey beards,

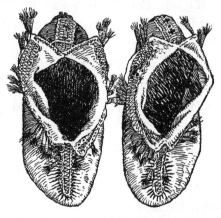

a shoulder sack or pocket of dyed deerskin, also embroidered, a couple of tufts of white down-feathers fastened to little wooden stems. There was not a skirt in the lot this time!

"I made everything," she said simply, "except the crest and the feather tufts. They are Thunder-Arrow's work."

I thanked them as well as I could and went outside with brimming eyes. I started across the square toward the river bank, intending to tell White-Deer the good news. As I approached the Big-House, I noticed an old woman sitting on the ground with her back up against the building not far from the path. I did not pay much attention to her at that moment, but after I passed her, she hailed me.

"*Hey*, In-the-Forest! Come hither!"

Foolishly, I turned and walked back. My heart missed a beat when I saw that it was Black-Medicine-Woman, the reputed witch. There was no mistaking that hawklike face under its mop of unkempt, gray hair. Moon-ha'kee's back bristled and he growled menacingly at her, until I made him stop. She studied me with piercing, deep-sunken, black eyes.

"You are happy now," she said, "but soon you will be unhappy."

"What do you mean?" I asked. I could not take my eyes from hers.

"You will be very sick, very sick, unless I help you."

"I don't understand." Now my heart was pounding.

"You have an enemy in the village who is trying to harm you. He will succeed if I do not help you."

"Why don't you help me, then?"

"First you must make me strong with gifts. Give me four strings of corn and two sacks of dried meat."

I could see it all now. The old crone was receiving gifts from Toad-Face to harm me; now she was playing with me to get more gifts. Without thinking of the consequences, I blurted out what was in my mind.

"How would Toad-Face like that?" I demanded. "He gave you presents first."

She scrambled to her feet, her lips drawn back in a sort of snarl that showed what remained of her teeth. They were worn down nearly to the gums. She fixed me again with those baleful eyes.

"You will be sorry," she answered slowly. "Beware the *Kook'hos*." She walked a few steps toward her cabin, then turned and faced me again. "*Nay Kook'hos*," she repeated solemnly.

I felt as if someone had struck me a hard blow. Deciding not to alarm White-Deer by telling her this new threat, I hurried back to the cabin. Thunder-Arrow had gone out, but Bowl-Woman and the baby were at home.

"What is the matter?" cried Bowl-Woman as I came in. "You look frightened."

"Tell me, what is a *Kook'hos*?" I demanded without answering her question.

"It is a bird with big, round eyes that flies at night. But why do you ask?"

"Black-Medicine-Woman has told me to beware of the *Kook'hos;* just now she told me."

"*Ee-kee'!* I am very sorry," Bowl-Woman said. "That means she is threatening to bewitch you."

"I was afraid that was what she meant. But what has the *Kook'hos* bird to do with that? We have them in England and call them owls. All they do is fly around at night and catch mice."

"Black-Medicine-Woman did not mean a real bird. They say witches can take the form of a *Kook'hos* at night and fly to the house of the victim they are going to bewitch. Maybe she was just talking; trying to scare you into giving her a present. I hope that is all it amounts to."

"If she is a witch, why is she allowed to live in the village? In England we burn them or hang them." Bowl-Woman did not know just what I meant by "hanging," as applied to a person, so I explained.

"The White-Faces must be a cruel people." Bowl-Woman shuddered. "If *I* were a witch, I'd rather be burned any day. As for Black-Medicine-Woman, people think she is a witch and fear her, but nobody can prove it. She takes advantage of the fear to make people give her presents. The only real way to kill witches and be sure you get the guilty ones, is to shoot them when they come in the form of an owl. When the owl dies, the witch dies, too."

When Thunder-Arrow came home that night, he made light of our fears. It was plain that he did not take witches very seriously, and so by the time I went to bed, I had about forgotten my scare. However in the night I awoke thinking I was being smothered and I could see, or thought I saw, a great black something hovering over me as I lay and holding me down with unseen bonds. I struggled, struggled and finally breaking loose, rolled off the *ha'soon* to the ground. As I scrambled to my feet, I heard an owl hoot in the big tree outside the cabin.

I was afraid to go to sleep again, so I got but little rest; yet in the morning I was ready when Thunder-Arrow said we must begin to prepare for the adoption. I told him about my nightmare, but he made no comment.

The first step, he said, was to be inside purification. He took some herbs and boiled them for a while in a little pot; then gave me the tea to drink. It made me very sick, and I am sure that within half a day there was nothing left inside me, pure or impure.

In the meantime he had cut eight poles six or seven feet long and had planted them in a circle on top of the bank just above the swimming hole. Then he bent the tops together and tied them so as to form four arches, meeting in the center, a dome-shaped frame. He ran two or three courses of basswood-bark string around from pole to pole, parallel to the ground, and finally covered the dome with pieces of old tent mats, completing the *pee-mo-a'kun*, or sweat house. I heard later that some villages had permanent sweat houses, built of logs and earth. The next step was to heat twelve round stones, each as big as my two fists, in a fire built near by; when they were ready, he rolled them inside with a forked stick, and we both crawled in naked, closing the door opening behind. Once inside Thunder-Arrow threw some tobacco on the stones, then began to sing and splash water from a bark bucket on them, and the steam rose so thick and so hot that I could hardly breathe. The sweat simply poured from me, everywhere.

At last it was over, and we plunged into the river. After we had swum around for a while, Thunder-Arrow caught hold of me and ducked me a number of times.

"*Hoh!* It is enough," he said at last. "Now you are completely clean, inside and out, ready to become a Lenape. You will have to bathe again every morning until the *Gam'wing*, but the hard part is over. As for myself, I feel almost as clean as you look!"

I felt pretty weak, but I ate a good meal, some stew that had been saved especially for us, and went to bed early, hoping for a good, long sleep. In the middle of the night I awoke again, smothering, and again I heard the owl call.

Thunder-Arrow, awakened by my cries, rushed out with his bow and arrows, but although the moon was shining, he could not locate the owl.

"I'll get her next time," he said. "You'll see."

He made me go to sleep again whilst he watched, and next day I felt fairly well.

Thunder-Arrow started the day by making two little tapering sticks about half a span long of cedar wood and smoothing them very carefully. Then he cut the strings of beads that poor Granny had hung from my ears and took them out, replacing the strings with the little sticks, after greasing them well.

"The sticks," he explained, "are to stretch the holes in your ears until you can wear ornaments more befitting a man. Every once in a while push them into the holes a little farther."

The next thing was my hair.

"I want you to wear a crest," he said, "and that means that most of your hair must be removed. There are three ways of doing this: one by cutting, which looks ragged; one by burning with a hot stone which is likely to blister your head, and the third by pulling the hair out, bit by bit. This is the best way, but it hurts, and only brave boys can stand it."

Since he put it that way, there was only one thing for me to say, although I dreaded the ordeal.

"Pull it out!"

He sat down by the fireplace, and I lay my head in his lap. He moistened his thumb and forefinger, dipped them in ashes and began. Once in a while he drew a grunt out of me, and I squirmed and sweat, but he kept

on until my poor head was picked like a chicken, all but
a strip, two fingers wide from the front to the crown of
my head, where there was a circular tuft three or four

fingers across. The strip he cut with a sharp flint flake
until all that remained was a crest of hair about two
fingers high; the tuft which was my scalp lock, he left
full length, and made it up into three thin braids. These
he decked with wrappings of dyed porcupine quills and
little tubes made of bird bone, strung upon the braids.
My head felt very strange and light without my hair and
it was very sore. Bowl-Woman suggested that I rub it
with that wonderful food and cure-all—bear's grease.
She carefully gathered all the hair that had been pulled
out and burned it, for fear it might fall into the hands of
the witch, who would then have double power over me.

That night I did not get to sleep very early, my head
being so sore, and I was awakened some time after midnight by a strange cry. I was sitting on the edge of the
ha'soon, rubbing my eyes when Thunder-Arrow came in,

carrying something. He held it in the shaft of moon-light from the smoke hole for me to see. It was a big owl, transfixed with an arrow.

Next day we heard that Black-Medicine-Woman had been found dead in her cabin. Everybody said that the killing of the owl took her life, too, but of course I can-not vouch for that. Her death may have just happened at that time. One thing, however, I *can* bear witness to. From that time to this I have never wakened again with that horrible smothering sensation nor have I seen that shapeless, black something hovering above me.

The following night was sleepless for another reason: the constant tum-a-tum of the water drum, the steady "heen-a-heen, heen-a-heen," of the chant made sleep out of the question. They were playing the moccasin game whilst they sat up all night with Black-Medicine-Woman's body.

X. A Full-fledged Lenape

I HAD taken my morning plunge and was standing on the bluff above the swimming place, looking down the river, when my roving eye lighted on some distant specks. They must be canoes! As I stood watching, they seemed to grow larger. After a while I could count them: there were five! Suddenly an idea struck me and I ran to the cabin.

"*Hoh*, Thunder-Arrow!" I puffed. "Give me some red paint."

"What's the matter? Going to war? Want to lose that new scalp lock so soon?" Thunder-Arrow fished around in a basket and found me a little deerskin bag of pulverized red earth, *o-lum' a-nay*.

"Not yet," I responded and then I explained my plan. Thunder-Arrow chuckled as he rubbed my head and face with the paint; then he took down his wooden feather case from the platform where the *Mee-sing'* was stored and selected a couple of eagle tail feathers, not his best ones, I noticed, and tied them on my scalp lock. He looked me over, handed me a new light robe of his own, and together we strolled over to the bluff.

Here we stood, dignified and aloof, whilst the five canoes approached, the paddlers whooped, and the usual crowd, mostly children, rushed past us down to the shore. Beaver-House's canoe was the last to arrive, as he was short-handed, and by the time he and Little-Bear were ready to mount the path most of the crowd had gone. Just as I expected, Beaver-House greeted Thunder-Arrow with a friendly, *"Hey!"* but passed me by with only a curious glance.

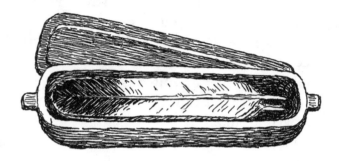

Now came Little-Bear, carrying a sack and a package.

He greeted his father, but looked at me out of the corner of his eye as if he were a little afraid of me.

"Where is In-the-Forest?" he demanded.

"Tak-ta'nee. He seems to have disappeared," Thunder-Arrow answered. "Maybe he flew away like those grains of corn the speaker always tells about at the Corn Dance."

"Don't joke about my friend," said Little-Bear. Then his voice fell to a whisper, and I knew he was asking who I was. I could hardly keep my face straight.

"You mean this man?" Thunder-Arrow pointed at me. "Oh, he is a visiting *Min'see* tribesman from up the river. He says he will give you ten deerskins if you will take him home in a canoe; he has walked a long way."

I could hold back no longer.

"Yes," I said. "We can stop on the way and catch a few sturgeons!"

"*Nee'tees!* In-the-Forest!" Little-Bear shouted. "Crest and scalp lock! All painted up! No wonder I didn't know you!" He turned to his father. "Before the *Gam'wing* I want my hair fixed that way."

"Better not," grunted Thunder-Arrow with a grin. "White-Deer won't know you."

"Did you bring me anything?" I asked Little-Bear.

"One sack of shells!"

I looked into the sack; it was full of large whelks, or conches, the Lenapes called *chee-kwo-a-la'leh*. Thunder-Arrow looked in, too.

"You can make a lot of *kay'kwuk* beads out of those," he remarked.

"*Wa-nee'shih*," I said. "They look fine. Did you bring me anything else?"

"A queer piece of wood," was the answer, as Little-Bear opened the mat wrapping of the package. I recognized it instantly. It was a piece of a hen coop that had stood on the deck of *Ye Portsmouth Maide*. I took it into my hands almost reverently.

"Did the coast people find many other pieces of my big canoe?" I asked.

"They said they found very little, but I think I know the reason."

"What do you mean?" I asked with a strange, tight feeling in my breast.

"The people of the villages south of the bay saw a great, winged canoe moving southward the day after that

storm when we found you a year ago. It looked somewhat damaged, especially the wings, but it was traveling
along quite rapidly. Maybe your big canoe was not so
badly broken on the shoal as you thought."

Perhaps *Ye Portsmouth Maide* had not been wrecked
after all! Yet, if my dear father still lived, he would
have come to seek me. Probably, then, the Indians had
seen some other ship or my father had been lost before the
Maide freed herself from the shoal. Thinking thus, I
thanked Little-Bear and tried to turn my mind to happier
thoughts. However I carried the piece of hen coop home
and stored it with my other possessions. It was my
sole link with the life I had left behind.

Little-Bear wanted to know if I had received a song,
and when I told him I had, he confessed that he had
received a vision two years previously with a song
included; but that he had never attempted to recite it
at the *Gam'wing* because he could not carry a tune. I
did not inform him that I was to be his adopted brother;
I would leave that to Bowl-Woman. Therefore when we
reached the cabin, I remained outside.

In a moment he came rushing out with shining eyes
and gave me a real brotherly hug, and I was much relieved
for I had feared that he might be a little jealous. To have
a boy for your friend is one thing; to have him taken into
the family on equal footing with yourself is a very different matter.

Thunder-Arrow sent me with a string of beads to
Roaring-Wings that afternoon for instruction in reciting
my vision, in singing, and in the sort of dancing necessary
for the *Gam'wing*.

My teacher led me away to a quiet place in the woods and there I went with him every day until the old man thought I could do my part very well. I was not so sure, although I had tried hard enough. Before we went home, he gave me the rattle which I had used to beat time for my singing. It was made of the shell of a box turtle. It pleased me very much.

While I was learning to sing, Little-Bear had been having his hair plucked, and I thought he looked brave and fine and I told him so; but he hardly heard me and I could see that his mind was on other things. He beckoned for me to follow him and led me across the common to the river bank; I trailed close behind, wondering.

Then he began:

"There is something I must tell you before you are adopted; perhaps you will not wish to be my brother when you know. *Ee-kee'!* Truly it is hard to tell you."

"Go ahead and tell me," I urged. "It can't be so very bad."

"I like White-Deer very much; moreover, I hope to marry her some day!"

Of course I really knew this all the time, so I was not taken by surprise. Long ago I had made up my mind not to stand in the way if the matter should come up, much as I thought of White-Deer. So I said, although I must admit it was not easy:

"*Yoh!* Be it so! And truly in my heart, I wish you well, my elder brother."

"*Wa-nee'shih!* If you really feel that way, perhaps you will help me," he said, apparently much relieved.

"*Kay'hay-la!* I'll help you. What shall I do?"

"Can't you teach me to play the *ah-pee'kawn*? I want to play a call for White-Deer tonight."

"There is not enough time; the sun is already half-way down the sky. But this is what I can do. I can go with you and play the calls; then I can run when we hear her coming out."

Little-Bear studied my face a moment, then he replied:

"Very well. The only thing is, it will be pretty hard on you." He never knew just how hard it was.

White-Deer's house stood on the low bluff above the river in the south edge of the village, and we planned to serenade her from the river bank below. The moon was shining brightly as we made our way along the shore, Little-Bear carrying his *ah-pee'kawn*.

As we approached our destination, we began to hear a curious, squawking sound, and tiptoeing quickly, we found that it was Toad-Face trying to serenade White-Deer himself!

"I am thankful," Little-Bear whispered, "that there is someone on this great island who plays worse than I." He stepped up to Toad-Face, whilst I remained in the background.

"What are you doing here?" he asked. "Trying to choke a duck? It sounds that way."

"I'll choke you," growled Toad-Face, "if you don't get out of here. I was here first." Seeing that he made no move to depart, Toad-Face made a sudden grab for Little-Bear's *ah-pee'kawn* and hurled it far out on the river. Before Little-Bear could take action, I sprang forward and snatched Toad-Face's instrument, throwing it as far as I could.

"So you're here, too?" Toad-Face sneered. "Two against one, eh? A brave pair you are, truly. *Ay-kay-saa'!* Very well, I'll go. But you wait; I'll get even," he said with a menacing glance as he slunk away.

We watched him out of sight; then I ran back to our cabin and fetched my own *ah-pee'kawn.*

I played three of my best calls over several times, and then Little-Bear made me stop. He had heard a voice from the cabin above. I handed him my *ah-pee'kawn* and scuttled out of sight, returning home by a roundabout route. I did not sleep very well; in fact I heard Little-Bear when he came home, and that must have been late.

Along toward morning I slept better; in fact I was still asleep when Bowl-Woman called me from outside the cabin.

"Fling-Her-This-Way is here and wants to see you," she said.

I knew that was White-Deer's mother's name but I could not imagine why she should come to see me.

"I know that it is not considered proper," she explained when I came out of the cabin, "and Bowl-Woman, here, thinks it is terrible, but my daughter wishes you to come over to our house as soon as you can. She is a good girl, In-the-Forest, but when she wants anything, she will not be denied."

White-Deer made a very pretty picture when we entered the cabin, sitting on the edge of her *ha'soon.* She had put on her best embroidered dress; her hair was very smoothly brushed and fastened with a pretty *ah-see-pe-la'wan* and an embroidered ribbon. As to paint, there was only a small red spot on each cheek, and a little streak of red showed in the part of her hair. She wore all of her beads and bracelets made of little oval white shells. She motioned for me to sit down beside her, which I did with some trepidation; then her mother considerately withdrew.

"I wish to talk with you," she began. "Little-Bear came here last night and played some very beautiful love calls on the *ah-pee'kawn*. I went down to the river's edge, and do you want to know something?"

I managed to ask, "What?"

"I expected to find *you* there, but it was Little-Bear instead. Oh, don't misunderstand me. I like Little-Bear very, very much. He is a wonderful boy and a very fine *ah-pee'kawn* player, but I was—I was—well—a little disappointed," she said shyly, looking at me in the old way, "that it wasn't *you*."

I dared not let her know how I felt; I could not say a word, my mind was in such a turmoil, so I stared dumbly into space.

"Little-Bear asked me to marry him," she went on. "I did not say, 'Yes' and I did not say, 'No.' I thought I should speak to you first. Tell me, straight from your heart, In-the-Forest, shall I say, 'No' or 'Yes' to Little-Bear?"

Finally I forced out the words, "Better tell him, 'Yes.' "

"Why? Don't you like me? I thought you did," she faltered.

"Like you? Of course I like you, better than any other girl I know. But Little-Bear is a man, a very fine young man, whilst I am just a boy. In my country I should have to be five or six years older before I would be allowed to marry," I explained with effort. "Truly, White-Face children grow up much more slowly than Lenapes."

She burst into tears, whilst I sat there stupidly, not knowing what to do or say.

"Go!" she said, giving me a push, "tell Little-Bear to come here tonight and play his third call. I shall be ready to give him his answer then."

When I reached home, I found Little-Bear under the shed talking to his mother. He looked at me strangely, but his eyes lighted when I gave him White-Deer's message. Then his face fell.

"Did she say 'the third call'? *A-kee'!* I don't even remember how it goes, let alone play it, or any of them, for that matter. What shall I do?"

"Listen, my elder brother," I said. "I'll play for you again tonight, but I can't keep on doing it forever. I advise you to pray to your *man-it'to* to give you power to learn how to play the *ah-pee'kawn*. Then I'll try to teach you. I can see trouble coming if you don't learn and learn quickly."

At last the great day came, the day of the *Gam'wing*, that meant so much to me. Thunder-Arrow awakened me before dawn and made me take my plunge in the chilly waters. Whilst we were eating our breakfast, he informed me that this time the ceremonies were to begin just after midday instead of in the evening as usual.

"We are going to enjoy a rare privilege," he said. "We shall hear the *Wa'lum O'loom*. Only once before have I heard it in this village, and everyone knows I have lived here," he hesitated, "a good many winters. I was going to say ever since this great island was created, but I was afraid you would not believe me!"

"What is the *Wa'lum O'loom?*" I queried.

"It is a set of flat, wooden tablets," he replied, "with a lot of little pictures painted on them in red. They tell the story of our Lenape tribe: whence we came and how we arrived in this country where we live today. Only the owner and his helper know just what the pictures mean, and they carry the tablets around from village to village and recite the story. Each picture reminds the owner of one part of it, so he cannot forget. I think he must have lost some of the tablets, though."

"What makes you think that?"

"In all that wonderful story no mention is made of the brave deeds *I* have done! They should fill up four or five tablets at least!"

Now came the time to put on my new clothes. The *sahk-koo-ta'kun*, or breechclout, had a broad stripe of red and yellow quill embroidery bordering the flaps front and back. The leggings were bordered to match across the bottom and were provided with long fringes at the sides, whilst the moccasins had the front seam covered with a quill design and the flaps decorated with a fine pattern in colored deer hair. To go with this outfit, Bowl-Woman had made me a light fall robe of two buckskins sewn together and decorated on the back with a large figure of a turtle done in little, oval, white shells, sewn on separately.

Thunder-Arrow fastened the red deer-hair crest on my head with his own hands. First he removed the

ornaments from one of my scalp-lock braids and pulled
the braid through the hole purposely left in the middle
of the crest until this rested on the top of my head.   Then
he threaded on the bone "spreader"; then he fastened
both in place by thrusting a bone pin through the braid.
I reached up and felt of them; they seemed firmly attached.
Next he painted my face with red and black, and finally
he pulled the stretching sticks from my ears and inserted
the wooden stems of the white-down tufts.

I could gain some idea of my appearance by looking
at Little-Bear, for he had new clothes very much like
mine, white ear tufts and all.   After we were dressed, we
went over to the creek to admire ourselves in a quiet
pool.   This was not so satisfactory as a real mirror
would have been, but I must admit I made quite a brave
picture.

Thunder-Arrow had painted a wide, red band across
the upper part of my face from ear to ear, with a narrow,
black border along the bottom and a large red spot low
down on each cheek, whilst the whole lower part of
Little-Bear's face was painted yellow.

By the time Little-Bear and I returned from the creek,
Thunder-Arrow and Bowl-Woman were dressed.   We ate
a little lunch and made our way to the Big-House in all
our finery, Bowl-Woman carrying the baby on his cradleboard.   This time I was allowed to enter unmolested.

We entered by the east door as was customary, and
immediately I noticed a group of women sitting to my
right not on the bare ground, but on a layer of dry grass
that had been spread for the purpose, along near the
north wall.

"Those are the *Took'seet* women," Little-Bear whispered. "The *Took'seet* men are just beyond."

I knew *Took'seet* meant "round foot" and referred to the Wolf Band of the tribe. We passed on to the right, and Thunder-Arrow left us to sit with this group of men. Bowl-Woman joined the women of the *Po-ko-un'go*, or Turtle Band, sitting all the way across the west end of the Big-House, whilst Little-Bear and I sat down with the *Po-ko-un'go* men on the south side near the southwest corner. The word *Po-ko-un'go* seems to mean "dragging along" and referred to the turtle's motion in walking.

"The *Pay-lay'* Band sits in the southeast corner," said Little-Bear. "There are not so many of them in this village."

I knew *Pay-lay'* referred to the Turkey Band, although the regular word for "turkey" was *chik'kun-num*, easy to remember because it sounded like the English word for "chicken." *Pay-lay'* seems to mean "does not chew" or something of the kind.

"Next largest in numbers is the Wolf Band," continued Little-Bear, "and largest of all is the Turtle. Father belongs to the Wolf, and Mother and I to the Turtle. You yourself will become a Turtle as soon as you are adopted."

"I have heard this spoken of as a *Po-ko-un'go* village, also as *Tool-pay-oo-ta'nai*, or Turtle-Town. Is that because there are so many Turtle Band people here?" I asked.

"I think that is the reason; besides, our village chief is a Turtle," he replied. Suddenly he seized my arm. "Look!" he whispered, pointing. Toad-Face was just entering. He had tried to arrange his hair like ours, but whoever had helped him, probably some boy his own age, had made a sorry mess of it. The hair had been cut off, not pulled, and remained all jagged and uneven. The crest was a joke, and even the braids were poorly done. As he walked along past the women, there was a sort of ripple of snickers, and the men passed remarks loud enough for him to hear. I could see his face darken,

but he kept on. As he sat down, he gave me a mysterious and malicious, almost triumphant, look, which I was at a loss to understand.

While I was puzzling over the look, a little procession entered the Big-House, led by the village chief himself, wearing a bearskin cap to which several eagle feathers were attached.

"The two men behind the chief," whispered Little-Bear, "are the chiefs of the Wolf and Turkey bands; the next three are the assistant chiefs, and the next the *ee'la-wak*, or war leaders, one for each band."

I recognized the three men armed with long poles and the three neatly dressed women who followed; they were the *ash-kas'uk*, or Big-House attendants. After these came a very small, dark-complexioned man with very long hair and a slight beard, dressed in clean, but plain clothing. He carried on his back a bundle wrapped in fine matting and, stepping closely in his tracks, walked the tallest and fattest Lenape I ever saw, his head completely plucked except one small braid in back for a scalp lock. This individual bore a small drum, which he beat vigorously every few minutes, giving vent at the same time to a long-drawn, penetrating call.

With measured tread they marched, making four full circuits of the Big-House; then the chief halted in the middle of the north side. The village officers and the attendants, passing him, took their seats beside their clansmen; but the chief stood waiting the coming of the short, dark man and his gigantic companion. When all but these three had seated themselves, the chief spoke:

"One time, long ago, when our ancestors resided in the North, there lived a man who believed that the story of our people should never be forgotten. Knowing that men are, by nature, forgetful, he tried to plan some way to make them remember. Finally, it is said, a method of doing this was revealed to him in a dream. Truly, he was instructed to prepare flat, wooden tablets and to paint upon them pictures in red which would call to mind the things he wished to remember. To begin with, he painted the stories of the first days of the world as they were told by the old men of his time; then, he painted pictures to represent important things as they happened. On his death the tablets and the work were carried on by his family until the present day. You see before you Talking-Wood, the present owner of the set of tablets, which we call *Wa'lum O'loom*."

The short, dark man stepped forward.

"Talking-Wood will now recite the story of our people," continued the chief. "When he stops to rest, those who wish may go out, returning again when his companion, Naked-Bear, beats the drum. When his story is finished, those who feel able should throw a few *kay'kwuk* beads, in the corn mortar standing just outside the door, as a gift to Talking-Wood. This is the second time that the *Wa'lum O'loom* has ever been recited in this village as far as I know." The chief walked around and sat down near us.

Naked-Bear lifted the matting bundle from his companion's back, whilst an *ash'kas* spread a large, white-tanned deerskin in front of him; upon this the precious package was laid and opened. I could not see the contents although I stretched my neck in hopes. Then Naked-Bear, rising, beat his little drum and sounded his curious call.

Kneeling again beside the bundle, he handed a little flat board to Talking-Wood, who immediately began to chant, looking fixedly at the board as an Englishman reads a prayer book. When one board was finished, he handed it back to his companion who laid it carefully aside and gave him another, whereupon the chant began again. Besides these short stops there were four real intermissions, if I recall, and by the time the story was finished, the autumn sun outside was low and it was almost dark in the Big-House.

Like so many of the Lenape songs, this chant was hard to understand but it had a sort of swing like poetry and was quite pleasant to the ear. The first part told of the creation of the world, but it was told in such hazy language I could not get the story straight, except that the earth rose from the waters and men and animals were created. All lived happily together for a while, but an evil snake, *man-it'to*, came in and spoiled it all,

by flooding the earth with water. At this time the people escaped to a great island formed on the back of an enormous turtle.

Later on the people seemed to be living in a cold, northern land; then they moved south, fighting with different tribes, but learning how to raise corn; then they journeyed east to the country they occupied when I lived among them. There were references to wars with tribes I had never heard of and also to a long line of chiefs.

When Talking-Wood finished, many people left their seats, some to speak with him, others to drop a gift of *kay'kwuk* in the mortar outside. Little-Bear and I squirmed through the crowd and succeeded in getting a glimpse of the tablets before Naked-Bear wrapped them up. They were about two spans long and three fingers wide, and the figures seemed to be scratched into the wood, red paint being rubbed into the scratches. He put the tablets in five piles, each of which he wrapped separately before placing it in the outer cover of matting. A strange thing about the figures was that very few of them seemed to be pictures of anything; they were merely signs, which no one could understand unless previously instructed.

We all went home for supper, for we knew we should be hungry before morning, but I had heard that the adoption was to take place before the ceremonies began and I was so excited that I ate but little. Hardly had we finished when we heard the call of the chief *ash'kas*, acting as crier, summoning everyone to the Big-House. When we arrived, the two fires were burning, lighting the interior much more brightly than it had been that afternoon where the only light had come in through the door and the smoke holes.

After all were seated, the chief took his stand at the middle of the north side.

"I am glad," he began, "that so many of us have lived to meet again in our Big-House as did our ancestors. Before we begin our ceremonies, there are several namings and one adoption for us to consider. The first naming will be the child of Bowl-Woman and Thunder-Arrow. Where is the child?"

"*Yoo'ta-lee*," cried Bowl-Woman, rising and stepping forward. "Right here he is." She had taken the baby from his *am-bee'son* and was holding him in her arms.

"Who speaks for this child?" asked the chief.

"I do," spoke up an old man, a stranger to me, rising and taking his place beside Bowl-Woman.

"Listen, ye chiefs and warriors of the Lenape," he began. "Listen ye, women. Hearken, boys and girls. The name of this man-child, the son of Bowl-Woman and Thunder-Arrow, is It-is-Approaching. Let him be called by that name forever. Now I pray that he may enjoy good health and live to be very old and, most of all, be happy." He escorted Bowl-Woman around the Big-House so that all could see the baby; then they took their seats, and I saw the little one being strapped upon his cradle again. Then came several more namings, three girls and another boy, if I remember; I could hardly wait until they were finished, so anxious I was for my own turn. Finally the chief spoke.

"Are there any more namings?"

There was no answer.

"Then we shall consider the adoption. Bowl-Woman and Thunder-Arrow wish to adopt a captive boy, whom we all know as In-the-Forest, to be their son. To this I was favorably disposed, but late last night a certain young man begged me not to permit this adoption on the ground that the captive is a dangerous wizard; his wizardry being shown by the fact that he can conquer boys much larger than himself, by crushing their faces in a painful and cruel manner. The young man suggested that we destroy the wizard by burning!"

15

A dead silence followed. Toad-Face hung his head. All eyes were upon him accusingly.

For a moment everything had gone black but now fear had passed. Then I heard Thunder-Arrow's voice, clear and strong.

"The young man was wrong," he said. "In-the-Forest's power is not wizardry, but skill, like shooting with the bow. He has taught his skill to my son, Little-Bear, who already is almost as skilful as his teacher."

I saw my chance and rose to speak.

"I shall be pleased to teach anyone who wishes to learn this manner of fighting," I said; "that is, almost everybody. There is one person I shall never teach."

"Who is that?" demanded the chief.

"The young man who told you I was a wizard."

"Let us go on with the adoption," replied the chief with a faint smile.

The Big-House swam around, then I saw that he was motioning me to step forward. Bowl-Woman, leaving the baby with a friend, came and stood beside me. I tried to keep from trembling, and the sweat was dripping from me. She took hold of my arm reassuringly.

"Do you wish to adopt this boy?" asked the chief.

"*Kay'hay-la!*"

"Among our people captives are adopted to take the place of lost relatives. Whose place does this boy take?"

"The place of my second son, who died in his first year," Bowl-Woman replied, to my surprise, as I had never heard of the child. "Little-Bear is my first son," she went on. "It-Is-Approaching is the third."

"Who speaks for this boy?" the chief inquired.

"I do," answered Roaring-Wings, rising from his place among the *Pay-lay'* men and joining us.

"Listen, ye chiefs and warriors. Hearken, women, boys, and girls. The name of this boy is In-the-Forest; let him be called by that name forever. From this day onward he is a Lenape, a son of Bowl-Women of the Turtle Band, and consequently himself a Turtle. I pray that he enjoy good health and live to be very old, and, most of all, be happy. Now I have finished."

Roaring-Wings escorted Bowl-Woman and me around the Big-House back to the chief's stand in the middle of the north side. As we passed the door, I saw someone going out; he turned and looked at me. It was Toad-Face, and his look of deadly hate I shall never forget.

Now we stood before the chief.

"I accept this boy, In-the-Forest, as a member of the Turtle Band," he announced solemnly.

There was a pause, and I could feel that I was supposed to say something.

"I am proud to be a member of the Turtle Band of the Lenape tribe," I said, "I shall try to prove worthy."

XI. Visions and a Wedding

FTER I had been accepted into the tribe, I walked to my seat with as much dignity as I could muster, paying no attention to the remarks, favorable or otherwise, made as I passed along in front of the seated throng.   One glorious fact filled my mind—I was no longer a captive.   I sank down beside my new brother. Little-Bear grasped my hand silently.

I noticed that two attendants, a man and a woman, were sweeping the Big-House with their turkey wings; and shortly afterward the chief began to speak again.

He preached a very fine sermon on thankfulness to the Creator and his helpers for all the blessings enjoyed by human beings on this earth and prayed that they be continued.   He spoke of the course of the worshipers around the Big-House as the "Beautiful White Path of the Great Spirit" and ended with these words:

"The worship that takes place here will raise our prayers to the Creator.   Our Bringer-in or Leader this time will be our old friend Runs-by-Night of the Wolf Band.   Now I have finished."

A gray-haired old warrior who had been sitting in the "round-foot" section arose and stepped quietly to where the chief was standing, followed by Thunder-

Arrow, and I noticed that each was carrying a small turtle-shell rattle. These they shook upon arriving. The chief then took his seat near me in the Turtle section.

Next, two men sitting on the south side struck three times upon a dry hide which served as a drum, whereupon Runs-by-Night announced, "I now must worship," and the people answered in chorus, "*Ha'oo, Kay'hay-la!*"

Runs-by-Night began to shake his rattle crosswise and to recite the story of his vision in a high, level tone and in short phrases. After each he paused a moment to give Thunder-Arrow and the two drummers time to repeat the same phrase in the same tone, which made a very strange effect. When he finished, the drummers beat rapidly on the dry hide calling, "*Hoooo*" several times.

Now Runs-by-Night bent his head and shook his rattle up and down, and at this the drummers began to recite the words he had just taught them. Then he and Thunder-Arrow danced, rattling, westward with a shuffling step along the "White Path" until the verse was ended, finishing with a whoop, "*Kwee!*"

At this time a number of people rose and lined up behind them, and I was bold enough to follow.

The leader now sang his dream song, line by line, whilst the drummers and Thunder-Arrow repeated them after him; then the dance started again as the drummers took up the song. I had learned the step from Roaring-Wings so I did not dance too badly, but I felt that everyone was watching me. In this way, reciting, singing, and dancing we circled the Big-House, stopping only a few minutes whilst Runs-by-Night stepped out of line to shake hands with the drummers. As we danced past them, I noticed that everyone took pains to face them, dancing sidewise, so I did the same. After circling the building, our leader danced us out so that we faced "our Grandfather," the great carved face on the west side of the center post; then around we went to face its mate. In each place we raised our hands and in so doing it was said that we raised our prayers toward the Creator.

As nearly as I could make out from Runs-by-Night's recitation and his song, his Helper must have been some *man-it′to* connected with snow and ice, and the special power given him was that of hunting and trapping in the winter time. His song ran something like this:

Among snowflakes
On river-ice
Under gray clouds
Bringing blessing
Cold white Being
Breath of the north
Skins of bear's grease
Thus he spoke
Kwee-ya′!

After the leader had finished, the attendants swept the "White Path" and another vision-singer took up the ceremony, a middle-aged man this time, and so on until nearly morning, when the leading turtle-rattle had gone all around the Big-House, and everyone wishing to lead had taken his turn. I danced behind all the leaders but one, which seemed to please Bowl-Woman very much. In the intervals the people smoked and chatted and at such times they could go out or come in if they wished.

When Runs-by-Night started his recitation, two men and two women, *ash-kas'uk*, went outside to prepare the feast and I could hear the pomp, pomp of the hominy mortars in the lulls of the singing for sometime after they left. When the last vision had been sung, the four returned, bearing great wooden bowls full of steaming *sa'pan*, which were set down at intervals in the middle of the Big-House. Large clamshells were now passed around to all.

At the chief's order twelve times we sounded the prayer word *Hooo*, by way of a blessing and then we gathered around the bowls and dipped in with our clamshells. I would have preferred my own bowl and spoon, but the *sa'pan* was good.

When it was all gone, the chief dismissed us, saying we should meet again the next night.

The sky was just paling when we filed out of the Big-House, bound for home and bed.

I woke late in the afternoon and, after filling my stomach with stew and corn bread, I went out and watched the games being played on the common. I bet one of the spoons I had made against a wooden deer call, which entitled me to play in the game of *tat'gusk*, or hoop and spears. Our side won, and I was quite pleased with my  prize, which made a sort of bleating sound when you blew it, until I learned that the deer call is used by the hunter to imitate the cry of a fawn. When the anxious mother-doe comes to the rescue of her child, the hunter shoots her. This did not seem like fair play and I dropped the call into my shoulder pocket in disgust, intending to bet it on something else. But I forgot it, and there it lay.

About the same ceremonies took place the next two nights, but the fourth morning Thunder-Arrow awakened me some time before midday to witness another sort of performance. As we left the house, I heard the familiar, *ho-ho-ho-ho* of the *Mee-sing'* and I was not at all surprised to see the hairy monster entering the Big-House ahead of us.

Six men, equipped for the hunt with bows, quivers, and knives were just rising from the remains of a feast. They formed in line, and I noticed that they seemed to be resting all their weight on the left foot.

Now the chief addressed them and told them that it was their duty to go out and kill deer for the Big-House and to think of nothing but this duty. Whilst talking, he stepped over to the west fire and threw in six pinches of tobacco, then to the east fire where he did the same. He continued, praying to *Mee-sing-haw-lee'kun* to drive up the deer so that the hunters could get them. As he dropped the last tobacco, he said:

"If you kill a deer right away, bring it in tonight; if not, bring all you kill day after tomorrow." Finally he gave the chief hunter some tobacco to make offerings in the fire when they camped. The *Mee-sing'* had been listening to all this and, when the hunters left, he saw them off on their journey. Later in the day he danced in the Big-House whilst the drummers sang.

That evening a number of old men were called up and given some shell beads to go out east of the Big-House where there was a pole to hang game upon, and there to sound the prayer call twelve times, I suppose for the benefit of the hunters. This night also the chief cut a string of *kay'kwuk* and scattered the beads on the ground between the east fire and the center pole; these the attendants were supposed to pick up and keep. They called it "picking berries."

On the seventh afternoon the village was quiet enough except for the laughter of some girls who were playing the "scatter game," something like "jackstraws," when we were startled by a long, shrill call from the forest, followed by three short whoops.

I did not know what was afoot; but the drummers who had been dozing on the sunny side of the Big-House jumped up and hurried inside.

I happened to look toward the trail leading northwestward into the forest and saw somebody coming. It was the hunters, and they were bringing three deer!

They gave the deer to the attendants and went into the Big-House, whilst the drummers sang a special song. Then a feast was brought in to them, after which their leader announced the names of those who had killed deer.

By the time I came out, the carcasses had been skinned and hung on the game pole. From that time on, we had venison with our *sa'pan* after the ceremonies every night.

Nothing unusual happened after this until the ninth night when the attendants opened the west door and carried out through it all the ashes which had gathered.

Then they started a new fire with a queer pair of fire sticks, different from anything I had seen. The upper stick had a wheel, a string, and a crossbar on it, and you

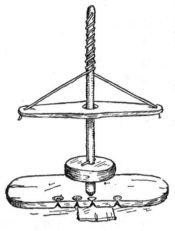

could make it turn rapidly by raising and lowering the bar much easier than by twirling the upper stick between your palms in the usual fashion.

Before this the drummers had used just common sticks for beating on their dry hide; tonight they brought out sticks with human heads carved on them, one representing a man, one a woman. These sticks were forked on the end, very old and polished from use. Besides this, they distributed twelve "praying sticks" about as big as my little finger and two spans long; six of these were painted with red stripes and six were plain. Those who received them, all elderly people, raised these sticks when the prayer call was sounded and carried them when they danced.

Now the chief called upon everyone who owned box-turtle shell rattles, such as were used in singing the visions, to bring them forward. I ran home and got mine, which I had not expected to use until the twelfth night, and placed it in line with the rest on the north side in front of Runs-by-Night. When all were in place, he measured the backs of all the turtles with strings of *kay'kwuk* beads, and left with each turtle, a string of the same length.

The turtle owners were then called to get their property, with the beads which represented their pay for bringing their rattles to the meeting. Each was supposed to shake his turtle as he picked it up; I shook mine a little awkwardly, being excited, and everybody laughed; but several others were laughed at, too, so I didn't care much; the fact was, I smiled a little myself.

Finally, before the regular vision singing began, the chief called up six elderly men, two from each band,

directing them to go outside and sound the prayer call, *Hooo*, twelve times, holding up their left hands. This was done thereafter every night until the end.

The additional ceremonies had taken so long that it was daylight before the feast was eaten and the people dismissed.

At last the twelfth day came; Thunder-Arrow woke me early in the afternoon and made me take another sweat bath and wash very carefully. He wanted me to be as clean as possible when I recited my vision. He took the ornaments off my scalp-lock braids, unbraided the hair, washed and combed it for me, then anointed it with bear's grease and rebraided it with great care, making it very smooth and shiny. Then he replaced the bone beads and quill bands, also the deer-hair crest. He renewed the white down on my ear tufts and finally repainted my face as it had been the night of my adoption.

In the meantime Bowl-Woman had cleaned some grease spots off my new leggings by rubbing with a sort of white earth which she kept for that purpose. When I dressed, all agreed that I looked very fine.

On this night things were begun quite differently, and I really feared there had been some mistake and that I would not be able to sing my vision. First of all, cedar branches were burned on the two fires to purify the house with their sweet smoke, and then two of the women *ash-kas'uk* went around with a little bark dish of *pa'kon*, red paint, and a dish of grease. They touched a little paint to the left cheek of every man, woman, and child present and placed a little grease on their heads. Two men did the same for all the carved faces on the posts of the building and applied paint and grease to the drumsticks, the drum, the praying sticks, and the turtle rattles.

When Runs-by-Night announced that the women should come forward and sing their visions, I was sure that, somehow, I had missed my turn. The Turtle chief was sitting right near me, so I dared not whisper to anyone to reassure myself. The first vision singer was a stout old lady; she had a man for a second singer and a line of dancers followed her. She went around the "Beautiful White Path" in good style, reciting and singing about some *man-it'to* connected with the herbs they used for medicine, and even stopped to shake hands with the drummers. There were a number of women who wanted to sing and by the time they had finished it was very late.

When the Bringer-in rose at last to speak, I feared he was going to direct the attendants to bring in the feast, to close the meeting, but, no, to my great delight he called for the young men and boys! My heart was pounding like the drum, but I felt that probably I should wait until others had taken their turn. As nobody seemed willing to start, Runs-by-Night settled it.

"There is here tonight," he began, "a boy who was recently blessed with a vision and a song. He is In-the-Forest of the Turtle Band. I shall ask him now to step forward and worship as our ancestors have done before us since this great island was created."

Now the longed-for moment had come. I was deathly frightened, but I rose and started for the leader's seat. After I had gone a few steps, I realized that I had forgotten my turtle rattle, so I had to go back for it. Finally I stood before the leader, facing west, trembling like the ague.

"Who will second for this singer?" For a moment nobody moved; then old Roaring-Wings rose leisurely. I was delighted, for he was the man who had taught me.

"I will!" he said and took his stand just behind me. "You can do it," he whispered, "be brave! Don't forget the starting words."

The drummers struck their dry hide three times.

"Now I must worship!" I chanted.

"*Ha'oo, kay'hay-la!*" shouted the people.

I shook the rattle sidewise and began walking and reciting:

"Among the rocks."

"Among the rocks," repeated Roaring-Wings and the drummers.

"Feeling sad," I continued.

"Feeling sad," they echoed.

Then I continued, and the drummers repeated:

"Needing help (needing help). There I sat (there I sat). Now they come (now they come). Bringing food (bringing food). Men and women (men and women). When they turned (when they turned). Then I saw (then I saw)! *Kwee!*" Now the drummers beat rapidly and shouted, *HOOO!* three times.

I paused, and a number of people fell in behind me, mostly young; I recognized White-Deer among them and Little-Bear. There were even some older folk, including Thunder-Arrow, Bowl-Woman, Beaver-House, and, to my surprise, Cross-Woman.

For one awful second I could not think what to do next, but Roaring-Wings whispered, "Dance!" I inclined my head, shook my rattle up and down, and the drummers began the recitation which I had just given them. I danced then with the shuffling step that Roaring-Wings had taught me along the "Beautiful White Path" and the line danced after me. I let the drummers repeat the recitation twice and then I shouted, "*Kwee!*"

Once more I paused, but now I was confident that I could go on. Once again I began to rattle sidewise and walk, singing my song, whilst Roaring-Wings and the drummers repeated it.

"Bringing food (bringing food). Men and women (men and women). Now I live (now I live). Live in plenty (live in plenty). Thin black legs (thin black legs). Thus he said (thus he said). Bringing blessing (bringing blessing). *Kway-hay-yay!*"

I paused whilst the drummers beat rapidly and sounded the prayer call; then noticing that I had reached a point opposite them, I walked over and shook hands with both drummers, then returned to my place.

Inclining my head and rattling up and down, I started the dance again as the drummers sang my song. It sounded good and it made me feel proud and happy to think that it was mine. The dance brought us around almost to the east door and then again I paused. Glancing back, I saw that almost the entire congregation was following me!

This was the time to recite again, but instead of repeating I gave them a new one:

"Little bundle (little bundle).   Sewing awl (sewing awl).   Little bundle (little bundle).   Chipper flint (chipper flint).   Little bundle (little bundle).   Tiny bow (tiny bow).   Little bundle (little bundle).   Tiny club (tiny club).   *Kwee!*"

By the time we had walked and danced that one, I had guided my dancers around west of the center pillar. Here we all faced east and sounded the prayer call, raising our hands "to lift the prayer," while holding praying sticks if we had them.   Again I sang my song and walked, which brought us around to the east side of the center pillar.   Here we faced west and again raised the prayer call.

The drummers beat rapidly as a signal that my part of the ceremony was ended.   I went back to my seat weary but happy.

Several youths then sung their visions, and I thought they did it very well, but somehow the people did not wish to dance with them as they had with me, and their followers were few.

Runs-by-Night spoke again:

"There is a young man here who was blessed with a vision and a song fully two years ago.   However, the gift of singing has not yet been granted him.   For this reason he has engaged an expert singer to act in his place, for which service he is paying one shoulder length of *kay'kwuk* beads.   The young man is Little-Bear of the Turtle Band; the substitute is Roaring-Wings!   Substitute, stand forth!"

Again Roaring-Wings rose.   "Little-Bear has chosen a second for me," he said.   "He wishes his brother In-the-Forest to accept that office."

Called upon again! I had no practice "seconding" or repeating the song of another, but I could not refuse either Roaring-Wings or Little-Bear. I took my place behind the leader, whispering as I did so, "Be brave, you can do it!"

"*Hoh!*" grunted Roaring-Wings.

My performance as a "second" was a little stumbling at first, but finally I got the knack of it. Little-Bear's

man-it'to was no less than a *m'bee'ahk*, a whale, and his blessing was in connection with fishing.

This was the last performance; after the feast most of the venison that remained was divided among the women who had sung their visions. The chief dismissed us with instructions either to return early in the morning or to sleep in the Big-House. Little-Bear and I went home after our robes, as the night was chill, but we were determined not to miss anything. As we returned, the *ash-kas'uk* were carrying the ashes out the west door.

It seemed as if I had hardly fallen asleep when some-one shook me. I opened my eyes sleepily. Daylight was shining in through the Big-House smoke holes, and an *ash'kas* was saying:

"Get up, boys, if you want to see the ending."

We rose and rolled up our robes, whilst a long line of women formed along the north side. Now some man standing beyond the women shook a rattle and cried, "*Kwee-yaaaa*," and immediately the women answered, "*Hoo!*" one after another down the line. Twelve times he called and twelve times they answered. Then two men began to sing and the line danced around toward us. As the women approached, we saw that there was a line of men on the other side, so we joined in. The leaders sang twelve different songs, during which we circled the "White Path" four times; then we danced around the center pole, and those who had praying sticks reached up and touched the carved faces. Finally the singers announced, "We shall pray," and all returned to their seats to sound the prayer call, *Hooo*, twelve times.

After the last feast was served, two women carried wooden bowls full of *kay'kwuk* beads around, and everyone took two or three as a remembrance, then the chief thanked the attendants for their work, paid them with *kay'kwuk*, and made a final prayer, spoken. All filed out of the Big-House and formed a long line facing east. Here we sounded the prayer call, *Hooo*, six times standing, and *Haaa* six times kneeling. The *Gam'wing* was over.

Everybody slept most of the time for the next three days, and meat racks became pretty empty and wood-piles low before the village came back to the workaday world again.

We had to hunt several days then to replenish the family meat supply, and Little-Bear, I noticed, paid very little attention to what we were trying to do. His mind was far away and he would hardly answer when I spoke to him, so, after our return, I decided to let him alone for the present.

One day I came back after a trip to gather arrow sprouts and found our cabin full of people, some of whom I recognized as Bowl-Woman's relatives. I started to go in, but my way was blocked by a stranger.

"You can't come in here," he said, "unless you belong to the *O-kay-ho'kee* clan."

"Let him in; he belongs," called Bowl-Woman's sister, Duck-Woman. "He was adopted the other day."

That was my first knowledge that I now belonged to this clan, which I later learned was one of a number composing the Turtle Band. The name meant "Bark Country." I soon found this was a sort of family council, and the subject of discussion was: Should a formal proposal be made on behalf of Little-Bear for the hand of White-Deer? Little-Bear was there to give his own views, but he was too absorbed in pleading his cause with a portly old matron of the clan to notice my arrival.

After talking a long time about White-Deer's character and ability, it was finally decided that she would make Little-Bear a good wife. Then they talked some more about gifts. I listened closely, so as not to miss anything, and learned that these were to go to White-Deer's mother, Fling-Her-This-Way. Different relatives offered skins, furs, and *kay'kwuk* until they made quite a respectable bundle.

"Whom shall we get to deliver these gifts and act as
go-between?" asked the man who had stopped me at the
door and who turned out to be a cousin.

"Why not try In-the-Forest?" suggested Bowl-
Woman's sister, slyly.

I looked at her, hard. I did not like what she said
and was about to make a heated answer, when I felt a
hand on my shoulder: it was Bowl-Woman's.

"Never mind, son," she said softly. "I know how
you feel. Duck-Woman was only teasing. You couldn't
do it anyhow. You see, the go-between should belong
to the third band. We are Turtles, and White-Deer is
a Turkey; we shall have to find a Wolf."

"How about Runs-by-Night?" someone suggested.

After a lot of talk he was chosen to carry the bundle
of gifts to White-Deer's cabin and lay them at her mother's
feet, formally asking her, in the name of Little-Bear, for
the hand of her daughter. This he did, and then without
waiting for an answer, he quietly withdrew. In the
meantime our family council broke up.

Later on in the day when I wandered down toward
the river, for no especial reason except that I felt restless,
I noticed a lot of people around White-Deer's home.
"Another council," I thought. Then, wishing I were a
few years older, I continued on down to the canoe landing and, picking up a stick of driftwood, I went and sat
moodily in a canoe. I drew a beaver-tooth carving tool
from my shoulder pouch and began to work on the stick,
hardly noticing what I was doing. After a while I was
startled to see that I had carved from the white wood the
head of a deer. Dreamily I stared down into the water;

and then gently let the white deer head slip from my fingers into the river.

Next day I went hunting, and when I returned, empty handed, in the evening, Little-Bear told me that the presents had been accepted and that White-Deer would marry him on the fourth day. Runs-by-Night had brought the word, stating that the girl needed that much time to get her clothes ready.

How should we pass the intervening days? I wanted to learn to make *kay'kwuk* beads to repay to Bowl-Woman and Thunder-Arrow the strings they had expended upon me; but somehow I could not apply myself, nor could Little-Bear. Finally he suggested that we get ourselves tattooed! That sounded really interesting.

We visited the tattooer, a middle-aged man by the name of Walking-Tree, who lived in a little thatched cabin on the west side of the village, taking with us some of the bowls we had made and four spoons.

His tools were very simple, little bundles of sharp-pointed needle-like slivers of bone and a clamshell full of finely ground willow charcoal mixed with some kind of grease. Some of the bundles contained more "needles" than others, according to the width of the lines he proposed to make.

"What patterns would you like?" he asked.

I had not thought of this before, so I said nothing, but Little-Bear had made up his mind, or White-Deer had made it up for him.

"Here on my breast," he said. "I want a turtle, the emblem of my band. I want a whale, too; but that, I suppose, should go on my stomach."

"If the young chief will pardon," said Walking-Tree, "I would suggest that the whale be placed above the turtle on your breast. The *man-it'to* might feel insulted if I placed his picture on your stomach. *Joo!* Now, what does the other young chief wish?"

It made me feel queer to be spoken of as a "young chief." I was trying to think what I did want, if anything, when Little-Bear spoke up.

"Go ahead and have a turtle, just like mine," he suggested. "You could have a picture of an ant above it, you know."

"I do not know as I wish to be tattooed."

"*Al-la'pee!* Come on! Don't desert me now. It would look strange for one brother to be tattooed, the other not." His voice was pleading.

"Very well, if I must. But you be tattooed first."

"*Mat-ta-ka'!* And have you back out? No, we shall be tattooed at the same time."

So Walking-Tree took a little brush, made by chewing the end of a stick, and drew on my breast, quite low down, the figure of a turtle, using the black stuff in the shell, and then he made another on Little-Bear's breast. He rubbed out parts of the turtles several times with a bit of buckskin and redrew them until they suited his fancy. Then he got out his little bundles of bone needles. They looked prickly and unpleasant.

"I don't think I want to be tattooed," I said, half in fun.

"No backing out!" Little-Bear growled. He ducked around behind me and pinioned my arms whilst Walking-Tree pricked my skin around the lines he had drawn and rubbed in more black stuff. It hurt, but not so much as I had expected. Then Little-Bear went through the ordeal himself, and after that came the whale and the ants. I decided to have two ants instead of one, because my *Man-it'to-wuk* had been both men and women, and so I came out a greater hero than my new brother after all, having three tattooed figures to his two.

Just to plague Little-Bear, I strutted back and forth in front of him, straight as an arrow and proud. He pretended not to notice.

On our way home Cross-Woman stopped us. "Have you seen Toad-Face?" she asked. "He has not been home since the first night of the *Gam'wing*. He has stayed out in the forest before, several nights at a time, but never anything like this. I know you boys do not like him; but you wouldn't *harm* him, would you? If I thought you had——" her eyes gleamed fiercely.

We hastened to assure her that we had not seen him either since that time, and she went away muttering.

We washed off the surplus black stuff that evening, and the places were pretty sore; but next morning they were scabbed over. It was eight or ten days after that the scabs fell off and the figures showed up clear and blue. I was quite proud of mine, but I never saw Little-Bear's until the following spring.

After we were tattooed, Little-Bear and I spent the remaining days with the *ah-pee'kawn*, for we knew how badly White-Deer would feel if she discovered that he could not play. Little-Bear must have prayed to his *man-it'to*, or something, for to my surprise and his, he really learned White-Deer's favorite call. Not satisfied

LENAPE WOMAN'S DEERSKIN
SKIRT WITH QUILL-WORK BORDER

RIGHT, WOMAN'S
DEERSKIN BELT

DETAIL OF THE
METHOD OF
QUILL WORKING

HAIR ORNAMENT
OF SLATE

WHITE-DEER'S
COSTUME

PATTERN OF
MOCCASIN

PUCKERING
THE TOE

WOMAN'S DEERSKIN
LEGGINGS WITH QUILL WORK

LEFT, DEERSKIN
GARTER

CLARENCE
ELLSWORTH

FINISHED MOCCASIN
SEAM COVERED WITH
QUILL WORK

LENAPE WOMAN'S DEERSKIN
CAPE WITH QUILL WORK
BORDERS AND FRINGED ENDS

DEERSKIN
HAIR RIBBON

WHITE-DEER'S WEDDING DRESS

with that, after he got the knack, he actually picked up a number of the others. As a reward, I gave him my *ah-pee'kawn*. I had no further use for the instrument.

On the wedding morning I did not feel like getting up early, but Bowl-Woman routed me out because she wanted to clean up the place. She fussed about and put everything to rights and got out a new mat for the bride and groom to sit on. Little-Bear dressed himself with great care and had his father paint his face; then he begged me to put on my *Gam'wing* clothing, but something wouldn't let me. I felt strange and silent. Suddenly I heard some boys shouting without. I braced up and stepped outside to see what was going on.

There was quite a crowd gathering in the Big-House square, and they stood so as to leave a wide passageway. Along this, as I looked, I saw a procession approaching. At the head, with eyes modestly downcast, walked White-Deer, beautiful in her festive attire. In her hands was a large wooden bowl.

My bow and quiver were hanging under the shed. I took them down hurriedly, called Moon-ha'kee, looked about and not seeing anyone watching, I made a quick dash out of sight, never slackening my pace until I had put miles of forest between myself and the scene that was taking place.

XII. Put to Test

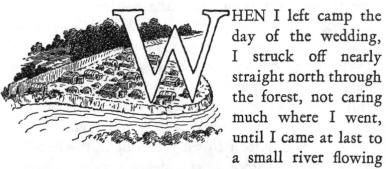

WHEN I left camp the day of the wedding, I struck off nearly straight north through the forest, not caring much where I went, until I came at last to a small river flowing southeastward. Following this downstream, I ran across, late in the afternoon, a plain trail going in my direction. Before I had traveled very far upon this, I heard a dog bark. I halted and listened carefully. I was sure I smelled smoke. A village must be near.

Should I walk boldly into the village or try to make my way around it? What if the people were enemies? I could not remember hearing of any hostile towns within a day's travel, but I could not be sure. It was risky! On the other hand I had eaten nothing since morning and early, too. The wind was raw and the sky gray and lowering, threatening rain or snow; moreover the night was coming on. I decided to take a chance and try the village. In a few minutes I came to the first garden clearings.

The village was much smaller than ours and had no Big-House; the cabins were clustered on a point of land overlooking the river; in fact the river ran on three sides of it. Across the fourth side was a high fence or palisade made of logs set on end, which seemed to have been newly built.

As I passed through the narrow gateway, the village dogs rushed forward and barked loudly, whilst poor Moon-ha'kee shrank down as small as possible and stuck close to my heels. A man stepped quickly out of a near-by cabin with an arrow nocked on the string. He looked me over suspiciously. I stood shaking inwardly.

"*Hey!*" I said, the everyday familiar greeting, which I tried to make sound natural.

"*Hey!*" he responded, lowering his weapon; then stood waiting for me to speak further.

"Are there any *O-kay-ho'kee* clan people here?" I ventured.

"Two houses!" came the quick reply. He pointed toward the river bank. "If they haven't room for you over there, come back here." He disappeared within his cabin before I could answer, and I drew a deep breath.

A few drops of cold rain sprinkled my bare shoulders as I approached the houses: one a fair-sized, arched-roof, bark-covered cabin; the other a small, dome-shaped, thatched hut. I raised the door curtain of the larger and stepped inside, Moon-ha'kee following very close behind.

"*Hey!*" I said.

"*Hey!*" answered the master of the house. Now in the firelight I could see him lying on the back *ha'soon* playing with a chubby two-year-old. He rolled off the platform and stood up to welcome me. His wife, who had been looking for something in a basket, laid that

aside and, bustling about, found me a clean mat to sit on.
Then she ladled me out a large bowl of warm stew.
Moon-ha'kee smelled it and whined, for which he received

a big bone with a lot of
meat on it.

After I had finished
eating, my host filled
and lighted a small stone
pipe for me.   For polite-
ness sake I drew a few
whiffs, then handed it back.   After he had finished
smoking, he spoke as if he had always known me.

"Was it raining when you came in?"

"A few drops," I replied.   "But judging from the
sound on the roof it has begun now in earnest."   I was
glad to be inside.

"That rattle sounds more like hail," he said and then
he began to talk freely, but with never a question as to
whence I came or what my errand might be.   It was not
until later in the evening that I learned his name was
Flying-Snake and that his wife, Red-Sunflower, was not
only a member of my clan, but a cousin of Bowl-Woman's.
Then I told him who I was.

"The little house next door belongs to another kinsman of yours," he said.   "I mean *Ka'wi-a*, the story-
teller.   You probably know all about him."

"I never heard of him," I replied.   "Of course I
know the animal called *Ka'wi-a*."   The word meant the
American hedgehog now named "porcupine."

"Porcupine is a very strange person," he went on.
"To begin with, he has no legs."

"No legs at all?" I cried aghast.

"His legs are very small, twisted, shriveled; he cannot use them."

"What happened to them?"

"They say that when he was a little boy, he went in swimming one time right after eating a hearty meal. His legs twisted all up with the cramps and, although another boy saved him from drowning, no one has ever straightened out his legs. They never grew, either; instead, they shrunk."

"How does he make a living?" I asked.

"I was coming to that. His head is queer, too, twice as large as an ordinary person's. And that big head is completely filled with stories. He makes his living telling them."

"What a strange man!" I exclaimed. "I should like to know him. Is he home?"

"No, he is away at present, telling tales in some other village. The story-telling season has begun. He stays home only in summer."

I would have asked more, but my hostess produced a bed mat and a fur robe.

"The young man is tired," she said to her husband. "We must let him rest."

I suspected that she was rather tired herself, but I said nothing. As I pulled the robe over my head, however, I resolved that some day I would seek out *Ka'wi-a*, the Porcupine, and hear some of his stories.

In the morning when I awoke, I found a nice bowl of hot *sa'pan* waiting for me, and Moon-ha'kee had some of last night's stew. Flying-Snake came out with us and he noted that, although the weather had cleared, there was a bitter wind blowing from the north. He went back into the house and fetched me a good fur robe.

"Wear this, son," he said. "Send it back or bring it when you have the chance. Better keep off the main trails going home."

"Why?" I asked, wrapping the robe around me.

"The *Sis-kuh-ha'na-wuk* are raiding again in this part of the country. Be watchful lest you meet a war party. We built our stockade because of this danger."

I had heard of this tribe, whom Captain John Smith called "Susquehannocks." They lived on the Muddy River, or *Sis-kuh-ha'na*, to the west, and were said to be kinsmen of the dreaded *Man'gway* Nation of the north, now called Iroquois.

Thanking the hospitable Flying-Snake, I set out. The villagers stared and the dogs sniffed, but no one

offered to molest me.   Once in the forest I set my course
southward by the sun, keeping it first to my left, then in
front, then to the right.   When the sun was half down
the sky in the afternoon, it occurred to me that perhaps
I was too far to the east, so I turned somewhat south-
westward.

At last I encountered a little creek, which I thought
must run into the Lenape River, and following this I came
upon a large mass of rocks.   They looked familiar; then
I recognized them.   The place of my vision! I built a fire
in front of my little cave and settled down on my grass
bed to rest, Moon-ha'kee at my side.   Between the fire
in front and my fur robe I was very warm and comfortable,
although of course, hungry again.

During my journey into new country and to a strange
village, my mind had turned to other matters, but now
near home, everything rushed over me, and I could see
White-Deer with her bowl coming across the Big-House
square.   How could I go back?

Finally I decided to camp right where I was.   I
wandered up the creek with Moon-ha-kee in search of
food and we were lucky enough to scare up a rabbit.

Before dark I had gathered a lot of dead wood, so when the fire burned low at night and the cold woke me, all I had to do was to throw on more sticks.

I had hung the neck and forequarters of the rabbit on a bush and in the morning I broiled them for our breakfast; but Moon-ha'kee looked up expectantly for more after he had devoured his share, and I was far from satisfied. My stomach cried for *sa'pan* and bread; and there was only one place to be sure of getting them, in Bowl-Woman's cabin. Somehow things began to straighten themselves out in my mind.

"Moon-ha'kee," I said. "Don't you think we are foolish to go wandering around the woods without anything to eat when there is no need for it?"

He looked up at me with his head on one side as if he understood all about it.

"Don't you think so?" I repeated. He barked twice as if to say, "*Eh-eh*" or "yes!"

"Isn't it foolish," I continued, "to feel bad about a girl when she's going to be your sister anyhow?" He barked again, "*Eh-eh*."

"Then we'd better go home, hadn't we?" He barked three times, and I am sure he meant, "*Kay'hay-la!*"

When we returned to the village, I found that Little-Bear and his bride had started out the day after the wedding for a winter hunt and would not be back until spring.

After we had filled our stomachs, I asked Bowl-Woman a question.

"Who performed the marriage ceremony, the chief or Roaring-Wings?"

She looked at me in astonishment.

"Why, Little-Bear and White-Deer performed it, of course."

"What do you mean?" I asked.

"White-Deer brought in a bowl of *sa'pan* that she had prepared and set it down before Little-Bear, and then she seated herself beside him on the same mat. He ate a little *sa'pan*, and then she ate some out of the same bowl, and that made her his wife."

Somehow I felt disappointment: I felt there should be more.

"Was that all the ceremony?" I pursued.

"That was all that took place here. They got up from the mat and White-Deer began to help me prepare food for the friends who had gathered, whilst Little-Bear talked with them. We missed you, son, but of course I know how you felt. When Fling-Her-This-Way reached home, she divided her presents among her kin-folk, and next morning eight or ten of them formed another procession and came here."

"What for?"

"They brought useful gifts for the couple: bowls, spoons, pots, baskets, strings of corn, sacks of dried meat, and a skin bag full of bear's grease."

"Where are the things?"

"You know we are rather crowded here, and Fling-Her-This-Way has a cabin all to herself now. They stored the gifts there until they come home in the spring."

It was lucky for them that they did so. That very night a horrible thing happened, or, rather early next morning.

17

I was awakened by a terrible clamor: shouts, whoops, and shrieks. Half awake in the gray light of dawn, I saw somebody dragging Bowl-Woman out the door; a painted warrior clad in furs followed, carrying the baby on his *am-bee'son*. I sprang to my feet, looking for a weapon. Now I saw Thunder-Arrow struggling with another stranger. Suddenly remembering the stone pestles, I seized one and brought it down on the head of his assailant with all my might. Immediately something struck my own head with a sickening crash.

The next thing I remember was Thunder-Arrow's voice saying weakly:

"Save—the *Mee-sing'*;—the—the cabin is burning." I tried to open my eyes and finally succeeded, though the pain in my neck and head was terrific. I was lying near the big tree, Thunder-Arrow beside me; our cabin was in flames. I could hear women wailing and children crying.

Now Roaring-Wings and several others came stumbling out of the burning cabin with their arms full of our belongings just as the roof caved in.

"The *Mee-sing'* was gone," said Roaring-Wings. "Those snakes have taken it."

"Bowl-Women—the baby—the *Mee-sing'*—*a-kee'*," Thunder-Arrow moaned and spoke no more.

I managed to sit up. He was lying back, bandaged in several places, pale and senseless. The sun was up. Several houses were burning in the village and the corner of the Big-House was smoking. People were rushing about with water buckets, trying to put out the fires.

A cool hand was placed on my throbbing head and a gentle voice spoke.

"How do you feel?"

I looked up; it was Fling-Her-This-Way.

"Where is Bowl-Woman?" I demanded.

"Those snakes, the Susquehannocks, they took her, the baby, too."

I struggled to my feet and stood swaying.

"I must go," I said. "I must bring them back."

"You can't," she answered. "You are wounded. Lie down now and let Roaring-Wings doctor you."

"*Ma'ta.* I must not lie down. I promised to defend them, and I failed."

"You saved Thunder-Arrow's life, is that not enough?" said Roaring-Wings, who was working over him. "I came in just as you swung the pestle. The Susquehannock was about to stab him to the heart with his big bone dagger. I saw that other snake strike you down with his war club, too. He ran off with my arrow sticking in his side. Don't worry about Bowl-Woman and her baby. Everything will be done to save them. The *ee'la-wak* are getting up a war party, now."

"It will have to be a strong one," said Beaver-House, who was standing near. "The raiders were many."

Runs-by-Night came by with a water bucket. "We have saved the Big-House," he said. "That was a strange raid. It seemed to be aimed mainly at Bowl-Woman's cabin. I wonder why?"

"They took the *Mee-sing'*," said Roaring-Wings. "How did they know where it was?"

The village chief joined us.

"I have examined everything," he said. "Travels-Far and North-Man are dead and five others are wounded,

including these here.   Bowl-Woman and her baby have
been carried off, this cabin has been burned, and several
others damaged.   As far as I know, that is all.''

"They took our grandfather, the *Mee-sing'*," Roaring-
Wings informed him.

"*Ka-yah'!*" cried the chief. "How did they locate it?"

"I wish someone would tell us," grunted Runs-by-
Night.

At that moment we heard drumming, loud whoops,
then a wild dance song from the Big-House square.

"The Turtle *Ee'la* is raising a war party," said the
chief.   "The war-dance is starting.   They will try to
rescue our missing ones and avenge our dead."

I looked—my bow and quiver were hanging under the
shed—overlooked by the raiders.   I took them down and
ran around to the other side of the Big-House.   If my
head hurt, I did not notice it.

Between the Big-House and
the river a pole had been erected
and painted red; from the top
fluttered a black wisp of human
hair, a scalp.   Pushing through
the crowd, I found an open space
in the center, between the pole
and the Big-House, on one side
of which stood two singers, one
of them beating a drum made of
a skin stretched on a hoop, like
a large tambourine.   Beside them stood the war captain
or *Ee'la* of the Turtle Band.   About the pole danced
painted men, carrying bows and war clubs.   As I watched,

another warrior broke through the crowd and struck the pole with his club. Instantly the dancing stopped.

"I join this party," announced the newcomer, "to rescue our missing friends and avenge our dead; to bring back our grandfather, the *Mee-sing'*."

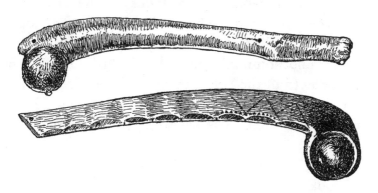

"*Ha'o, kay'hay-la,*" said the *Ee'la*. "Now will anyone else volunteer?"

I was about to step forward when a hand detained me. I looked and saw Roaring-Wings. The dance had started again.

"Paint yourself first," he advised. "I have some war paint with 'brave medicine' mixed in it. Here, let me paint you." Standing there in the crowd, he applied red and black and yellow from little bags he carried in his shoulder pouch. "Now go," he whispered.

I stepped out and struck the red pole with my bow. The singing and dancing stopped. A strange exhultation filled me.

"I am joining," I shouted, "to rescue my mother and my brother, to bring back our *Mee-sing'*, to avenge our dead."

"*Ha'o, kay'hay-la!*" responded the *Ee'la*. "Now who else? We need about twenty." After a pause, they began again. I soon caught the step and danced with the best of them, weaving in and out among the others about the war pole.

Suddenly a woman rushed out of the crowd and struck the pole with a club. Dance and song stopped short. It was Fling-Her-This-Way.

"I am not joining," she said. "I wish I could. But I am giving to In-the-Forest this war club which belonged to my late husband slain by the Susquehannocks. In-the-Forest, I call upon you to avenge the death of my husband!"

"*Ha'o, kay'hay-la!*" said the *Ee'la*.

I took the club which was carved of one piece of wood and painted red.

"If I can, I shall avenge him," I answered.

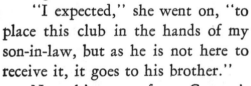

"I expected," she went on, "to place this club in the hands of my son-in-law, but as he is not here to receive it, it goes to his brother."

Next thing, one of poor Granny's daughters brought me a bag of *ka-ha-ma'kun* in memory of her mother; the other sister two pairs of moccasins and their brother, Beaver-House, gave me a long, keen, war knife made of flint, with a wooden handle. Each one struck the pole before he made his gift and stopped the dance, just as if he were volunteering for the war party. A boy whom I hardly knew gave me a prisoner tie—a stout rope made out of the native hemp. Thus I was fully equipped as a warrior.

Many volunteered, and gifts were given to other warriors; finally the war captain called a halt. We had all the men and supplies we needed. Then he made us a speech:

"Warriors!" he began. "As you know, it is customary, in making up a war party, to dance all night and feast, then to travel a certain distance and camp and dance again, then set forth in earnest.

"However, this occasion is different. The enemy who struck us this morning are doubtless now returning to their palisaded villages on Muddy River. They are carrying at least four wounded, and have had to bury one or two dead. They are moving more slowly than usual and there is hope, if we start at once, that we may catch up with them before they reach shelter. It is now midday; let every warrior eat a good meal now and take a shoulder pocket full of *ka-ha-ma'kun* for provision on the road. Each man shall take also his weapons, his dream bundle, two extra pairs of moccasins, a fur robe, and some tobacco. We shall start when I give the call."

The warriors scattered to their cabins. With aching head and neck and empty stomach, not to speak of a heavy heart, I wandered over to the heap of smoking ashes. There was a pile of our belongings rescued by the neighbors lying under the shed, and I was rummaging among these hoping to find a wooden bowl, or at least a gourd, to mix a little *ka-ha-ma'kun* in, and had luckily found my dream bundle, when Fling-Her-This-Way appeared.

"Come to my house and eat," she said. "Thunder-Arrow is there, and I shall care for him until you return."

I went with her to the well-remembered cabin, and there he lay on White-Deer's *ha'soon*. He was sleeping when I entered, but before my bowl of stew was finished, he awoke. He reached out a weak hand.

"You'll bring them back, won't you, Son?" he whispered.

"I will if I can," I answered, giving his hand a squeeze.

"If your Helper speaks, be sure you listen," he added.

A loud call from the Big-House square put an end to further words. I gathered up my things and departed. As I went out the door, Moon-ha'kee joined me; he had been waiting outside. Probably he had been away mouse hunting at the time of the raid.

When I reported to the war captain, he looked askance at Moon-ha'kee.

"You will have to leave your dog behind," he cautioned.

A feeling swept over me that I *must* take Moon-ha'kee, so I answered:

"My Dream-helper tells me that I should take this dog."

The *Ee'la* looked at me doubtfully. Finally he spoke.

"*Hoh*! In that case we shall have to take him. But do not let him bark."

We left the village singing our war songs; that is, everyone sang except me. I knew no war songs, but I could whoop as well as anybody.

Before night the *Ee'la* was glad that we had brought Moon-ha'kee, because he followed the enemy's trail without any trouble, and much time was saved where their tracks were hard to read. Their general course was northwestward.

When we camped that night, the leader and then each one of us burned a little tobacco in the camp fire and prayed that our journey would be successful. We slept in the open with only our robes for cover, and I felt cold enough before morning. Luckily there was no rain or snow; instead the moon was shining brightly. Two guards were posted and these were changed several times during the night, but I was not called upon to take a turn.

In the morning we had a hurried breakfast of *ka-ha-ma'kun* mixed with cold water and we pressed forward on the enemy's trail as fast as we could. That night again we burned tobacco and again posted guards.

I found it hard to sleep; I had a feeling that the enemy was very near. Finally I dropped off and was dreaming that a huge black ant with red paint on his face had just handed me a war club, when Moon-ha'kee awakened me by scratching my shoulder and whining. He kept running out into the forest, then back to me again, and I knew he wanted me to follow. The guards would not let me go without the *Ee'la's* permission, so I woke him and explained that my Dream-helper wished me to press forward. To this he finally agreed, but said that I would have to go scouting alone, as he could not risk his other men.

"Be cautious," he said. "If you learn anything, come right back and report."

Now Moon-ha'kee moved forward, nose to the ground, slowly so that I could keep up, and I followed him into the moonlit forest. We had not gone more than

252 PUT TO TEST

a mile when he stopped suddenly and bristled, then went ahead even more slowly. In a moment he halted again, uttered a low growl, and looked up at me. My heart nearly stopped beating, when peering ahead, I spied the glowing coals of a camp fire in a little glade and somebody moving about, dimly seen in the moonlight.

Whispering to Moon-ha'kee to keep silent, I crept about through the trees until I got a good view of the bivouac. I could see dark figures lying about the camp fire; the man moving was a guard.

As I stood trying to plan what to do, I heard a baby's fretful cry and a woman's voice, Bowl-Woman's voice, speak soothingly. Thanks to the Creator, they were both still alive!

Now a plan took form in my brain; if I could only decoy the guard out of camp far enough so that the commotion would not wake the others, I might put him out of action and rescue Bowl-Woman. But how could I do it? How could I call him away and at the same time not warn him of danger?

Suddenly, like a lightning flash, the answer came! The deer call! I was wearing two shoulder pockets, the right full of *ka-ha-ma'kun*, the left containing my tinder, my beaver-tooth chisel, and other things. I reached into it. Sure enough, there was the deer call, forgotten since I won it in the *tat'gusk* game at the *Gam'wing!*

About two hundred paces from the camp was a clump of evergreens and beneath these, in the sheltering darkness, I took my stand. Not knowing whether or not my stratagem would work, I began to bleat softly with the deer call, imitating a lost fawn's cry, then bleated again,

watching the camp and prepared to run for my life if
necessary. Moon-ha'kee crouched silently by my side.

When I had just about given up hope that the scheme
would be successful, I saw the guard, clear in the moon-
light, coming with some hesitation in my direction. I
suppose the fellow was wondering at a fawn's bleating so
late in the year, or perhaps he expected to find it an easy
victim and fresh venison for breakfast. The instant he
stepped into the black shadow, I swung my war club. The
man dropped like a felled ox and lay perfectly still. However, taking no chances, I bound him hand and foot with
the prisoner tie, which I carried wound about my waist,
then I gagged him with a piece of his own breechclout.

With my heart in my mouth, I made my way into the
camp. All were sleeping. Cautiously I looked about
among the sleepers. I soon found Bowl-Woman, but I
also discovered that her release was not, as I had expected,
simply a matter of slashing skin thongs or fiber ropes.
They had cut a stout forked stick and driven it deep into
the ground with the fork over Bowl-Woman's ankle in
such a way that she could not withdraw her foot. I
noticed with dismay that the stick was far too thick to
cut quickly with a flint knife. What could I do? The
first step was, of course, to wake Bowl-Woman.

Creeping up beside her, I placed my hand over her
mouth and shook her gently. She gasped and quivered;
then I whispered:

"This is In-the-Forest. I have come to rescue you.
Make no sound." She nodded her head.

Then I took hold of the stake and tried with all my
strength to pull it up. It would not budge.

My only hope seemed to dig out the ground under Bowl-Woman's foot between the prongs of the fork, until she had room to work herself free. When I started to dig with my flint knife, I found to my horror that the Susquehannocks had thought of that and had planted a large stone between the prongs before they drove the stake. Now I was desperate indeed.

Looking about for something with which to pry the stake up, I spied a rude litter made of stout poles and robes which they had made for carrying their wounded. Hurriedly cutting loose one of the poles, I tried to insert it in the fork above Bowl-Woman's foot, but there was not enough room. Finally I rove a loop of thongs from the litter through the fork and ran my pole through that until it had a good purchase, then I lifted with all my might. Gradually the stake moved—it was coming! Bowl-Woman withdrew her foot and rose stiffly. Silently she embraced me in her motherly way.

"Where is the *Mee-sing'*?" I whispered.

She pointed. I stepped over and saw the familiar bundle beneath the head of a gigantic, sleeping warrior. I was tempted to give him a taste of the war club, but better judgment prevailed. Such an act would put Bowl-Woman and the baby in great danger.

Bowl-Woman picked up the cradleboard, or *am-bee'-son;* the baby started to cry. One of the warriors stirred—and sighed.

"Down, lie down, quick!" I whispered. We threw ourselves flat and lay very quiet. I could see the warrior sitting up, looking about sleepily. My grip tightened on my war club; every muscle was tense.

Now the baby stopped crying; the warrior yawned and settled down again, pulling his robe up over his head in a satisfied way. I lay still a few minutes, sweating from every pore; there was no further sound but the heavy breathing of the sleepers.

Nudging Bowl-Woman, I helped her up whilst she lifted the *am-bee'son* very carefully; then we tiptoed away with Moon-ha'kee creeping close to our heels.

Approaching our camp, I hailed the guards from the thicket, so that they would know who we were. I had no desire to be seen first and perhaps stop a Lenape arrow.

When I told the *Ee'la* what I had done, he roused the whole party and before them all he took his own eagle feather and tied it upon my scalp lock. Then he sent me back to our village with Bowl-Woman and the baby.

"Tell the chief," he said, "that thanks to In-the-Forest and Moon-ha'kee we shall return in a few days with the *Mee-sing'*, also prisoners and scalps. Now go!"

I was glad enough to go, because I knew that the attack on a camp full of sleeping men would not be a pleasant spectacle. Yet I also knew that the Susquehannocks started the trouble and would deserve all they got.

We traveled all night, guiding our course by the stars. About the middle of the morning I found a sunny spot on a southern slope, hidden by brush from hostile eyes, and here I made Bowl-Woman rest, whilst I went hunting. Returning with two rabbits, I gathered the driest wood I could find, to avoid smoke. She broiled them and we had a feast.

After another rest we pressed on again and camped for the night in a deep thicket. I took off my feather and hung it on a bush whilst I slept; from then on I took pride in caring for it. The following afternoon Bowl-Woman taught me the long, hailing call to sound as we approached the village, the "death yell," meaning that I had struck the enemy, and still a different call meaning that I had rescued a Lenape from captivity. As we approached within earshot, I sounded all three.

The whole village turned out to welcome us and escorted us to Fling-Her-This-Way's cabin, where we found Thunder-Arrow somewhat better. Then the people dragged us bodily to the chief's house, where we told our story, after which they gave us a grand feast. Some boys got hold of Moon-ha'kee and, after painting his face red, they tied a bunch of eagle down on top of his head and set him on the chief's *ha'soon* beside Bowl-Woman, the baby, and me. They knew and he knew that he deserved every honor that could be given to a dog.

Returning late to our temporary home, we lost no time getting to bed. I fell asleep wondering what the rest of the war party had done and when they would come in.

XIII. The Man of the House

THE war party came in the second afternoon. I was hunting for Thunder-Arrow's stone pipe head in the ashes of the cabin when I heard the hailing call. They were coming in by the river trail instead of from the northwest where I had expected them. Seven times they gave the death yell, by which we knew that there were scalps or prisoners or both.

Everybody rushed to the Big-House square, myself among them. The war party had halted at the northeast corner near poor Granny's abandoned cabin and again they gave the hailing call and the seven death yells.

Now the people ranged themselves in two long rows forming a narrow lane reaching from where the warriors stood to the Big-House. I thought to honor the warriors, but when I joined them, I saw that everyone was armed with a stick, a handful of stones, or some sort of weapon. I picked up a stone, not knowing what it was for.

Suddenly there was a shout, and a naked man came running down the lane; everybody yelled and tried to hit him. Many succeeded, but he finally reached the Big-House and stood panting, leaning up against the closed door. Even from where I stood I could see that he was bruised and cut in many places.

257

Another man came dashing down the lane, but he did not fare so well. Somebody tripped him and before he could get up and stagger on to the Big-House, he had received a terrible beating.

The third runner was little more than a boy; he was wise enough, however, to run as fast and as straight as he possibly could, and because of this he got by with hardly a scratch.

By this time I realized that the runners must be prisoners and the scene I had just witnessed was their welcome to the village. Somebody announced there were no more; so I went up to speak to the *Ee'la* and inform him of my safe return with Bowl-Woman and the baby. Then I saw for the first time that four of my warrior comrades carried slender poles. Attached to the end of each pole was a small hoop upon which a scalp was stretched. Each scalp was a circular piece of the skin of a man's head three or four fingers across, painted red on the flesh side, with the long hair still attached, and I knew without being told that each represented the death of an enemy—one of the Susquehannock raiders. A fifth comrade proudly bore the bundle containing "Our Grandfather," the *Mee-sing'*.

The *Ee'la* insisted that I hold one of the scalp poles, and I took it with a very squeamish feeling; then he whispered to me what to do. First I gave the death yell and then I shouted:

"Fling-Her-This-Way! Come hither! Come before me!"

"*Oh'ho!*" she answered. Soon she worked her way through the crowd and stood in front of me.

"Are you mourning the death of your husband, slain by the Susquehannocks?"

"Yes!"

"Here is a Susquehannock scalp to dry your eyes with!" I gave her the pole and glad I was to be rid of it.

Now the widows of North-Man and Travels-Far were called and each given a scalp; the fourth went to a man whose wife had been killed in a raid years before.

Next the leader demanded that I march next to him at the head of the war party and the scalp carriers. I called Moon-ha'kee who was still wearing his original paint and feathers with later additions, and he walked along beside me with head and tail up as proudly as could be, whilst we paraded the whole village, carrying the scalps and singing war songs.

The *Ee'la's* grim face softened and his lips twitched when he spied Moon-ha'kee with all his decorations. He said nothing about keeping him out of the parade.

We stopped at Fling-Her-This-Way's cabin long enough to deliver the *Mee-sing'* bundle to Thunder-Arrow, who was very grateful.

Evidently some cooks had prepared for the party's return, starting to work as soon as the warriors sounded their first hailing call, for by the time we got back to the square we were called to a feast in the chief's house, venison stew made with hulled corn, berry bread and baked squash. Moon-ha'kee was not neglected, for he had a bowl of stew and a little round loaf of bread.

The Turtle Chief now called upon various members of the party to tell of their adventures, beginning with the *Ee'la*. From his story I learned that the Susquehannocks were all awake when the attack was made, and so instead of exterminating the whole raiding party the Lenapes killed only four and took three prisoners, counting the guard I had tied up under the tree.

Then I had to tell my own experience and I took pains not to forget Moon-ha'kee's part in it. By the time other warriors had their say, darkness was falling beneath a stormy-looking sky.

Two large fires illuminated the Big-House square, one to the north and one to the south. In the middle of the west side in front of the Big-House stood the two singers who had served in the first war dance, with the same flat drum, which now I noticed was decorated with five red spots, one in the middle and four at regular intervals around the edge.

They struck up a stirring dance song, which was greeted with whoops. The warriors and scalp carriers then formed themselves in a long north-and-south line and danced eastward almost to the river bank, then turned around and danced back to the Big-House again, then again to the river bank and so on back and forth. Now I noticed that the scalps were changing hands and I learned that anyone who felt glad that the raiders had been overtaken and punished was entitled to carry a scalp for a while in this kind of war dance.

We might have danced all night, but sometime around midnight, I suppose, a driving snow began to fall, and we were glad to find refuge in the warm cabins. When the dance stopped, the scalps were all delivered to the *Ee'la*, and I saw him untying them from the poles, but I have no idea what he did with them.

Fling-Her-This-Way's cabin was now a crowded place, with Thunder-Arrow, Bowl-Woman, the baby, and myself added to the family, together with White-Deer's wedding gifts and such of our own belongings as had been rescued from the fire, not to mention Moon-ha'kee. What this large family would mean to me, I did not realize until the following morning when I asked for a little bear's grease to eat with my sa'pan.

"I am very sorry," said Fling-Her-This-Way, "but the grease bag is empty, and for that matter the meat rack, too. My brother has supplied these things to White-Deer and me since my husband was killed, but he has a family of his own to support and it may be some time before he can spare us any more grease or venison."

At that moment it dawned upon me that I was now the man of the house. Thunder-Arrow was wounded, Little-Bear absent; who was there but myself to feed the family? Certainly we could not expect Fling-Her-This-Way's brother to support us.

I talked the matter over with Thunder-Arrow, and he felt as I did.

"Truly," he said, "we cannot continue to eat up Fling-Her-This-Way's supplies nor use the food that was given to White-Deer and Little-Bear."

"We have some provisions of our own," said Bowl-Woman. "Of course our dried pumpkins, our dried berries and beans were all burned, also our dried meat, but our corn crop is still hanging on the drying pole in the garden and we have a pitful of pumpkins and squashes."

"Hoh! For that we should be thankful," said Thunder-Arrow. "Besides I hope to be making arrows again before very long. The stabs in my arm are healing fast, although I must say the hole that Susquehannock snake punched in my leg is not doing so well. I do not get much sleep on account of it!"

"Perhaps I can bring in enough venison to keep us alive," I suggested, "but I don't know about grease. How do you hunt bears?"

"After bears have holed up for the winter in hollow trees, in caves, or in brush piles where trees have been blown down, all you have to do is find out where they are, scare them out, and shoot them."

"*Ay-kay-saa'!* Is *that* all you have to do? What do you mean by 'holing up for the winter'?"

"Pretty soon now, when the winter sets in with full force, the bears will all find sheltered places for themselves," Thunder-Arrow explained, "and there they will sleep until spring, unless someone disturbs them. They do not even eat for several moons."

"*Ka-ya'!* Truly that is strange. How do you find out where they are?" I persisted.

"On a big tree that is easy. You can tell from the scratches on the bark that a bear has gone up. In windfalls and caves better get Moon-ha'kee to help you; dogs can smell a bear a long way."

"How would you get a bear out of a hole in a tree?"

"Climb up to the mouth of the hole and throw in fire or punch the bear with a long pole until he gets mad; then he'll come out. It's too early to hunt bears yet," Thunder-Arrow concluded. "As for grease, don't worry about that; we do not really need bear's grease now. The deer are fat at this time of year."

The very next day I brought in a fat young buck, whilst the womenfolk visited the corn-drying pole and the pumpkin pit. For a while at least our food worries were over.

Fortunately the sack of shells that Little-Bear had brought me from the sea had lain out in the shed and had thus escaped the fire, so my material was at hand when the chance came at last to learn the art of making shell beads, or *kay'kwuk*, under Thunder-Arrow's instruction.

The first step was to break the outer whorls off the shells, which were a species of large sea snails or conches, until only the center core or column was left. This had to be done bit by bit with great care so as not to break the cores. I then ground these with bits of sandstone until they became round, smooth bars of shell, in length from half a span to a span and in thickness a little less than a quarter inch. The grinding was a very tedious task, then I had to mark each bar into quarter-inch lengths, a little more or less, and saw the pieces off by grooving around and around with a flint flake. Each core made twelve to sixteen little shell cylinders. Now the ends had to be ground off flat on sandstone slabs; then came the hardest part, the drilling.

Thunder-Arrow, although his right arm was still almost helpless, showed me how to clamp each bead to be drilled in a split stick which held it like a vise. The actual boring of the holes I did with a fine flint drill mounted on a wooden shaft like an arrow, but thicker, and this I rotated between my palms in the manner of a fire stick. The hole had to be started with a sharp bit of flint held in the hand; but after this was done, the actual drilling was simple but very slow. When the bead was pierced half through, I turned it over and drilled from the other side. A copper drill used with water and fine, gritty sand was sometimes used for boring; and I have seen beads made of hard shell fully two inches long that had been pierced in this way. However that sort of work was much too slow for me.

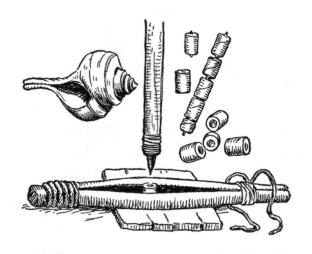

I was grinding cores one evening by the fireside when the *Ee'la*, or war captain, came in. He watched me for a while, then he spoke.

"Tomorrow will be a great occasion," he said, "and I should like to have all my warriors, especially the members of the last war party, take part."

"What are you going to do?" I asked.

"We are going to burn one of the Susquehannock captives," he replied simply.

My shell and my grinding stone fell from my hands. I stared at him with horror.

"Burn a captive!" I cried. "What are you going to do that for? Is he a wizard?"

"*Ma'ta!* Not that I know of. The thing is this: We must show those Susquehannocks that they cannot raid our villages and kill our people and escape the consequences. We shall make his death a hard one!"

"When," I asked with a shudder, "are you going to burn the other two?" He was astonished at my ignorance.

"Probably never, unless they try to escape," he replied. "Both have been spoken for by families who have lost relatives. If they prove worthy, they may be adopted some day."

"Why did you select this one for burning?" I persisted.

"Somebody recognized him as the raider who killed Travels-Far! I shall look for you tomorrow, soon after midday on the Big-House square."

"*Hoh!*" I grunted. I did not wish to say, "No," yet I could not promise to take part in the burning of a human being.

I slept little that night, thinking of the time when they burned the witch in our village in England. The smoke in the street, the shouts, the yells of the crowd, yes, the shrieks of the tortured sorceress—I remembered them all.

As soon as dawn came, I decided that the meat rack must be empty; I should go hunting. Now that I was the man of the house, I could not let my family starve, *Ee'la* or no *Ee'la*.

As I left, I looked at the meat rack. Nobody was watching, but if they had been, they would have seen me throw about fifteen pounds of good venison into the river.

For some reason, deer were hard to find, and I did not come back until nearly dark. As I crossed the Big-House square, I saw a pile of smoking embers with the charred remains of a stake rising out of the middle, which told its own story. Although I had been out all day without food, I had no appetite for the *sa'pan* Bowl-Woman warmed for me.

Something inside me seemed to say that the Creator does not like to have his children burned, even witches or murderers, whether in England or in America.

Now I went ahead with the bead making and, by the time all of my material was used, I had become quite skilful. I repaid to Bowl-Woman and Thunder-Arrow all the *kay'kwuk* they had expended upon my training and my adoption and had several strings left.

During the time I stayed home bead making or going hunting only when we needed meat, I found out something that disturbed me. Bowl-Woman and Fling-Her-This-Way were not getting along very well! I suppose it was only natural, as the house belonged to one and the family to the other.

When Bowl-Woman wanted to cook *sa'pan* for breakfast, Fling-Her-This-Way thought *soo'tay-yo* would be better, and so it went. Usually Thunder-Arrow or I would stop the argument by saying that we wanted whichever happened to be Bowl-Woman's choice, naturally. Then Fling-Her-This-Way would sulk the rest of the day and would not talk to anyone.

Fling-Her-This-Way had decided ideas of her own on how babies should be cared for and did not like Bowl-Woman's methods at all. One day she told her so very frankly, and Bowl-Woman got up without a word and walked out of the cabin, leaving the baby with Thunder-Arrow.

Quite a while later I had occasion to go down to the river bank and I found her sitting on a rock, with her robe pulled up over her head. I addressed her as "Mother," and asked her what the trouble was, but she made no answer. Worried, I gently lifted the robe from her face and found that she was weeping.

As head of the house I felt that, boy though I was, I must do something to prevent these two good women from becoming enemies, not only for their own sakes, but on account of Little-Bear and White-Deer, It was a tough problem.

The night after I found Bowl-Woman crying I sat up late, thinking what to do, until everyone was asleep. Then I threw twelve pinches of tobacco upon the fire and prayed as I had been taught. That night I dreamed that a crew of huge ants were helping me to build a house.

Build a house! Of course, that was the answer. A separate home for Bowl-Woman, Thunder-Arrow, the baby, and myself. We would move out and leave Fling-Her-This-Way in peace.

I brought up the subject at breakfast, and Thunder-Arrow was delighted, although he lamented that he was still unable to help. The women did not say much, but I thought that they both looked relieved. Later on I heard them talking together in a very friendly way, quite like old times.

Bowl-Woman gave me her ideas that afternoon when Fling-Her-This-Way was out gathering wood. She wanted her home built on the same ground it had stood upon before and of the same kind of substantial gable-roof bark house, but she wanted it a little larger to allow room for two more bed platforms. This I knew would take a long time to build, and a quick change was needed.

"Why not build a mat tent to live in until the house is finished?" suggested Thunder-Arrow. "All you need would be sixteen poles about twice as tall as a man; I mean good poles to stand upright around the circle. The crosswise poles can be willow switches or almost anything."

"What will we do for mats to cover the frame?" I asked. "All our tent mats are burned."

"We can borrow some for the present," replied Thunder-Arrow. "Almost everybody has them. It is too late to gather rushes this year, for they have to be cut green and cured. Of course we could thatch the frame with uncured rushes, but that would take a lot of time and work."

I went up the creek to a swamp some distance above the rock pile where I had my vision and found plenty of limber ash poles about three fingers thick at the butt and twelve to fourteen feet long. With an English ax it would have been a joke to cut these poles, but with only a stone-bladed ax and a flint knife it took me fully two days to cut them, trim them, and fetch them home. The stone ax bruised the wood instead of cutting it.

There was a vacant spot just south of the big tree in front of the burned cabin and here we decided to build our temporary lodge. I found Roaring-Wings and he helped me bring Thunder-Arrow over to watch my work

and give advice, wrapping him in a warm robe and setting
him with his back to the tree. The old man looked at
the wound in Thunder-Arrow's leg, which was still
running matter, and shook his head.

"When you get moved into the new home," he said,
"I'll come and doctor it if it has not stopped running by
that time."

I marked out a circle about twelve feet across with a
sharp stick and then set on this circle little stones about
two feet apart until I had laid sixteen, which just about
completed the circle. These I shifted to and fro until
they were about the same distance apart, then I was ready
to set the poles, one for every stone.

To make holes for the poles, I used a stout *see'meen*
wood stake upon which I had worked a sharp point,
which I hardened in fire.

Luckily the ground was not yet frozen, and I was
able to drive my stake into the ground a foot or so with
the aid of a stone, then rock it from side to side a little,
then pull it out, thus making a hole into which I set a
pole, afterward tamping down the earth around it.
When the poles were all set, Thunder-Arrow told me how
to bend them all in toward the center of the circle and tie
them together with strips of *len-nik'pee*, or basswood inner
bark. When finished, the dome was about six and a
half feet high in the middle. The next thing was to tie
on four or five courses of slender willows encircling the
frame, beginning about two feet above the ground.

I was just lashing the topmost course of willows,
standing on a roll of robes, when the Turtle Band chief
appeared and asked me what I was doing. I explained

and added that I would now have to look for somebody
to lend us some tent mats.

The chief shouted for his crier and in a few minutes
everybody in the village knew what we needed. People
came with large rolls, and soon I had to tell one good-
hearted woman after another not to bring any more mats
for we now had plenty for our *wik'wam*.

Next morning Bowl-Woman tied the mats, which
measured about three by six feet, on the frame in a certain
way so as to shed water. Whilst she was busy with this
task, I dug a little bowl-shaped hole in the middle for a
fireplace and gathered poles to outline the beds, of which
there were three. She pulled some dry grass to lay back
of these poles to keep our bedding off the ground, and by
dark we had everything moved over.

That night we sat around a fire of borrowed wood
and, although it seemed strange not to have platforms to
sit upon, it was wonderful to be in a home of our own
again. We slept warm, close to the bosom of "our
Mother, the Earth," whilst the late November wind
whistled through the bare branches of our favorite tree.
Of course Moon-ha'kee insisted upon sharing my bed.

The next night Roaring-Wings came over to doctor
Thunder-Arrow. He was wearing the skins of several
kinds of birds tied on his scalp lock and in his hand was
a curious-looking little knife made by setting a very keen
flint flake crosswise in a small, wooden handle. This he
used to enlarge the wound so that he could clean out the
matter with a swab made of some fine, almost white
fiber attached to a stick. Then he washed it out with
water, afterward chewing some sort of herb in his mouth

and squirting the juice, mixed with water, into the wound.
Finally he put a poultice made of herbs on the outside,
tied in place with a deerskin bandage.

I thought this was the
end of the doctoring; but no,
it was only the beginning. All
night long Roaring-Wings
sang over the invalid, keeping time with a rattle made of
deer hoofs attached by short strings to a thong, and this
to a handle.

Now that I knew a little about Lenape singing I
could understand what he was driving at, although the
songs were mainly made up of musical syllables without
any meaning, with a real word stuck in here and there.
Roaring-Wing's song ran something like this:

> You promised
> To help me
> Cure sick men
> Cure wounded
> Now I need you
> Keep your promise
> Come help me
> Cure this man.

He did not state to whom this appeal was addressed, but it was, of course, his Dream-helper. The monotonous song repeated over and over and the clash-clash-clash of the rattle put Thunder-Arrow to sleep after a while, and I dropped off myself not long after. Roaring-Wings noticed this, stopped his song, and woke me. In this class of doctoring nobody may sleep except the patient. Day was breaking when he finally brought this ceremony to a close, leaving us all exhausted, except Thunder-Arrow who still slept peacefully, the longest rest he had enjoyed since he was wounded. I gave Roaring-Wings a string of my new beads for a fee, which pleased him very much, especially as I had made the *kay'kwuk* myself, although I suspect that ordinarily the fee would have been thought rather small.

He talked with me whilst we were eating our breakfast, and when I told him I was now providing venison for the family and that later I proposed to kill at least one bear for the grease, he promised to fix me up some hunting medicine and to make a tiny, wooden mask representing *Mee-sing-haw-lee'kun* for me to carry as a charm.

I walked with him over to his cabin, and on my way back someone stepped up behind me and grabbed me by the arm. It was Cross-Woman.

"I want you to tell me where Toad-Face is. Have you done away with him?" She tried to shake me, but I pulled away from her grip.

"Be careful," I warned her, "I allow no one, not even a woman, to jerk me around."

"Tell me, where is Toad-Face?" she insisted. I looked her full in the eye.

"I do not know where Toad-Face is and I do not care if I never see him again. However, if I knew, I would tell you; you are his mother and have a right to know."

She studied my face a moment.

"You never did lie to me," she said, "and I do not think you are lying now. Furthermore, I believe that you would tell me should you learn anything. Will you?"

"If I can," I answered.

We were hardly settled in the new home when a woman who had lent us about half the tent mats wanted them back again, as she and her husband had suddenly decided to go out on a winter hunt, starting within a few days. Naturally, after all she had been through, Bowl-Woman was discouraged and wept. Then she decided our house should be thatched after all. Nobody could then come and take the roof from over our heads.

Her first act was to call another meeting of our clan, the *Oh-kay-ho'kee*, and state our predicament. Every woman offered her tent mats, but she was firm.

"*Ma-ta-ka'*, no, indeed. I thank you, but I want no more borrowed roofs. Will you help me gather rushes or not?"

"*Ka-tuh!*" shivered Duck-Woman, her sister. "Swamp water is cold on the legs at this time of year."

"Very well," retorted Bowl-Woman, "if you are such a delicate flower, we shall leave you out. Won't anybody help me or must I do it alone?"

Grudgingly, with half-joking groans and grimaces and shivering *ka-tuhs'*, five women volunteered, including Duck-Woman.

"*Kay'hay-la shee'kee.* It's very fine," she grumbled, "but if that cold water makes my legs stiff, Sister, you'll have to carry me around from now on." Everybody laughed, because she was about twice Bowl-Woman's size.

They started in that afternoon, whilst I went out hunting for a deer to feed them. They pulled the rushes and trimmed them with big knives made of a fine-grain black stone found near the river some distance above the first rapids. It is not so shiny nor quite so hard as flint but it makes good knives for cutting rushes, skins, and meat.

I got the deer the first afternoon, so the next day I went up to the swamp, the same place where I had gathered my poles, to watch them work. The women took off their leggings and moccasins and stepped bravely into the icy water and mud. When they had gathered a back load of rushes, they rubbed their legs and feet dry with grass and put on leggings and moccasins again before starting back to the village.

Next afternoon the thatching was finished, my only part in it being to cut more willow switches and get additional basswood inner bark. Beginning at the bottom, they leaned the rushes up against the frame of the *wik'wam*, clamping them fast with horizontal willow poles sewed through to the frame inside with strips of bark. Bowl-Woman did the sewing with a big wooden needle. Then a second course of rushes was fastened on in the same way above but overlapping the first, like shingles, and so on until the dome was covered, all but a small opening in the middle which was left for a smoke hole. I insisted on plastering the edges of this hole with mud so that the thatch would not catch fire. One fire was enough for me.

A thatched round cabin like this was called *me-ay-khas-kwee'ga-mek* in Lenape, and it made the warmest kind of winter lodge. We returned the borrowed mats with thanks, and Bowl-Woman only laughed when the woman who had wanted them back changed her mind again and decided not to go on her trip after all. If the sister got stiff legs from the cold swamp water, we did not hear of it.

The night after the cabin was finished we had our first heavy snow. It must have been early in December. Still the ground was not frozen and I was able to build part of the frame of the new large house and between times keep the family supplied with meat. Thunder-Arrow was still too weak to work, but thanks to Roaring-Wings' doctoring, was now able to walk around and advise me.

I cut two stout, forked posts for the main uprights, about ten feet long, and, planting them in holes some eighteen inches deep, I wedged in stones around them and tamped them well. These stood nine feet apart as nearly as I could guess it, and were intended to support the ridgepole, which was fifteen feet long.

The corner posts were sturdy and forked, and were set to outline a rectangle fifteen feet long from east to west and twelve feet from north to south, with the forks about four and a half feet above the ground. In the middle of each long side I set a similar forked post to support the middle of the side poles or plates. When all these had been set in place, I cut sixteen rafter poles about eight feet long, but I did not start the roof. I

19

simply tied them in bundles and laid them aside to season, along with the ridgepole and the plates, on Thunder-Arrow's advice. We could not finish the cabin until spring anyhow for lack of the necessary elm bark, which will not peel in winter. Basswood bark might have answered the purpose and may be peeled at any time; but there were no trees large enough within reach of the village, as I discovered after several days' search.

Now the time had come to go bear hunting and one day I went over to Roaring-Wings' cabin to see about the things he had promised me. He hung the little *Mee-sing'* hunting charm on a deerskin thong around my neck. It was a fine piece of wood-carving and a perfect copy of the full-sized mask. He also gave me some medicine to carry in my shoulder pocket and chew which he said would kill my scent which so often alarmed the deer before I could get within bowshot. For these things I paid him five deerskins from animals I had killed, skins tanned soft by Bowl-Woman.

I was just returning home when I met two men carrying a strong pole from which hung a sort of sling made of tanned skin, containing something heavy and round. They halted and all at once two powerful arms shot up out of the sling, the hands grasped the pole, the arms bent, and a huge head rose into view, crowned with a bushy thatch of stiff, black hair. A pair of fine, brown eyes surveyed me.

"*Hey, ne-gwees!*" said a deep voice.

"*Hey, nohk-han!*" I replied. If this strange creature was willing to call me "Son," I would be equally polite and call him "Father."

"Where does Bowl-Woman live?" rumbled the voice. "I am a kinsman of hers."

Then I realized who he was—no less a person than *Ka'wi-a*, the Porcupine, famous, legless story-teller of the *Oh-kay-ho'kee* clan.

XIV. Winter Tales: Moon-ha'kee Growls

BOWL-WOMAN is my foster-mother," I replied. "I am now on my way to her house. That is where I live."

"*Woo-la-mo'wee shee'kee,* truly fine," rumbled Porcupine. "You lead and we shall follow."

He let himself down into the sling again and his bearers turned about and followed me. I halted before the new thatched *wik'wam.*

"Here it is," I said.

The bearers let the sling down to the ground. Porcupine swung himself out, resting his weight on his hands. His clothing was a sack made of deerskin, with his head sticking out of the top and two holes for his arms just below it. The bottom was solid, hiding the shriveled legs he was said to possess. He could take off this garment in a minute by simply slipping his arms out of the holes and pulling his body out of the sack.

"*Hoh!*" he said, "*Shee'kee!* I am glad it's a thatched *wik'wam.* I don't like to climb up on a *ha'soon.* I thought all the time that Bowl-Woman lived in a bark house."

Bowl-Woman heard the talk and came out to see what was going on.

278

"*Kweh! Ka'wi-a! N'a-lun-goo'mak!*" she cried. "It's my kinsman, Porcupine! Come right in! I am glad you have lived to see this day!" The strange story-teller swung himself along like a man on crutches and the rest of us followed, the bearers bringing in two fur robes and several bags including one embroidered with quills, that had been carried in the sling along with Porcupine.

The bearers spread his robes on the grass bed across from mine, and the cripple swung himself into the middle of them, his companions seating themselves near by. Thunder-Arrow had been asleep; now he awoke and greeted the new arrivals, whilst Bowl-Woman warmed the stew pot.

After they had eaten, the bearers, who were strangers to me, took their leave.

"They are from South Fish Village down the river," Porcupine explained. "They wish to return home before dark."

"Don't they work for you all the time?" I asked, filled with curiosity as to how the story-teller managed his affairs.

"*Mat-ta-ka'*. No, indeed. When I finish in one village, I have no trouble in finding young men to carry me to the next one. You see, I make my living telling stories; people like to listen and give me food and shelter or whatever else I need."

"I have heard that you stay at home in the summer time and tell stories only in the winter. Why is it?" I asked.

"Ho-ho-ho!" he laughed. "I thought every child knew that. In the summer I tell no stories because there are many little creatures, such as snakes and bugs roaming about, who might hear what was said about them and get after me; or they might repeat my words to some powerful *man-it'to* and then I would be in trouble. In the winter time all the little villains are asleep!"

"That is true," put in Thunder-Arrow. "Nobody tells stories in warm weather, except perhaps the speaker at a feast will tell how the celebration was first held long ago by our deceased ancestors."

"I am glad this is winter, then," I said. "When are you going to tell some stories?"

"Tonight I shall begin," rumbled Porcupine. "I see there are only three of you here. Why don't you ask in a few friends?"

"Better get Roaring-Wings," Bowl-Woman suggested, "also my sister, Duck-Woman, and of course Fling-Her-This-Way. You might ask Beaver-House, too, if you do not object to Cross-Woman. She will probably come if he does. You may want to invite two or three of your boy friends also. But do not ask too many: the *wik'wam* is small."

I started out, going first to Roaring-Wings, but he could not come on account of doctoring a sick woman that night. Then I went to Duck-Woman's house and invited her and her husband. Then I got Fling-Her-This-Way and finally sought out two young fellows who had been playmates of mine—one named Breaks-Everything and the other Catches-Two. I put off asking Beaver-House until the last, because I had not entered that cabin since I left it nearly a year before and I dreaded doing so.

Finally I screwed up my courage and raised the door curtain. Alas, the familiar dwelling that I had left so clean and tidy was all dirt and disorder again. *Wee-sao'suh*, the dog, sprang up and approached me, wagging and fawning; he, for one, was glad to see me.

"*Hey*, Beaver-House! You have seen another day!" I said politely.

"*Hey!*" he replied. "Wife, it is customary to spread a mat for our guest and to set food before him."

Cross-Woman, who had been lying on the rear *ha'soon*, now rolled over and rose to her feet. When she saw who I was, she sat down again suddenly and stared. Her hair was hanging loose and tangled as if she were in mourning, and her broad face was smeared with charcoal.

"Have you brought me news of Toad-Face?" she asked in a hoarse whisper. I really felt sorry for the woman and hated to disappoint her.

"No," I said. "I am sorry. Bowl-Woman simply sent me over to invite you and Beaver-House to come to our *wik'wam* this evening. Porcupine is going to tell stories. But who is dead? I see you are mourning."

"I am mourning for Toad-Face," she replied. "I know that if he were alive he would come home to his mother. Tell Bowl-Woman I do not feel like going out tonight."

Beaver-House however, promised to come, and I left the cabin thinking that perhaps I knew Toad-Face even better than his mother did. "He must be up to some mischief," I said to myself.

After dark the invited ones gathered and seated themselves around the flickering fire. When the last had settled himself, Porcupine began:

"Now I shall tell some of my stories. Do not interrupt me or go out or come in whilst I am speaking. Between stories you may ask questions or go out if you desire. Do not disobey these rules, because if you do, I shall become very angry, and story-telling will cease. I always start with the story which we believe to be true, of how this great island where we live was created. Has anyone here heard the *Wa'lum O'loom?*

"It was recited in our Big-House last fall," said Thunder-Arrow.

"*Kay'hay-la shee'kee.* Then you know something about what I am going to tell you.

"It is said that in the beginning *Kee-shay-la-muh'-ka-ong*, the Creator, made the world in the form of good, dry land and placed various creatures upon it. Among them was a huge Toad, to whom was given the management of the waters, which he kept in his body and let out only as they were needed to water the earth.

"One day, it is said, an evil monster appeared and quarreled with the Toad. This was a great horned serpent with only one horn. They fought, and the Toad tried to swallow the snake, but the monster gored the Toad in the side with his horn and the waters gushed forth and soon began to overflow the earth.

"At this time a powerful person named *Nan'a-push*, or *A-men'a-push*, was living on the earth and he, when he saw the water rising, went to the highest mountain he could find, thinking that there he would be safe. The waters continued to rise, however, until at last there remained only a little plot of dry ground on the top of the mountain with a cedar tree growing upon it.

"The water came nearer and nearer, and it was plain that the land would soon all be covered. *Nan'a-push* picked up all the animals and birds he could of those that had gathered on the mountain top and put them in the bosom of his girded robe, then he started to climb the tree. As he went up, he broke off branches from the tree and stuck them under his belt; finally he reached the top.

"Now the waters rose still higher and nearly touched his feet. He began to sing and beat time with an arrow upon his tight bowstring which sounded like a drum. As he sang, the tree began to grow and continued to grow as the waters rose, so that the waves never quite reached *Nan'a-push*.

"Tiring of singing, he threw upon the water the cedar branches which he had plucked as he climbed upward, and they became a large, strong raft. Upon this he embarked with all the creatures he had saved, and they floated about until all the mountains were covered and nothing alive remained on the earth except *Nan'a-push* and the creatures on the raft.

"After a while *Nan'a-push* decided that a new earth should be made, a task he knew he could perform through the power that had been granted to him, providing he could get a little material from old earth to start with.

"So he employed different water creatures to dive down and try to get a little mud from the bottom of the great water. The first was the loon, *me-tay-wee-lay'on*, who dived down bravely and stayed a long time, but when he came floating up, he was dead. *Nan'a-push* breathed upon him and he came back to life. Next the otter, *kwen-a'mohk*, tried to reach the bottom and he stayed longer than the loon, but he also failed and, coming up

dead, was revived by *Nan'a-push*. Next the beaver, *ta-ma'kwa*, tried it with the same result.

"Finally *Nan'a-push* chose the muskrat, *ta-mask'-was*, to make one last attempt. He stayed down much longer than any of the others and floated up dead, but in his mouth and paws was a little of the precious earth from the world that had been. *Nan'a-push* revived the muskrat and blessed him, promising that his tribe would never die out.

"Now *Nan'a-push* called upon someone to receive and carry the earth, and *tahk-gohk'*, the turtle, responded. The mud was placed upon the turtle's back, and *Nan'a-push* blew his breath upon it. It began to grow and grow until it became the great island where we live today.

"Truly, it is said that *Nan'a-push* sent a wolf every so often to see how large the new land had grown. The first time the wolf traveled to the far edge of the island and back in one day; the second time it took five days to make the trip; the third time, ten; then a moon, then a year, then five years, then twelve. At the last it is said that *Nan'a-push*

sent forth a young wolf on this errand, but it died of old age before it could return. Then, indeed, *Nan'a-push* decided that the world was large enough and commanded that it stop growing.

"Now, they claim, *Nan'a-push* lives in the far north. He sleeps all winter like a bear and before he goes to bed he smokes his big stone pipe. When you see the air all smoky in the fall, that smoke comes from the pipe of *Nan'a-push*. Now the story is finished."

"*Hoh!*" said Thunder-Arrow, "that was a good story!" He turned to me. "You have often heard me speak of the 'great island where we live.' Now you know what I meant."

"There is one thing I don't understand," I said. "You talk all the time about *Kee-shay-la-muh'ka-ong*, the Creator, and call Him sometimes *Kit-tan-it-to'wet*, Great Spirit, yet now Porcupine tells us that *Nan'a-push* created the world we are living in today. How do you account for that?"

"It appears that you are one of those who wishes to know everything," answered Porcupine. "There are some things nobody knows, but I think I can answer your question. *Nan'a-push* was created by the Great Spirit in the beginning, to be one of His helpers. As you know, the great Creator works through His helpers, such as the sun and the winds, not directly; yet His power is back of them all."

That was a big thought, and I asked no more questions for a while. The men lighted their pipes and smoked, and the women gossiped. Finally Porcupine's pipe was smoked out; he cleaned it and laid it aside.

"May I ask one thing more before you tell another story?" I asked. Porcupine grunted his assent.

"According to your story the big Toad who controlled water was killed by the horned snake. What power, or *man-it'to*, is in charge of water now?"

"That is a good question," said Porcupine, "but I thought everybody knew the answer. The Thunders, or *Pet-ha-ko-way'yuk*, whom we call Elder Brothers, have charge of the rains that water the earth and make our crops grow. However, the great waters, since the death of the Toad who was their guardian, have become the abode of evil monsters, such as horned serpents. The Thunders are always on the watch for these serpents, and, when one appears, they shoot their crooked, fiery arrows at them. Thunders and horned snakes are enemies by nature."

"How many Thunders are there and what do they look like?" I pursued. "We don't have them in my country."

"There are said to be three companies of Thunders, with three Thunders in each company; but I think there must be more than nine; I should say twelve at least. They are spirits, of course, but when they take visible form, they are both manlike and birdlike. For this reason they are sometimes called 'Thunder-Birds.' It is the roar of their wings that makes the sound that we hear; the lightning flashes are their arrows. Are you satisfied?"

"Just one more question. Where do the Thunders live?"

"Far to the north there is a short river which joins two great lakes, lakes so large that they are almost like seas. In this river is an enormous waterfall, and under the fall is a cave where some of the Thunders live. Other Thunders are said to live in distant mountains to the west. Do you wish to ask anything more?"

"*Ma'ta.*"

"Very well," said Porcupine. "Besides the stories we believe, such as the one I have just related to you, there are others we tell for pleasure, not knowing whether they are true or not.

"It was strange, the beginning of this kind of story-telling," he went on. "One time a hunter was returning to his village in the evening when he heard a little voice singing. He tried to locate it and finally found that the voice was coming out of a curious hole in the ground indeed not much larger than the home of a furry nut chewer.

" '*Hey*, you down in the hole,' said the hunter, 'who are you?'

"The singing stopped, and the same little voice answered, 'I am a grandfather; if you wish to learn more, give me some tobacco.'

"So the hunter wrapped some tobacco in a leaf, tied it with a blade of grass, then dropped it quickly into the hole.

"Soon he heard the little voice again. 'Truly with tobacco you are stingy,' it said. 'Go back and tell your people that I will tell a story to anyone who gives me tobacco or a bit of bread. Now listen to this.' Then the little grandfather told the hunter the best story he had ever heard, ending with the words: 'If you wish to hear another story, be not stingy with your tobacco.' Such was the beginning of stories told for pleasure. Now my story about stories is ended."

"I wish that story had been longer," I said. "The little grandfather must have been a fairy." I used the English word "fairy" because I did not know the Lenape term.

"What is a *pa'lee*?" asked Porcupine. Evidently he could not pronounce the sound of *f* or *r*.

"Fairies are little people who live out in the forest," I replied. "Many stories about them are told in my country."

"Your *pa-lee'uk* must be like our *way-ma-tay-gun'is-suk*. They, too, are little people who live out in the woods. They help *Mee-sing-haw-lee'kun* to take care of the deer.

"One time when a certain man was out with several others hunting, his friends wandered off and left him alone, but finally he was lucky enough to kill a young buck. He dressed it and packed it on his back, then went on looking for his friends. After a while he whooped to call them, and somebody answered; it seemed close by, just across the hollow. He ran to catch up across the hollow but he saw nobody. Then he whooped again and somebody answered from the side of the hollow he had just left, and the same thing happened several times.

"Then the hunter became angry; he threw down the deer and chased the person who was answering him. When he caught him, he found that it was one of the little people, carrying a bow with the bark on it.

" 'I'll teach you to answer when I am calling my friends,' the angry hunter said. 'For that we'll have a fight right here.'

" '*Kay'hay-la!*' said the little man. 'I'll fight, but wait until I take off my jacket.' He took off a jacket made of cornhusk; then the hunter was ready to fight.

" 'Wait, I'll take off this jacket, too,' the little fellow said and stripped off another one. He kept on taking off jackets until there were twelve in all. Each time he took off one he became smaller and when the twelve were off, he was so small that the hunter was ashamed to fight him.

" 'I won't fight you now,' said the hunter. 'But I'll give you a name. When you get home, tell your folks that someone named you *Noh'koo-mi*, Answer-Me. And now I want you to 'answer me' this. Why did you try to fool me?'

"The little man laughed.

" 'I just wanted to see how strong you were; how far you could run carrying that deer.'

"Now, indeed, this short story is finished."

"*Hoh*! A good story," Beaver-House said. "However, I wish you would tell us a longer one. I was just beginning to enjoy that when it ended. I know you have a lot of long ones in your story bag."

Porcupine took his decorated bag which was made of deerskin and covered with little figures of men and animals done in dyed quills and deer hair, a fine piece of work.

"This is my story bag," he explained to me. "Inside are different things which represent all the stories I know. I reach into it, and the first thing I draw out informs me which story to tell."

He put his hand into the bag and drew forth a little wooden ball.

"*Hoh!*" he said. "That means the story of Ball-Player. You should like it, Beaver-House, because it is one of my long stories. However, it will be the last one for tonight. When a story-teller begins to put people to sleep, it is time for him to stop. Already Bowl-Woman is yawning, holding her hand in front of her face so that I won't see it."

"*Saaa!*" cried Bowl-Woman. "Shame on you! I'm not yawning and you know it. Don't go making up stories about *me*!"

"Stop scolding and listen," chuckled Porcupine. "I am beginning the story of Ball-Player. Do you all want to hear it?"

"*Kay'hay-la!*"

"Long ago a family went out into the wilderness to hunt: the father, the mother, and six boys. They found a place where there was plenty of game and there they made camp. The old lady built some shelves to put the meat on; the older boys started out hunting.

"The youngest boy never went hunting, but played with his ball all day; for this reason they called him Ball-Player. His ball was a strange one, the skull of a bobcat, and if ever he hit a tree, the ball would stick to it; the skull seemed to bite into the tree and stick fast.

"They stayed at that camp a long time, going hunting every day and bringing in a great deal of meat, which the old lady dried for future use. The boys hunted, east, north, and south, but never to the west because their mother had warned them not to hunt in that direction.

"One day the oldest boy thought he would go to the west in spite of the warning. After a while he came to a lake and, looking out upon it, he spied a young woman sitting in the water combing her hair which floated out all around her. He called to her and they talked together a while. Suddenly she disappeared. The boy liked her looks very much; truly, thoughts of her so diverted his mind from hunting that he never killed anything that day. He went home thinking, 'I shall try to see that girl again tomorrow,' but he never told his mother.

"When daylight came, he started off to the west. Coming near the lake where he had seen the girl, he began to call upon his Dream-helper, saying over and over, 'Whirlwind, my friend, Whirlwind, my friend.' When he reached the edge of the lake, he said, 'Whirlwind, my friend, help me to win that girl.' He broke a stem of grass which a whirlwind carried right to where the girl was sitting, and through the swirling of the waters it finally returned to the boy, bringing with it a strand of hair from the girl's head. The boy took this home, laying it on the back side of the bed.

"Somehow his mother knew what had happened, because she said, '*A-kee'*, my son; I know you have seen that girl!' The younger brother said nothing but kept on playing with his skull ball. When he struck a tree, the skull would bite in and stick.

"Next morning the girl came to camp, bringing a big bowl of bread, which pleased everyone, as they had eaten little but meat for a long time.

" 'I will marry you,' she told the eldest boy, 'but I am afraid there will be trouble. An ugly old wizard with only one eye, named Red-Feather-on-His-Head, has been after me, but I refused to marry him. Now he is

threatening to take me by force, as he has taken several
other women already.'

"The young man quieted her fears, and they were
married. Afterward she found the lock of hair and put
it back on her head. She had very pretty hair, all shining
green and blue.

"The hunters brought in plenty of meat and skins,
so that the family never wanted for anything; but after
a while the old parents grew tired of living and departed.

"The youngest boy grew bigger every day. Now he
sometimes wandered a long way from camp, playing with
his ball and making friends with animals, sometimes not
returning until late. The oldest brother warned him not
to go far from camp when the hunters were away, but to
stay near by to take care of his sister-in-law.

"One morning when the older boys were off hunting.
Ball-Player forgot this and wandered away from camp.
That was just the time Red-Feather arrived, looking for
the girl. As she was all alone, he had no trouble. Whilst
he was carrying her off, she kept grabbing hold of the
bushes, pulling some of them up by the roots, but he
went on, never thinking that she was marking a trail for
her husband to follow.

"When the boys reached home that night, they found
her gone. When Ball-Player came in long after the rest,
he felt very much ashamed that this had happened because
he had been forgetful.

"In the morning the older brother said, 'I am going
to look for my wife.' Picking up his *ah-pee'kawn*, or flute,
he blew it. 'If they kill me, within two days blood will
flow out of my flute.'

In two days the boys looked at the flute.

"'*Ee-kee'!*' said the next older boy. 'There is blood on the flute. I shall follow where our brother went.' He blew on the *ah-pee'kawn*. 'Look at the flute in two days; if blood flows from it, they have killed me.'

" 'Better let me go along; I can bring our sister-in-law back,' said Ball-Player; but the others would not believe him.

" 'You are too little,' they said.

"In two days when they looked again at the flute there was blood on it. The third brother followed the two that had gone before, refusing Ball-Player's help, then the fourth went and then the fifth.

"The fifth brother followed the trail of the bushes which the girl had pulled as she was being carried away, finally coming to Red-Feather's camp. He raised the curtain and entered the *wik'wam*. There sat the wizard and four women, one of them the girl he was seeking.

" 'Why have you come here?' asked Red-Feather.

" 'I am looking for my brothers who came this way, also for my sister-in-law.'

"'Very well,' Red-Feather replied and turned to the girl.

" 'Cook for this man,' he commanded. 'He is very tired and hungry; he must have come a long way.'

"The girl broke some bear ribs. After cooking them, she put them in a bowl, which she handed to Red-Feather. He held it out to the boy, but when he started to take it, Red-Feather snatched it away.

" 'Do you think I am going to give it to *you*? I am going to feed it to my *ya'kwa-hay*.' He untied his fierce, naked bear, or *ya'kwa-hay*, and said:

" '*Ya'kwa-hay*, eat this. When you are through, crush this boy's skull. He has been talking bad about your sister-in-law.'

"When the beast had finished the ribs, he attacked the boy and soon killed him. Dragging the body off, he left it in a ditch.

"Two days later Ball-Player looked at the flute; as he had expected, there was blood upon it. Now there was nobody to hold him back.

"He went down to the brook where they got their water, taking with him his father's otter-skin pouch. Now he whooped and called for his friends. Soon a lot of different animals were gathered around, for the boy had been friends to them all.

" 'Toad,' asked the boy, 'what can you do to help me?'

"The toad began to breathe hard and every time he puffed, fire came out of his mouth.

" '*Hoh!*' said Ball-Player. 'That is good enough. You shall be my pipe.' Reaching down, he picked up a snake.

" 'You, Snake, shall be my pipestem.'

"He took the otter-skin tobacco pouch and shook it.

" 'What can you do, Otter?'

" 'I can bite his spinal cord and break him down!'

" 'That is good enough.'

"Now Ball-Player turned to *Soun'-gweh*, the weasel.

" 'What can you do, Weasel?'

" 'Oh, I can go down his throat and cut his heart off while he is fighting.'

" 'That is good enough,' said Ball-Player.

"Having now enough help, he went up on the hill and built a fire. Then he made six arrows and every time he made one he would throw it in the fire. When it had burned, he would pick up the ashes and rub them between his hands, at which it became a good arrow again. Ten times he did this to each arrow; then he gathered up his ball and his other things and started for the house of Red-Feather, following the trail of the bushes which the girl had pulled up.

"Reaching the *wik'wam* of Red-Feather, he walked in.

" 'What did you come for?' asked Red-Feather.

" 'I am looking for my brothers,' Ball-Player replied.

" 'My *ya'kwa-hay* killed five little boys, and I threw them out there in the ditch. Maybe they ate your brothers,' Red-Feather answered, then turned to the girl.

" 'Cook for him, woman,' he ordered. 'Maybe he is hungry and has come a long distance.'

"While the girl was cooking the bear ribs, Ball-Player took out his pipe and tobacco pouch and started to smoke. Every time he drew a puff, the pipe said, 'We will kill him!'

" '*A-kee'!*' said Red-Feather, 'Your pipe sounds bad!'

" 'That is the natural way for it to sound,' replied Ball-Player.

"Just then the weasel came out of Ball-Player's shoulder pocket and climbed all over him. Red-Feather saw it.

" 'You have a pretty little pet,' he said. 'Let us fight our pets. Mine can crush the head off yours in a little while.'

" 'Very well,' agreed Ball-Player. 'My pet has never been whipped.' By this time the girl had the ribs cooked.

"Red-Feather offered Ball-Player the bowl of ribs, but he refused.

" 'I came to hunt my brothers, not to eat,' he said.

"So the *ya'kwa-hay* got the ribs, and Red-Feather said to it:

" 'When you are finished eating, crush that weasel's head; the little villain has been talking bad about your sister-in-law.'

"The *ya'kwa-hay* started to fight, but when it opened its mouth, the weasel disappeared into it. Then the otter-skin tobacco pouch came to life and began to chew on the *ya'kwa-hay's* hind legs. Every time the otter got a mouthful, he would spit it out and go after the legs again until the *ya'kwa-hay* had to sit down to fight. Finally even the little toad got in front and began to throw fire at the *ya'kwa-hay*.

" 'Take them off,' cried Red-Feather. 'They will kill my pet.'

" 'No, let them kill one another,' Ball-Player responded.

"In a minute the weasel came out of the *ya'kwa-hay's* mouth carrying its heart, and the fierce, naked bear fell dead.

"Now Ball-Player set his pets on Red-Feather. He himself threw his skull ball at Red-Feather's head, hitting him on his only good eye. There the ball stuck and Red-

Feather could not get it off. He could not see to fight, so they killed him in a few minutes and cut off his head.

" 'You have not really killed him yet—be careful!' warned the woman.

"Ball-Player went outside and built a fire, whilst the women helped him all they could by bringing wood. He threw Red-Feather and the *ya'kwa-hay* on the fire. They burned a while, then Red-Feather's head popped out of the fire to the north. The weasel followed and dragged it back. It popped out four times in all, but the weasel got it every time. The last time it popped it fell in the edge of the grass that grew around the *wik'wam*. Ball-Player picked it up and threw it back into the fire and it could pop no more.

" 'You have killed him now,' said the women.

"The women all wanted to go with Ball-Player, but he would not let them; he took only his sister-in-law. They went then to where his brothers were lying. He strung his bow and shot one arrow into the air.

" 'Look out, I might hit you!' he shouted.

"When the arrow hit the ground, his oldest brother jumped up, alive and well. This he did for each of his five brothers until all had been brought back to life; whereupon they all went home, taking the wife of the eldest with them.

"In this way, it is said, the boy named Ball-Player conquered the evil wizard, Red-Feather-on-His-Head. This, now, is the length of the story."

"*Wa-nee'shih!* Thanks!" said Thunder - Arrow. "Now tell us another one!"

"Tell us about the Flying Skeleton," begged my friend, Catches-Two. "That's a worse monster than the Naked-Bear even."

"*Say-hay!* He's a *man-it'to*, not a monster," responded Porcupine. "I don't dare tell stories about *him*. Anyhow, the story bag is closed for the night."

I went to sleep thinking of the tales I had heard and I was dreaming of a fight between the Thunders and a horned serpent when a growl awakened me. I sat up—it was Moon-ha'kee. I listened. Now I could hear faint sounds outside the back of the *wik'wam*. Whispering to Moon-ha'kee to be silent, I slipped out the doorway, war club in hand, and tiptoed around. In the cold moonlight I saw a dark, fur-clad figure bending low. In a moment there was a tongue of flame. Someone was setting fire to the *wik'wam;* the rushes were catching!

With a warning shout of "*Tin'dai*, fire!" I charged. Taken by surprise, the man sprang to his feet and fled, Moon-ha'kee after him. It took but a moment to put out the fire with snow. Now I saw the man had fallen; Moon-ha'kee had hold of his leg. I rushed up with my war club and then I saw who it was. Toad-Face!

XV. The Doom of Toad-Face

YES, it was Toad-Face who had been trying to burn our *wik'-wam:* Toad-Face, dressed in furs like a Susquehannock and armed with a sharp bone dagger. He was about to stab Moon-ha'kee with it when my war club knocked it spinning across the snow.

I grappled with him and I had to use my club. Now people came running out of the houses. Somebody sent for the *Ee'la*, thinking that I had caught a Susquehannock; and he, when he saw who my captive was, sent for the village chief. Standing there in the snow, under a winter moon, I told my story and showed them all where the fire had been started and the burned rushes. They bound Toad-Face with stout thongs and carried him to the chief's house to lie until morning. The chief told me to appear there and help to decide then what should be done with him as soon as possible after daylight.

On my way home I noticed Cross-Woman's bulky form in the outskirts of the crowd. She had her robe pulled over her head.

Next morning came the trial. It might have ended with merely a payment of *kay'kwuk* beads and other valuables to Bowl-Woman if it had not been for the

Susquehannock captive—the boy who had run so fast and straight when he was brought to the village. This boy had come in to clean ashes out of the fireplace for the chief's wife when he spied the prisoner. He pointed at Toad-Face and jabbered excitedly in his own tongue, but he did not know enough Lenape to make himself understood. The chief sent at once for an old woman who had been for years a captive among the Susquehannocks and could speak their language perfectly. Then the whole amazing story came out.

It was Toad-Face who had been responsible for the Susquehannock raid upon our village. When he had left the Big-House at the time of my adoption, he had evidently gone straight to the enemy villages and found an interpreter.

Then he had told the Susquehannocks the secret of the Lenapes' great success in hunting: their possession of the sacred bundle containing the mask of Our Grandfather, *Mee-sing-haw-lee'kun*, guardian of all wild animals. All that the Susquehannocks had to do to gain this power was to capture the bundle; then Our Grandfather would help them and not the Lenapes.

He had then offered to reveal where this bundle was kept, providing the war chief of the raiding party sent to capture it would agree to two things: first, to burn the cabin where the bundle was stored; and second, to kill or capture its occupants.

The agreement was made, and the Susquehannocks carried out their raid, the results we knew.

"If it had not been for *him*," said the young Susquehannock bitterly, pointing again to Toad-Face, "I would be safe at home enjoying life instead of working here as a slave cleaning out somebody's ashes.''

The revelation put a different view on the whole matter. The chief said solemnly:

"Toad-Face has betrayed us, his own people, to the enemy. There is only one thing to do with a traitor.''

"Burn him,'' ordered the Wolf chief. "He belongs to my band, but I say burn him.''

"Agreed,'' said the Turkey chief.

"Is there anyone here who disagrees?'' the village chief asked.

There was a commotion at the door and Cross-Woman forced her way in through the crowd.

"I disagree!'' she cried. "Don't burn him; he's my son, my only son!''

"We shall have to hear a stronger reason than that,'' said the chief. Cross-Woman seized hold of his arm.

"*Ma'ta!*'' she cried. "You can't burn my son!'' her voice rose to a scream. "You shan't—you shan't—I won't allow it——'' The assistant chief and the *Ee'la* dragged her struggling and crying from the house. In a few minutes I saw her slip back in again, silent this time.

"Does anyone else disagree?'' the chief continued.

Something moved within me and I stood forth.

"I disagree!'' I said. Everyone stared.

"You who captured the guilty one! You who might have suffered from his evil acts!'' The chief could not understand it.

"It is my belief,'' I said as calmly as I could, "that the Creator does not wish us to burn his children even when they are traitors, murderers, or witches.''

The chiefs talked in whispers for a moment; then the village chief spoke again.

"We respect your belief, In-the-Forest, and shall not ask you to take part in the burning. However, we shall burn this traitor tomorrow." He turned to his assistant chief. "You will see that a suitable stake is made ready."

"Go ahead and burn me," said Toad-Face. "Have it over with. Nobody ever liked me, anyhow."

Cross-Woman spoke up.

"*I* always liked you, Son," she said.

"You don't count," he answered and turned his face away.

When I got home from the trial, I found Porcupine making friends with Moon-ha'kee.

"You have a wonderful dog here," he said.

"Thanks to him they are going to burn Toad-Face," I replied. "I feel sick about it."

"You should think of the other side," said the story-teller. "If Moon-ha'kee had not wakened you, we would all have been burned—roasted to death in a burning *wik'wam*."

"I am glad he saved us, of course," I said, "but still I do not see why anybody need be burned."

That evening none of us felt like listening to stories, so Porcupine got me to carry his things over to Duck-Woman's whilst he swung along beside me. As a reward, he showed me the contents of his story bag. I do not remember, of course, the many things that were in it, but I do recall a bit of crystal which looked like ice, which reminded him of a story about the Ice Spirit; a bear claw which represented a tale of a lost boy who was raised by the bears; and a bit of slate with a zigzag line scratched on it as a symbol of lightning, which brought to his mind the story of the girl who joined the Thunders.

That night I could not sleep at all for the thought of Toad-Face being burned on the morrow, enemy though he was. I got up and went out several times during the night. Flying clouds hid the moon, but once in a while its pale face would break through. It was a night for strange and desperate deeds, and I was not at all surprised when I heard in the morning that Toad-Face had escaped.

During the night someone had cut a slab of bark loose from the outside of the chief's house, had crept under the *ha'soon* where people were sleeping, had cut the thongs that bound him, and Toad-Face had followed his rescuer to freedom. Great care had been used, for the tracks in the snow that might have told the story had been erased.

The village was buzzing like a nest of hornets. Who had freed the prisoner? Why had he been freed? Suspicion was cast upon his mother, and some said she should be burned in his place, for in this village it was a rule to burn any person who had set free a prisoner doomed to burning. Others argued that Cross-Woman was too fat to crawl under a *ha'soon* without waking everybody. And so amidst all the argument nothing was done, and the stake stood in the Big-House square without a victim, until someone lifted it for firewood.

A few days after the escape I decided to start out on my long delayed bear hunt. Rising before dawn, I slung my little mask hunting charm about my neck, slipped a packet of lucky herbs, the gift of Thunder-Arrow, into my shoulder pocket, and chewed a little of Roaring-Wings' hunting medicine which was supposed to keep animals from scenting me. There was not much snow on the ground, but the sky was gray and threatening.

Moon-ha'kee and I had no sooner arrived at the clan hunting grounds when I spied a fine deer, and more from habit than reason we took after it and followed it until I was finally able to bring it down. Then I was disgusted with myself for using so much precious time on a deer when I should be hunting for a bear tree. Still, the deer must not be wasted, so I found a bushy place where it would be hidden from observation and hung it from a projecting branch. Then we went on up the valley, which contained many large elms, searching for one with a hole big enough to furnish lodging for a bear. In the meantime, I unstrung my bow so that I would not be tempted to take another shot at a deer.

There were no caves in that part of the country and no windfalls that I knew of, so trees were my only hope. When I was just about despairing, I spied a huge tree with an opening about thirty feet above the ground and, when I reached it, I could see scratches on the bark. Moon-ha'kee sniffed them and growled, so I was sure a bear must be in the tree. I had brought Thunder-Arrow's ax which had been rescued from the fire with me and I pounded on the tree with it, but there was no response.

There were just two possible things to do: either I must climb the tree and poke the bear with a pole until he came out or throw fire in to drive him out. The first would be rather close quarters to fight with an angry bear, and I could see no way to climb the tree anyhow. I had heard that it was often necessary to fell a small tree that could be climbed, against the larger one, but there were no such trees near; nor could I find one that I could cut and drag thither to set up for a ladder. Maybe I did not hunt with any too great diligence.

As for fire, there was the problem of getting it into a hole thirty feet above the ground. First of all, I searched out a rotten, fallen tree and pulled the outer bark from it; the bast inside was quite dry. This I made up into a number of loose bundles, two spans long more or less and two spans round. Next I built a fire, which was none too easy, because my fire sticks were a little damp, but I got it at last. Now I lighted one of my bundles and tossed it at the opening. It missed and was too badly burned to use again. The fourth blazing bundle went in the hole.

I knew that it takes a bear some time to come out, and I was leisurely preparing to string my bow, thinking how good bear's grease would taste again, when a growl above made me look up. A huge, yellow beast like a lion was coming out of the hole! It slid down the tree in a flash, and Moon-ha'kee put for it. One blow from its paw knocked him flying over and over in the snow.

Now it came for me, like a cat stalking a bird. I was trying, fumbling vainly to string my bow and watching the creature at the same time, when I saw it gather itself for a spring. I thought I was doomed, but I grabbed for my ax. Just then it snarled and turned quickly; good reason, Moon-ha'kee had it by the tail. To save Moon-ha'kee, I rushed at it with the ax; it heard and turned toward me again just in time to receive a stunning blow

between the eyes.   Before it could recover, I swung the
ax once more and crushed its skull.

Not until then did I realize that we had slain a
kweh-neesh-kwoo'nai-yas, or long-tail, now known to the
English as "panther."   I rested a little while, then started
to skin the animal.   Before I finished, I became aware
that not only had the fire gone out, but that it was snowing very hard and getting dark.   We should have started
for home long before.

Before we had gone far, it was pitch dark; I could
not see which way to travel.   Then I realized that our
only hope to keep from freezing was to keep moving, it
mattered little which way.   If we could thus keep alive
during the long hours of darkness, when daylight came,
we might find our way home.

Fumbling around blindly among the huge trees, I
touched one with my outstretched hand.   "This," I
thought, "will be a good tree to walk around and around
until daylight."   Walking and feeling part way around,
I came to a place where the bark was broken.   Investi-
gating, I found that the tree was hollow, with an opening
big enough to squeeze into.   I went in and Moon-ha'kee
followed.   Still feeling, I found that there was a cavity
in there, floored with soft, rotten wood perhaps a yard
across and high enough to stand up in.   A ready-made
wik'wam!   We were saved!

There was a light covering of snow on the rotten
wood of the floor, so I scraped it all up with my hands and
threw it out.   How would I keep more from coming in?
I pondered a while—then propped the panther hide up
against the opening with my bow; this carried most of

the weight. Finally I pinned the edges out with arrows stuck through the hide into the soft, rotten wood. I felt with my hand. No more snow or cold air was coming in. I curled up on the floor and covered myself with my fur robe. Even with Moon-ha'kee beside me I was cold. I got up again and danced in the narrow space until I felt warm—a hard task in the dark, as I had to keep from stepping on Moon-ha'kee and from knocking down the arrows. At last I again curled up with Moon-ha'kee under the fur robe. This time I stayed warm and went to sleep. The last sounds I heard were the dismal moaning of the wind outside and the howling of wolves. They had found the carcass of the panther.

Where was I? Waking with a start, I could not imagine. There was not a sound; not a ray of light. Struggling to my feet, I struck against the arrows. Then I remembered. Pulling them out, I let down the panther-skin curtain. No light yet! Was it still night or had I gone blind? I reached my hand out the opening; snow! We were drifted in.

Now I took my bow and thrust it outward and upward into the snow outside. It broke through! When I pulled it back, I could see daylight. In a few minutes Moon-ha'kee and I had dug our way out.

The sky was clear and cold; a snow knee-deep covered the forest; drifts changed the looks of hill and dale, but I now knew that I could find my way home.

As we approached the bushy place where I had hung my deer, Moon-ha'kee gave a warning growl. I skirmished cautiously about and nearly jumped out of my skin when I spied a huge bear standing on his hind legs

21

trying to pull down the carcass! He was a formidable-looking monster, and my courage nearly failed me; in fact I had to take myself in hand.

"You came out to hunt bears," I said to myself. "Well, there's a bear, why don't you hunt it? Are you afraid? You who won an eagle feather in war? *Ka-ta'-tee!*" I put my hand on my little mask—my hunting charm; to be sure it was still there, and then I started. I scouted around—the bear was too busy to notice me—until I got a fair shot at his left side. I let fly.

The bear gave a roar, clapped his paw to his side, then he spied me and charged. I marvel to this day how I ever got out of his way in the loose snow, but of course Moon-ha'kee was nipping at his heels all the while, when not dodging his paws, which gave me a little time to circle around trees and plant two more arrows. Still he came after me, like a monster in a nightmare, until finally, almost exhausted, I managed to climb a tree and get out on a slender limb where I hoped he dared not follow. That bear climbed halfway up before his strength began to ebb; then he slid down and walked a dozen paces, sinking at last with a very human groan.

Even Moon-ha'kee did not dare come too near at this time, and I stayed on my freezing perch until I was sure it was safe to come down and finish the bear with the ax. He was enormously fat and had evidently been looking for a winter resting place when he saw my deer. He was much too heavy for me to carry.

I was just planning to butcher the bear and hang up the greater part with the deer whilst I carried the rest home, when I heard the hail, "*Yoo'hoo!*"

"*Oh'ho!*" I answered.   In a few minutes there came a rescue party of five men and three dogs, led by old Roaring-Wings.

"I dreamed you were out here needing help," he said. "As usual my dream came true."   Then he saw the bear.

"*Ka-yah'!*" he cried.   "That's the biggest bear that has been killed hereabouts in ten years.   The little *Mee-sing'* hunting charm I made you must be a good one!"

Then I showed him the deer and the panther skin. Before we got home, one member of the party had offered me ten strings of *kay'kwuk* shell beads for that *Mee-sing'* charm, but I would not part with it.

We approached the village after the fashion of a returning war party; Roaring-Wings gave the hailing call and three yells; then we marched in, Moon-ha'kee and I in the lead.   I was wrapped in my panther skin, wearing it outside my regular robe.   Then came Roaring-Wings; after him were two men carrying the deer on a pole, and finally two carrying my bear.

After parading through the village in the regular way, we stopped in the square just east of the Big-House so that everyone could look at the panther skin, which was bigger than usual, and the bear, which everybody vowed was the largest seen in many years.   I killed several other bears before the winter was over, but never one that approached it.

Almost every evening for a long time after that first bear hunt, some middle-aged man or woman would step in to the *wik'wam* on the pretense of talking with Thunder-Arrow or Bowl-Woman, but after a while the conversation would always switch to the visitor's daughter or niece, how smart she was and pretty and good-hearted and what a wonderful worker. I would be straightening my arrows in the firelight, or something of the sort, and pretended not to listen, but I knew that the visitor was watching me to see if I were impressed. Nearly every day someone tried to buy or borrow my hunting charm.

At last the long winter, my second in Turtle-Town, drew to a close. The days were much longer, the snow was melting and it froze only at night. One morning the crier announced that the sap was running; the time had come to make tree sugar. The previous year at sugar time, I had been Cross-Woman's servant and not at liberty to go where I pleased, but this year I resolved to learn how this delicious food was made.

Thunder-Arrow was not yet strong enough to undertake anything so tiring, so I went out with Bowl-Woman's sister, Duck-Woman, and her husband, New-Horns. They left their little boy and their two girls with Bowl-Woman. Each clan, it appeared, had its own sugar trees, and these grew, in our case at least, within the boundaries of our own hunting grounds. In these groves certain groups of trees were considered to belong to certain women of the clan and conveniently for us, Bowl-Woman's trees and Duck-Woman's made up one little grove. They were *ah-sin-na-min' shee-uk*, rock trees, known to the English as "maples."

Adjoining this grove they had built a small, low bark cabin without sleeping platforms, but provided with an extra large smoke hole, kept covered when not in use. It had a bark door, too, sewn on a frame of poles, like the Big-House door, and tied in place with strips of basswood bark to keep out any animal not of the gnawing kind.

Grass beds ran along the sides and four huge clay pots sat upside down, in the middle, upon a long fireplace. On the wall a big ladle hung beside a stout, wooden paddle, and stacks of small bark troughs and little boxes of bark nearly covered the beds. In the back stood two large barrels of elm bark made tight with pitch, a stout, large tray and four water buckets, also of elm bark.

We helped Duck-Woman carry all the bark vessels outside and to loosen up the grass bedding, searching for sleeping snakes which she said sometimes took refuge there for the winter. The bark vessels were in good condition except for a few that could be mended with a little pine pitch.

We had brought a piece of burning slow match, or punk, with us, but for some reason it had gone out, so I had to get out my sticks and make a new fire. Duck-Woman brought in some wood, we spread our bedding, and then we felt quite at home. Before dark, New-Horns and I had fetched in a deer apiece, so now we were sure of a food supply, especially as Duck-Woman had brought a pack basket of shelled corn and *ka-ha-ma'kun*, with a small skin bag of grease. She always kept a little mortar and pestle in the cabin, with the necessary hulling and sifting baskets, and a few spoons and bowls to eat from.

Next morning we started in to make sugar, the gathering of sap being the first step. A diagonal cut had to be sawed into the bark of each tree with a flint knife, and at the lower end of each cut was driven in a little flat stick split out of wood to lead the sap out, and under this was set one of the bark troughs. When the troughs were filled, New-Horns and I poured the sap into our

buckets to be carried back to the cabin and dumped into the bark barrels, which made a reserve supply.

Duck-Woman boiled this sap in the clay kettles and when it had simmered down to a sirup, she strained it through a basket sieve and heated it again over a slower fire. When it became very thick, she poured it out into the big bowl and worked it with a wooden paddle as it cooled until it became like coarse meal. This was tree sugar. Then she packed it in the bark boxes and sewed a bark cover on each, and in this shape it was ready to be carried home and used.

One day she gave me some hot, thick sirup in her ladle and told me to carry it around to the north side of the cabin and pour it in a snowdrift which still remained there. When I picked it up, it felt just about like tar, but not quite so sticky.

"Now give a piece of it to Moon-ha'kee," she directed.

Moon-ha'kee seized it eagerly and started to chew it—and then it stuck to his teeth. The poor little fellow

could neither swallow it or get rid of it, although he pawed at his mouth desperately, even rolling over in his misery. New-Horns and Duck-Woman laughed themselves to tears at his antics, but I felt sorry and started to help him.

"Wait," advised Duck-Woman. "You will see what happens."

By dint of prodigious chewing and pawing Moon-ha'kee finally conquered the morsel and swallowed it, and I thought surely one experience with the cruel joke would be enough.

Not at all. After a brief panting spell he demanded more and would not stop barking until I had given it to him and then, of course, the whole silly performance was repeated. Moon-ha'kee liked tree sugar.

By the time another new moon appeared in the evening sky, we decided that we had made enough sugar for the two families. The clay kettles were cleaned and turned bottoms up in the cold ashes, the troughs and buckets washed and put away, the smoke hole covered, and the door tied. The sugar was heavy, and we were glad indeed when we reached the village. Although Duck-Woman's family had supplied two workers and Bowl-Woman's only one—myself—the boxes of sugar were equally divided.

The season had now come when elm bark will slip, so I raised the ridgepole of the new cabin, which had lain seasoning all winter, so that it lay in the crotches sticking out some three feet beyond the uprights. Next I laid the side poles, or plates, in the crotches of the corner posts and put the seasoned rafter poles in position as is shown in the illustration, lashing them in place with strips of basswood inner bark, Thunder-Arrow helping.

In the meantime, Bowl-Woman and five of her friends belonging to our clan were bringing in sheets of elm bark. They selected trees four or five spans round, straight and free from low limbs. Then they threw

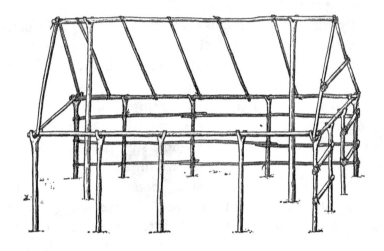

tobacco at the roots, telling the tree why they were about to kill it and praying that the house to be covered with the bark would stand a long time and shed the rain and wind. The next step was to reach up as high as possible and saw through the bark with a flint knife around and around until the tree was completely girdled. Then they girdled it again just above the roots and connected the two crosswise cuts with a vertical one. With a broad-bladed, crooked, wooden chisel they pried up the bark along this last cut, following it around until the bark sprang loose from the tree. Each piece of bark was laid in the creek, flattened out with stones, to keep it pliable until the time came to use it. The pieces were two or three feet wide and five or six feet long.

With lighter poles they now filled in the frame as the illustration shows and tied everything firmly together with bast. The next thing was to cover it with bark. The side pieces were put on first, the slabs overlapping like shingles. Upright and horizontal poles 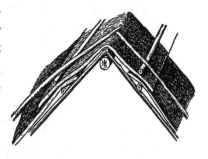 were set to hold them in place, and these were stitched fast to the frame inside with strips of bast, the holes in the bark being bored with a big bone awl.

The roof was laid next, the sheets of bark running up and down, and these were held in place with slender, horizontal poles stitched through to the frame. In the middle of the ridge, of course, a hole was left for the escape of smoke.

Last of all we built the platforms of poles set on stout forked posts and floored with smaller smooth ash poles laid crosswise and lashed fast. Sometimes the Lenapes will make a *ha'soon* floor of slabs or boards split out of wood, or half poles with the flat side up, but this takes a long time, and I wanted to see the house finished before Little-Bear and his bride returned. I saw to it that the posts for the east platform were high enough to build a second platform or bunk above, like the one in our old cabin, strong enough to sleep upon, but really intended for storing the bundle containing "Our Grandfather," the *Mee-sing'*.

To decorate the walls as well as to keep out the cold, I suggested that we hang some mats before we moved in; but Bowl-Woman could not wait; besides, she said, she had no mats. The night after the last *ha'soon* was finished, we were in the new home, and Bowl-Woman was happy.

When the first fire had burned down to coals, Thunder-Arrow threw on some branches of cedar as incense to

purify the house, and we all stepped up in turn and bathed our bodies with the sweet smoke. Then he prayed with tears trickling down his face, that the cabin might withstand the storms for many years and that the people dwelling within it might live long and happily, enjoying good health.

Next day Bowl-Woman gave a feast for the clan sisters who had helped us, and four of them brought mats as gifts: pretty, fresh rush mats with patterns in red, yellow, and black. The fifth brought Bowl-Woman a nice new cooking pot. The mats she hung against the walls on both sides, but the bark behind her own *ha'soon* remained bare.

I had heard that a certain old lady by the name of Snipe-Woman, who lived a little way from Granny's one-time home, was an expert mat maker, so I went to see her, hoping to get a good mat to fill the vacant space. She lived alone in a bark cabin with a platform on one side only, the other being taken up by her weaving frames.

"No, my son," she said when I explained my errand. "I have traded all the mats I made last summer for food during the winter, and now I have none."

"Can't you make me one?" I inquired. "If you will make me a pretty mat to hang back of Bowl-Woman's new *ha'soon*, I shall kill two deer for you."

"*Tak-ta'nee*," she said, "I don't know. You see, the new bulrushes are not ready until midsummer——." Suddenly she brightened up. "I remember," she cried, "my sister has some cured rushes in her outhouse left over from last year; maybe I can get them from her and we will divide the venison." So it was arranged.

I went over to watch how the work was done. Snipe-Woman first sprinkled her rushes with water, then hung two stout cords made of bast (basswood inner bark) about six feet long for a foundation across the top of her weaving frame, and on these she fastened the rushes one by one bending the tips over and inter-weaving them to form a border about two fingers wide. At regular intervals she hung a certain number of dyed rushes, but most of them were the natural tan color. When the foundation was filled with pendant rushes, she fastened it at short intervals to the pole which

formed the top of the weaving frame, to keep it from
sagging.

"You say these rushes are 'cured,' " I said, "what
do you mean by that?"

"What do you want to know for?" Snipe-Woman
demanded. "You are a boy, and men and boys are not
allowed to make mats."

"My Dream-helpers gave me the privilege to make
mats if I wish, as well as hunting and war power," I
assured her, thinking of the sewing awl in the little
bundle.

"*Ka-ya'!*" she cried. "You don't mean it? Well,
that is different, and I'll tell you. We boil the rushes to
make them tough!"

"Boil them? You are trying to fool me. There is
not a clay pot in this village big enough to boil rushes
in."

"We don't boil them in pots, stupid. If we have a
lot of rushes to cure, we boil them in a log canoe; if
just a few, we dig a trench in a clay bank or dig one anywhere and plaster the inside with clay."

"I still think you are joking. How could anyone
boil water in a canoe or in a hole?"

"*Ka-ya'!* How little you know! You boil water in
a canoe by dropping in hot stones. When it is boiling
hard, you throw your rushes in and push them down with
forked sticks. The other way you put your rushes in the
trench and pour hot water from kettles over them until
the trench is full. If it leaks out afterward, no harm
is done, as the rushes need to be boiled just a little. Then
we hang them up in small bunches and dry them."

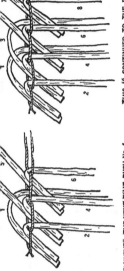

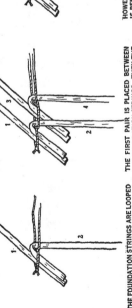

THE FOUNDATION STRINGS ARE LOOPED OVER A PEG AT LEFT AND STRETCHED TO THE RIGHT IN FRONT OF A POLE OR A SMALL LOG (SEE LOWER SKETCH) AND FASTENED LOOSELY TO ANOTHER PEG. THE REEDS OR RUSHES, KEPT WET BY SPRINKLING, ARE APPLIED IN PAIRS FROM THE TOP.

THE FIRST PAIR IS PLACED BETWEEN THE FOUNDATION STRINGS. THEN THE FOUNDATION STRINGS ARE GIVEN A HALF TWIST AND THE FRONT OR RIGHT-HAND RUSH IS BENT DOWN BETWEEN THE STRINGS. TWO MORE RUSH ENDS ARE APPLIED AND THE STRINGS GIVEN A HALF TWIST BACK AGAIN.

HOWEVER, THE NEXT TIME, RUSH No. 1 IS BENT DOWN BETWEEN THE STRINGS BEFORE APPLYING THE NEXT TWO RUSH ENDS, AND THEY ARE APPLIED BETWEEN THE TWO DOWN-HANGING RUSHES NOS. 1 AND 4.

THIS IS CONTINUED TO THE END OF THE FOUNDATION STRING OR FOR AS LONG AS THE LENGTH OF THE MAT. THE DRAWING DOES NOT SHOW THE FOUNDATION STRINGS DRAWN TIGHTLY, WHICH OF COURSE WOULD BE THE CASE IN THE FINISHED MAT. NEXT, THE WARP STRINGS ARE WOVEN IN AND THE MAT IS COMPLETED.

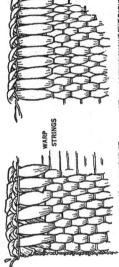

WARP STRINGS

THIS DRAWING SHOWS THE WRONG OR WORKING SIDE OF A SECTION OF A FINISHED RUSH MAT AS MADE BY THE LENAPE INDIANS.

THIS DRAWING SHOWS THE RIGHT SIDE OF A SECTION OF A RUSH MAT AS MADE BY THE LENAPE INDIANS.

DETAIL OF A LENAPE RUSH MAT

"When you dye rushes, you have to boil them again, don't you?"

"Yes! We boil the dye first in a kettle; *took'kwim*, walnut, shells for dark-brown or black; *pa'kon*, blood-root, for red and *wee-sa'awk*, a kind of oak bark, for yellow. Then we put the rushes in and boil them until they have taken the color."

"I thought you said you didn't boil rushes in a pot."

"I meant green rushes. You can boil cured rushes in a pot, a few at a time," Snipe-Woman explained. "All you have to do is dampen them so that they won't break, then coil them up and tie them loosely."

After all this talk she had to moisten her rushes again by blowing a spray of water from her mouth over them, then she went to work. Tying a stout cord to the original foundation cord on the left, she allowed it to hang down just beyond the last rush, then she placed another at the right; these were to form the selvages at the ends. Now tying a six-foot cord to the left-hand selvages just below the border, she wove it rapidly over and under the rushes to the right until she reached the end, where she tied it to the selvage cord there, and then she repeated the process.

To make diamond-shaped, colored figures she gradually worked the dyed rushes out of their natural places to the right and left and then back again, and to make little squares, she ran her strings over two rushes and under two, instead of the regular over-one and under-one weave.

I did not see the mat completed but went out to hunt deer to pay for it. When I came to get it, I noticed that she had finished the lower edge the same as the upper, with a sort of interwoven border. Such mats were called *a-na'kan-a*. I took it right home and tied it on the wall back of the *ha'soon* where Bowl-Woman and Thunder-Arrow slept. It was the prettiest mat of all.

Tent cover mats were made of a larger, coarser kind of rush, called "cattail" by the English; they were begun in much the same way, the tips interwoven with two foundation cords, but the rushes were sewed together, not woven, with a long, flat bone needle with an eye in the middle, made from the outer shell of a deer rib, used with strips of bast or cord. The best tent mats were made double. Single or double, the rows of sewing were about ten inches apart.

By this time the ice had broken up in the river. Late one afternoon I was sleeping on my *ha'soon* after a hard hunting trip when Bowl-Woman woke me. "There is a canoe coming down the river," she said. "It may be Little-Bear and White Deer. Let's go down to the landing."

XVI. The Ship from Jamestown

THUNDER-ARROW and I, with Moon-ha'kee, hastened to the bluff to view the approaching canoe, and Bowl-Woman, carrying the baby, followed. It was a strange-looking craft, sitting very low in the water, and seemed to be carrying two persons.

"Why do you think they may be Little-Bear and White-Deer?" I asked. "Didn't they go away on foot?"

"Perhaps they built a canoe to come home in," explained Thunder-Arrow. "Our people sometimes stay out hunting and trapping until the ice breaks up in the spring; then a canoe is the easiest way to bring home their skins."

The travelers recognized us before we did them, for they waved their paddles and shouted; then, of course, we knew their voices. We hurried down to the landing where Fling-Her-This-Way joined us.

Eager hands seized the canoe and ran it high on the beach, and for a while there were so many tears and embraces that I stepped back, embarrassed. White-Deer spied me then, and I came in for my full share, both from her and from Little-Bear, whilst Moon-ha'kee danced about, barking for joy.

Both looked different, somehow, from the boy and girl I had known; they were weather-beaten, more serious, suddenly much older. I caught White-Deer staring at me.

"What," she queried, "is my brother-in-law wearing on his head?"

Not grasping at first what she meant, I reached my hand up to feel; then I understood.

"*A-ta-koo'*; nothing at all; nothing but a *mee'kwin*, an eagle feather."

"Where did you get it? Surely not in war!"

"It is a long story," I answered. "There are others who might tell it better than I." I walked down to the water's edge again to get a better look at their boat, which I now saw was made of skin.

"That's a funny-looking canoe," I remarked. "Where did you get such a thing?"

"I'll acknowledge it's not so good as a dugout or even an elm-bark canoe," laughed Little-Bear. "It was easy to make, though, and you will have to admit it fetched us home. I am responsible for that crooked pole frame, and White-Deer sewed the six deerskins for the queer-looking cover."

"You have quite a load there," I said, scanning the piles of cargo carefully covered with deerskins.

"Oh, yes," said Little-Bear. "We brought back a few things—not very much. Only some dried meat, some fresh meat, three skins of bear's grease; a good back load of tree sugar; some furs, maybe twenty-five or thirty beaver, otter, and fox; and I don't know how many deer and bear skins."

22

"Let's go to the house," White-Deer broke in. "I'm hungry. I hope there is plenty of *sa'pan* in the kettle. I don't care if I never see another piece of meat."

As we rounded the corner of the Big-House, Little-Bear spied the thatched *wik'wam*.

"What's that frowzy-headed hut doing under our tree?" he growled; then he saw the new cabin. "*Ka-yah'!* he shouted. "We've got a new house! It's a lot bigger!" He turned to his father. "What has happened here, anyhow?"

We fed the returned wanderers all the *sa'pan* and bread they could hold and then we told them everything— all about the raid, the war party, and Bowl-Woman especially brought out the part that Moon-ha'kee and I played. To hear her tell it you would think it was something wonderful. Anyhow it drew many wide-eyed "*ka-yah's*" from my new sister-in-law and grunts of "*Hoh! Shee'kee!*" from Little-Bear.

Especially were they amazed when they heard of Toad-Face's return, his attempt to burn the thatched *wik'wam*, and the revelation that he had betrayed us to the Susquehannocks.

"They burned him, I hope," Little-Bear growled.

"No, they did not," I replied. "They intended to burn him, but he escaped, and I am glad of it."

"Glad of it! Why?"

"I do not believe the Great Spirit wishes us to burn any of His children. The religion of my people teaches that the Creator will punish the souls of the wicked after death. If He wishes then to burn Toad-Face, He is the one to judge."

"You have some strange thoughts," Little-Bear grumbled.

"I think In-the-Forest is right," said his wife.

"*Tak-ta'nee;* perhaps. But Toad-Face will do something else, remember what I say."

Their own story was interesting enough, if not so exciting as ours. Carrying only their weapons, a few small tools, their fur robes, a clay pot in a pack basket, and a sack of *ka-ha-ma'kun*, the newly wedded pair had started north, camping under overhanging rocks or building little shelters of basswood bark when bad weather threatened. Little-Bear found enough game along the way to keep them supplied with meat. Arriving at last at a *Min'see* village in the edge of the mountain district, they had traded the deerskins picked up on the way for more *ka-ha-ma'kun* and had learned of a place not far from the river not claimed by any family or clan as hunting territory.

Here they had built a very small basswood bark *wik'-wam* in which they spent the winter very happily, hunting and trapping, and, when the sap started running, making tree sugar.

"Little-Bear was perfectly contented," White-Deer said, "until after we finished the sugar; then he began to get restless, going down to the river every day or so to see if the ice had broken up."

"I wasn't the only one," he chuckled. "What did you do? You started in right away to sew deerskins together for the canoe cover; and every time I came home at night, you always asked if the ice had gone out yet and worried for fear it might not go out at all this year.

"We nearly lost everything coming down through that big rapids where In-the-Forest and I turned back on our fishing trip," he continued. "If it had not been for my old woman here, we might not have come out alive."

"Don't you call me 'old woman,'" White-Deer scolded. "Besides, I did not do much. When a big rock showed up suddenly right ahead, I simply jabbed my paddle into the water and jerked the bow of the canoe to one side, and my old man," she gave Little-Bear a mischievous glance, "did the same for the stern, so we shot by the rock like an arrow, just grazing it, with the rapids boiling all around us."

"I am thankful that you are both safe," said Bowl-Woman with a shudder. "That is all I care about."

The fresh meat which they had brought had to be eaten, which gave me a rest from hunting, also a chance to learn how the Lenapes tanned their deerskins, something I had never found time to observe before.

In this task Bowl-Woman, Fling-Her-This-Way, and White-Deer joined and I volunteered to help them, on the ground of the sewing awl in my dream bundle, which

I maintained gave me the right to do that sort of work if I wished. The women agreed rather doubtfully.

We selected a level bit of ground near the mouth of the creek for our tannery and here we carried the skins of the deer I had killed during the winter, those Fling-Her-This-Way's brother had provided and those which had formed part of the canoe's cargo. White-Deer even took the cover off the canoe itself, cut the skins apart, and added these to the pile. I was sorry to see it destroyed but she explained the reason.

"A skin canoe is good for a few days' use," she said, "but after that the skins would soon spoil."

The first step in tanning is to soak the hides until the hair begins to slip but not long enough to rot them. We picked out a near-by shallow pool in the creek and sank them in it, weighted down with stones.

After two days, the usual time, Bowl-Woman tried the hair, but it was still tight. The fourth day it slipped easily, and then the real work began. Each of the three women had a sort of draw knife made of a deer's leg bone, with part of the center cut away and the ends left for handles, and Bowl-Woman rummaged about and found a fourth one for me. In the meantime I cut for each worker a smooth log about four feet long and two spans round, peeled them and set them slantwise in the ground.

Now we laid the wet skins hair side up on these logs, and I found it an easy matter to scrape off the hair with my bone draw knife, although some spots needed a little more effort than others because the hair had not loosened equally. Cleaning the tissue from the flesh side with beveled-edge flint scrapers came next, and this I found

very much harder.   Once cleaned, we hung the skins up
to dry for a few days.

Thunder-Arrow's canoe had been launched sometime
before; now Bowl-Woman made me pole it from the

landing upstream into the creek, and here, with the help
of Little-Bear, we dragged it up to our tannery and half
filled it with water.

I could not imagine what they were going to do with
it, and nobody would tell me, until I threatened to dump
the canoe if they did not.

"We are going to make some delicious soup," White-
Deer giggled.

I almost believed her when the women brought
baskets full of little flat, brown cakes and emptied them
into the water, until I picked up a cake and examined it,
and then I remembered.   The women usually saved the
brains of deer and other large animals, mixed them with
moss and dried them in the form of just such little cakes.
I had seen them made often without knowing they were
used in tanning skins.

When the brain "soup" had been thoroughly stirred
and mixed, we threw in all the skins the liquid would
cover and worked them around with sticks until soft,
then wrung them out and rolled them up to await the next
stage.   Of course more brain cakes and more water had to
be added before another batch could be run through.   When
all were finished, I took it upon myself to give the canoe
a good cleaning and returned it to its place on the beach.

Now Bowl-Woman instructed me to build four frames of poles to stretch the hides upon, maybe six feet long and four feet broad, and then we each punched holes about a span apart around the edge of a hide and laced it on a frame with a heavy leather thong, stretching it just as tightly as we could. The next job was to clean the flesh side very carefully again with a stone scraper so that every shred of tissue was removed; then we scraped the skin on both sides with a wooden tool with a wedge-shaped blade until it dried soft, which was very tedious indeed.

Before I had my third skin half dry, I was ready to give up.

"*Ee-kee'!*" I grumbled. "I'm sorry now I killed so many deer."

"You mean to say you are sorry you offered to do woman's work," teased White-Deer.

"Oh, the boy wanted to jump right in and help us," added her mother. "He even told us his Dream-helper gave him the privilege of doing such work if he wants to. Now he sees how much a privilege it is. Tell me, In-the-Forest, shall I fetch Roaring-Wings to doctor you?"

"*Hoh!*" I grunted. "Have a care, or someone else may need a doctor!" Gritting my teeth, I went ahead whilst they laughed, but I stuck to it until I had finished six skins in all.

Most of the skins were to be smoked, which made still another task. Fires were made with rotten wood in small holes in the ground, whilst the skins, roughly stitched together to form little high tents, were suspended over the holes. When one side was sufficiently smoked, we simply turned the little tent inside out and hung it over the smoke again. Smoked buckskin had a fine, rich color, from golden to brownish, and a pleasant smell; and, best of all, it dried soft after wetting, which was very important for clothing, especially moccasins.

The skins were divided according to the number of people in the families. In this way Bowl-Woman received twelve, White-Deer eight, and Fling-Her-This-Way four, the extra skin of the twenty-five also falling to her.

Now I dragged my big bearskin out of the thatched *wik'wam* where it was hidden and carried it over to our tannery.

"*Ay-ka-yaaa'!*" cried White-Deer. "What do you call that? It can't be a bear; it's too big! Is it a *sis-see'lee-ya?*" This was a sort of wild cow, now called "buffalo" by the English, that lived on the other side of the mountains to the west.

"*Ma-ta-ka'*," grunted Little-Bear disgustedly. "A *sis-see'lee-ya* does not look like that; it's brown and curly; I saw a skin once. In-the-Forest is playing a joke on us; he's sewed four bearskins together!" Little-Bear grabbed the skin and turned it over; when he saw that it was all in one piece, he nearly let it fall; then he silently showed it to White-Deer.

"Where did you say you got your hunting medicine, Younger-Brother?" he asked me very respectfully.

"From Roaring-Wings, Elder-Brother."

"Maybe I can get him to make me one like it!" He chuckled and patted my head. "Perhaps we shall make a hunter of you yet, My Younger-Brother!"

"When I was your age," put in Thunder-Arrow, "way back about the time this great island was created, I never hunted anything smaller than *ya-kwa-hay'ak*, monster naked bears! The smallest of them was much bigger than a buffalo!" At this Moon-ha'kee, who had been sleeping in the sun, woke up suddenly and barked; then everybody laughed, except White-Deer.

"Let's talk about something else," she suggested faintly; then we laughed again. The bride was not yet accustomed to her father-in-law's jokes. I was glad to hear him joke again, for I knew by that he was getting well.

"What are we going to do with my bearskin?" I asked. "It is as stiff as wood, and I want it nice and soft for a bed mat next winter."

"We shall have to bury all the bearskins in damp sand on the beach until they are soft enough to work; soaking in water is not good for them," explained Bowl-Woman. "We'll have to put big rocks on them so that they won't wash away in case the river rises, and we'll have to watch them very carefully and not leave them too long, for the hair soon loosens and they are ruined."

The smaller skins, such as beaver and otter, had been pulled off whole, the only cut being from one hind leg to the other across the stomach. White-Deer had stretched them, fur side in, on U-shaped frames made of willow switches and had cleaned them as well as she could at the time. Now she buried these also in moist sand to soften them for further working.

The second day the bearskins were ready and the four of us, with Thunder-Arrow and Little-Bear to help, stretched them as well as we could and pegged them down to the ground flesh side up. It was real labor to clean the tissue, including large sheets of parchment-like stuff, off those skins with flint scrapers, until they were entirely free from it. Bowl-Woman and I spent one entire day on my bearskin alone, including the softening process, which meant to work the skin with the wooden scraper on the flesh side until it was dry. The other bearskins were easier, and, of course, the smaller skins easiest of all.

I was very proud of my bearskin and spread it at once on my *ha'soon*. The nights were still cold and it was fine to sleep on. It was well that I did not postpone my enjoyment of it until the following winter, for fate had other plans for me.

The first intimation of what might be in store came one fine afternoon when I was playing *pah-sa'ha-man*, or football, on the Big-House square with the young people of the village. In this favorite spring game, which they claim was learned from the *Sha-wa'no-wuk*, now called Shawnees by the English, a team of boys played against a team of girls; but the boys were obliged to kick the ball, never touching it with their hands, whilst the girls might handle it and throw it at will.

At each end of the field were set two goal posts about six feet apart. The ball was thrown up in the middle, and each team strove to kick or throw the ball between their own goal posts, for when that happened the team gained one point, and twelve such points won the game.

It was great fun, with much shouting, giggling, and screaming, and I had just kicked the ball for a goal when I happened to spy a stranger coming into the village on the run, panting and sweat-streaked. He headed toward the chief's house, and something told me I should follow. Calling Catches-Two, who was standing near, to take my place in the game, I hurried after the runner.

I arrived in time to see some of the village officers entering the cabin, but they lowered the curtain after them, and I durst not enter without permission, although I stood near by, straining my ears to make something from the murmur of voices inside.

Suddenly the curtain was lifted and the chief's crier or messenger appeared in the doorway.

"The chief wants you immediately," he said. "I was about to search for you."

A curious tight feeling gripped my heart as I entered. The council was assembled and the runner, sitting on a mat to one side, was refreshing himself with a bowl of stew.

The village chief spoke first.

"This runner," he said, "comes from a village far to the south of us. He says that a great winged canoe is moving up the river and that several times a puff of smoke and a thunder noise has issued from it. All along the villages are arming, because there have been so many stories of war between the White-Faces and the Indians. However, no warlike move has yet been made; they are waiting for the White-Faces to act first, should their errand be hostile.

"Now, In-the-Forest, you have won an eagle feather for bravery in war, and we trust you. Because of this, even though you are still only a boy, we shall ask you to advise us at this time. You know your own kinsfolk, the White-skins, better than we, of course. Tell us, do you think their intentions are peaceful?"

"Probably they are simply looking at the river," I answered, "perhaps to make a picture of it and not to cause trouble. However, I am not sure."

"What would you advise us to do?"

"If they land here, I would receive them in a friendly manner," I replied, "but have your arms ready in case of attack."

"Are they likely to steal anything?" the chief pursued.

"Food and furs are the things they most desire, and they will trade you for these, unless for some reason there is trouble. Then they will seize what they can."

"What about their weapons?" asked the *Ee'la*. "We have heard that they have magic thunder sticks; that all they need do is to point the stick at a man and thunder and lightning comes out of it and the man dies. Is that true?"

"Yes," I replied, "only the thunder stick is not worked by magic. They pour a black powder into the stick, which is hollow; then they put in one or more pellets of a material something like copper, only softer and lighter in color; then they touch fire to the powder and it turns suddenly into smoke, and the smoke drives the pellets a long way with great force."

"*Ay-ka-yah'!*" cried the *Ee'la*, "if that is not magic, what do you call it?"

I thought a moment and then I replied:

"Maybe it is magic, but it is magic anyone can work who has the thunder stick, the powder, and the pellets."

"Whatever works it, the bow and arrow has little chance against it," he growled, and I knew in my heart his words were true. However, I added:

"The bow and arrow is better in one way. You can shoot many arrows quickly, one after the other. The thunder stick shoots only once and then it takes some time to prepare it to shoot again."

In dread of a clash of arms I hoped the ship would not stop at our village; but in another way I hoped it would, for then I might perhaps learn details of the fate of *Ye Portsmouth Maide* and of my poor father—might even get tidings of my mother in faraway England.

After the council the village hummed with excitement. Many carried their food and furs out into the forest to hide them, in fear lest they be stolen; others built mat tents in hidden places away from the village for the safety of their women and children.

As for myself, I was as excited as the rest, or worse. I could not settle down to do anything or make up my mind to go anywhere. Obeying the *Ee'la's* orders to his warriors, I carried my war club stuck in my belt behind, my long knife in its embroidered sheath hung from my neck, my quiver slung, and my bow in my hand; but my advice had been followed and no one painted himself. To be so armed against English people made me feel like a rebel against King James, and yet I knew the necessity of it.

The younger boys in camp stationed themselves on the bluff above the landing to watch the river for the

winged canoe, and some even climbed a tall tree in order
to see farther. It was a little boy not more than seven
years old who had climbed the highest, who first sighted
the fateful white sails and sounded the alarm.

I think every man, woman, and child in the village,
not to speak of the dogs, gathered upon the river bank
to gaze in awe-struck groups. The ship moved slowly
and majestically before a light, southerly breeze, gradually
drawing nearer and nearer, growing larger and larger.
For a while I thought she would pass the village; then I
saw the anchor splash into the water; the yards swung
round, the sails fluttered limply.

Of a sudden a puff of white smoke shot out from her
bow and a thunderous "BOOM!" resounded across the
water. Women and children screamed; many ran to
hide themselves in the forest; others stood fast. As one
man the warriors answered the seeming challenge; but
whether our lusty *ko-wa'mo*, or war cry, was heard on the
ship we could not tell. A quick look around showed me
that no one was injured; perhaps the cannon had not been
aimed at anything.

Now a long boat appeared around the stern of the
ship and pulled rapidly toward our landing. At this
another group of timid ones took themselves to the woods;
the rest of us lined the river bank, hardly breathing as we
watched.

The boat grated on the beach, its crew, disembark-
ing, drew her up to safety, keeping a wary eye upon us the
while. There were eight sailors in charge of a bearded
officer. All were armed with cutlasses and four carried
the dreaded "thunder sticks."

How strange they looked, yet how familiar! The sound of English speech was very sweet, and I could understand it, although I had heard not a word for nearly two years.

I was about to step forward and make myself known when the chief directed us to fall back so as to receive them in front of the Big-House. As the village officers grouped themselves near the Big-House door, the chief beckoned me to a place at his side.

Now the landing party mounted the bluff, cutlasses drawn and firelocks at the ready, marched toward the Big-House and halted. Their commander formed them into line not twenty paces distant; then he scanned us. I thought surely I would be recognized as English; but no, he looked squarely at me without a thought that I was other than the Indian I seemed.

"We know you have in your possession a captive white boy," the officer announced. "If you do not give him up immediately, we shall burn the village," he added fiercely, flourishing his blade.

Nobody but myself understood a word of this, but they grasped the hostile tone and gesture; the whispered word ran around for the warriors to be ready; the women and children fell back. It was a perilous moment; my heart was pounding wildly.

As nobody made him an answer, it finally dawned upon the doughty commander that perhaps he was not understood, so he tried again in a milder tone, but contemptuous enough.

'Does any savage among you speak English, perchance?''

I was angered by the man's attitude, entirely uncalled-for toward the people who had rescued and cared for me, so I decided not to reveal myself yet. Then the spirit of devilment possessed me.

"I talk it, little bit," I ventured.

"You! Where did you learn it?" he demanded.

"One night I dream it," I said. "Next day I talk it pretty good."

He glared at me.

"You tell your king," he growled, "that we know he has a captive English boy here. If he does not give him up, it will be the worse for him."

I translated his words to the chief, omitting the threat, however. The chief's mouth twitched, but it would not do to grin.

"You tell the funny white man with the fur on his face that we rescued a boy from the sea two winters ago; that we held him as a servant for a while, but that now he is a member of our tribe."

This I interpreted in broken English.

"Where is the boy? Bring him forward!" the bearded one commanded. The time had come.

"I am the boy," I said simply.

"You! I do not believe it. Come hither!" I stepped forward.

"Blue eyes! True for you. What is your name?"

"*Day'kay-ning;* that is, I mean Richard Sherwood, commonly known as 'Dickon.'"

"Master Sherwood," he replied, "we are here by order of His Excellency, Sir Thomas Dale, Governor of Virginia, to rescue you from captivity and deliver you to your father." He barked a command. The men lowered their weapons.

"My father!" I cried. "Why, I thought he was dead!"

"He is very much alive!"

"But the ship—*Ye Portsmouth Maide*—it was lost!"

"No, the ship was washed off the shoal before much damage was done."

"Why did my father not come to seek me before this?"

"Everyone certainly thought you had been drowned, until——"

"Until what?"

"Until an Indian youth brought us a word a fortnight ago that a white boy had been rescued from the sea by his people and was now living on this river."

A sudden suspicion seized me.

"What did the youth look like?" I demanded.

"I did not see him, but they say he was most ill-favored, with a great, wide mouth."

Toad-Face! The youth could have been none other. Toad-Face had indeed "done something else."

"Did he come all the way to Jamestown to bring you that message?"

"No, but he must have been on the road. One of our exploring parties met him on the shore of Chesapeake Bay! Your father was sure the boy must be you."

"Why did not my father come this time to find me?"

"A ship from England is expected any day, now. Your mother will be aboard, and your father wishes to be at Jamestown to greet her. They say she has been in

23

poor health, through grieving over your supposed death. Perchance when she sees you, it will make her well again."

I could hardly speak.

"God grant it!" I murmured.

The chief had been waiting patiently during all this conversation; now he asked the meaning of it, and I explained in full, loud enough for all to hear.

"You are a fine young man," he said. "You have strong power for hunting and for war. The whole village will be sorry to see you go. However, you have won the right to do as you please."

Chokingly, I made them a little speech, thanking them all for what they had done in my behalf, especially, of course, Little-Bear, Thunder-Arrow, and finally, Bowl-Woman.

She burst into tears, throwing her arms about me.

"Your first duty," she sobbed, "is to your real mother, of course, but don't forget your—your second mother, will you, Son?"

"I shall never forget," I promised, "and what is more, I shall return again some day." Thunder-Arrow and Little-Bear embraced me silently. The more an Indian feels in his heart the harder it is for him to speak. White-Deer was so moved that she tried to talk to me, could not—drew her robe over her head and left the village and I saw her no more. The men from the ship watched all this with amazement.

With my brain awhirl, I started in to take leave of my other friends, to get my things together. Moon-ha'kee I could not find, although I called and whistled.

Whilst I was calling, Cross-Woman stepped up to me.

"Before you leave us, I must speak to you privately," she said in a low voice. "Come with me to the cabin."

"Watch out for her, she may be dangerous," Little-Bear whispered as we passed him. I went on, nevertheless, for I knew Cross-Woman.

Once inside the cabin, Cross-Woman lowered the curtain and led me up beside the fireplace where the light from the smoke hole was strong. Then she laid her hands on my shoulders and looked into my eyes.

"I think you know who freed Toad-Face," she said slowly and solemnly. "You know, but you are not telling anyone. Am I right?"

"I think you know who freed Toad-Face," I replied, using her own words and tone. "You know, but you are not telling anyone. Don't forget that part of it!"

Her eyes brightened and her wide mouth flashed a real smile. Pulling me into her arms, she gave me a squeeze that nearly broke my ribs.

"I wish the Creator had given me a son like you," she whispered. Releasing me, she stumbled over to her *ha'soon*, wiping her eyes with the back of her hand. As she turned, she saw me still standing there.

"Go on, you young puppy! Get out of here!" she shouted. "Nobody has ever seen me make a fool of myself, and I don't want you to be the first one!"

Of all my treasured possessions, the only things I kept were my dream bundle, my eagle feather, my bowl and spoon, the ear beads which Granny gave me, and my bow and quiver of arrows, all of which I have until this day.   The rest I divided amongst my friends and kinfolk: my hunting charm and war club especially going to Little-Bear and my big bearskin being left for White-Deer.

Many tried to hand me parting gifts, but I refused all with thanks, except a little sack of *ka-ha-ma'kun* which Fling-Her-This-Way brought me for the journey at the last moment.

At last I found myself in the boat, bound for the ship, and we were perhaps a hundred yards from the crowd upon the beach when someone shouted, "Look behind!"

Looking back, I saw a little head sticking up from the water.   It was Moon-ha'kee, swimming valiantly to catch up with us.   The rascal must have been off digging for mice whilst I was searching for him.

"Stop the boat!" I cried to the rowers.   "We must wait for my friend, Moon-ha'kee."

THE LENAPE LANGUAGE

The Lenape, or Delaware language, was spoken in three main dialects: the Unala'htko, or coast language; the Min'si, or Munsey, spoken in the hill country; and the Una'mi, or Delaware proper, which has been used in this book.

Lenape is very difficult to write in English letters so that the average reader can pronounce it, but I have done my best in the preceding pages to represent the Indian sounds. For those interested in pronouncing the words more correctly, I have prepared this list, in which may be found: first, each Lenape word as it appears in the book; second, the correct form, and third, the translation. The plural ending is given with most of the nouns.

To represent the two principal sounds found in Lenape but not in English, I use the capital letters X and L. X is a very harsh h, really between and k, like the German ch. L is a sort of slithered l made with the tongue in the same position as for ordinary l, but without voice. ' represents breathing. The vowels, marked and unmarked, are pronounced as follows:

a as in father
ä as in cat
â as in all
e like a in fate
ě as in met
i as in machine
ĭ as in bit

o as in note
u as in flute
ŭ as in but
û as in put

Scientific students use additional symbols and markings to record Lenape sounds even more accurately, but the markings given here will answer our purpose.

A

Form Used in Book	Correct Form	Plural	Translation
h-pee'kawn	a'pi'kân	a'pi'kâna	flute, flageolet
h'pees	a''pis	a''pisa	pack strap
h-pon'	a'pon'	a'po'na	bread
hk-wo-an-ee'kan	aXkwoani'kan	aXkwoani'kana	brush net
h-see-pe-la'wan	a'sipela'wan	a'sipela'wana	woman's hair ornament

343

Form Used in Book	Correct Form	Plural	Translation
ah-sin′na-min-shee	a′sin′aminshi	a′sinamin′shiuk	rock-tree (maple)
ah-weh′	a′wä′		ouch!
a-kee′	aki′		alas! oh, dear!
a-la′kwee	ala′kwi		what a pity!
al-la′pee	ala′pi		do it quickly
al-lo-ka′kan	aloka′kan	aloka′kanuk	servant
a-man′ga-mek	aman′gamek	amangame′kâk	water monster
al-lun-sin′oo-tai	alunsin′utai	-a	quiver
a-ma-na′tak	amana′tak	amana′taka	fishing line
am-bee′son	ambi′son	ambi′sona	cradle board
A-men′a-push	Amĕn′apûsh		a mythic hero
a-na′kan	ana′kan	ana′kana	rush mat
an′go-oo	an′gou		blessing
Ap-ah-too′hkway	ApaXtu′Xkwe		White-Deer (name)
a-pee-chay-ka′wan	apicheka′wan	apicheka′wana	shed, arbor
ash′kas	a′shkas	ashka′sŭk	attendant at Big-House
as-huk′tet	asXuk′tet	asXuk′tetŭk	thou miserable brat
a-ta-koo′	ataku′		nothing at all
at′hoon	ät′hun	äthu′na	skirt
at′ta	a′ta		not
ay′ka-li-uh′	e′kalĭŭ′		go away
ay′ko-han′	e′kohan′		yes
ay-kay-saa′	ekesa′		shame on you!
ay-ka-ya′	ekaya′		exclamation of surprise
ay-ko′kwa-lis	eko′kwalis	ekokwali′sŭk	raspberry

C

cha′chees	cha′chis		snow-snake (game)
Chah′kal-wush′-king	Cha′Xkalwŭsh′-kingw		Toad-Face (name)
chee-kwo-a-la′leh	chikwoala′le	-ak	conch shell
chee′pai	chi′pai	chi′paiŭk	ghost
cheet-kwe′se	chitkwe′se		you shut up
che-mŭm′es	chemŭm′es	chemŭm′sŭk	rabbit
chik′kun-nŭm	chi′kenŭm	chi′kenŭmŭk	turkey (bird)

D

ORM USED IN BOOK	CORRECT FORM	PLURAL	TRANSLATION
-shoo'kee	dashu'ki		I am very poor
ay'kay-ning	Te'kening		In-the-Forest (name)

E

-kee'	iki'		alas! oh, dear!
'la	i'la, i'lao	i'lawâk	war-captain or leader
-eh	e-e		yes (lazily)
ɩ-hawn'is	emhân'is	emhân'sŭk	spoon

G

ɩm'wing	Gam'wing		Lenape annual ceremony
ɩns-hay-woo-lon'- kwan	GansXewulon' kwan		Roaring-Wings (name)

H

-ka-nak'ha-ko- wee	Xakanak'hak- owi	-â	green and white striped large squash
-kee-sa'pi	hakisa'pĭ	-ia	bowstring
ɩ'lah-pees	ha'lapis		Indian hemp
'soon	Xa'sun	Xasu'na	sleeping platform
-ta'pe	hata'pe	-ŭk	bow
y!	he!		hello!
ɩway	-Xkwe		feminine name ending
ɩ!	ho!		exclamation
ɔ!	hu!		exclamation of joy
ɔ'ma	hu'ma		Granny
ɔ-paw'kun	hupâ'kŭn	hupâ'kŭnak	smoking pipe
ɔs'kweem	Xus'kwim		Indian corn
ɩun-ak'hakw	X'kunak'hakw	X'kunakha'kâ	gourd

J

!	ju!		exclamation of joy

K

ɩha-ma'kun	kahama'kun		parched corn
-hay'sa-na	Kahe'sana		Mother Corn
Kas'kweem	Xa'skwim		(a Lenape goddess)

Form Used in Book	Correct Form	Plural	Translation
k'ahk-peek'soo	k'aXpik'su		thou flea-bitten one
ka'kuhn	ka'kûn	kakûn'a	legging
ka-kuh-ka-ta'tum	käkûkata'tŭm		what do you want?
ka-ta'tee	kata'ti		be willing!
ka-tuh'!	katû!		It's cold!
ka'wi-a	ka'wĭa	kawĭa'ŭk	porcupine
ka-yah'!	kaya'		exclamation of wonᵈ
kay'hay-la	ke'hela		yes, indeed! truly!
kay'kwuk	ke'kwuk (sing. kekw)		shell beads
kee-nee'ta	kini'ta		you can
Kee-shay-la-muh'-ka-ong	Gishelamŭ'-kaong		the Creator
keet-chee'	kitchi'		certainly
ke-kah-moot-keh'tet	kĕkamutkĕ'tet	-ŭk	you little thief
kes-kund'hak	keskûnd'hak	keskûndha'ka	sweet (cheese) pumpkin
king-kas-kund'hak	Xingkaskund'-hŭk	Xingkaskund'-hŭk'a	big, yellow pumpkɪ
king'wee-ka-on	Xing'wikaon		ceremonial house (Big-House)
kin'te-ka	kĭn'tĕka		dance
kit-ta-hik'kan	kitahi'kan		ocean
Kit-tan-it-to'wet	Kitanito'wet		Great Spirit, God
k'nay-ha'sin	k'neXa'sin		you be careful
k'nees'gahk-gay-loon'en	k'nis'gaXge-lun'en		you nasty liar
k'nis'kay-wŭsh'-king	k'nis'kewŭsh' kingw		thou dirty-face
kook'hos	kuk'hos	kukho'sŭk	owl
ko-wa'mo	kowa'mo		war cry
ku-les'ta!	kŭles'ta!		listen!
k'pet'ching-weh-hĭh	k'pet'chĭng-wĕXĭ		look you here
k'tuh-shing'huh	k'tŭshing'Xŭh		you are disobedienᵗ
kway!	kwe!		exclamation

Form Used in Book	Correct Form	Plural	Translation
wee-kwin'gum-hkway	Kwikwin'gum-Xkwe		Duck-Woman (name)
wee-pe-la'nai	kwipela'nai	kwipela'naiya	hoe
weh!	kwĕ!		exclamation of joy
weh-neesh-kwoo'nai-yas	kwĕnishkwu'nayas	-sŭk	panther
wen-a'mohk	kwĕna'moX	-ŭk	otter
woch?	kwoch?		why
w'sha'tai	kw'sha'tai		tobacco

L

-lay-nee'kan	laleni'kan		scouring rush (equisetum)
l-ha'kwo-kan	lalha'kwokan	-na	scraper
'pee	la'pi		again, once more
y-nas-kund'hak	lenaskûnd'hak	-ha'ka	scalloped summer squash
y'na-wee tay-ma'hee-kan	le'nawi tema'hikan	-a	man's ax
y'nee Lay-na'pay	Le'ni Lena'pe	-wŭk	Lenape Indian (real man)
y-na'pay-wee-see'poo	Lena'pewisi'pu		Lenape River (Delaware River)
y-nee-lee-kwes'-suk	lenilikwe'suk		common ants
-hok'sin	lenhok'sĭn	lenhoksĭ'na	moccasin
-nik'pee	lenik'pi		basswood bark
kas	lo'kas	-a	dish or bowl
'kas-hkway	Lo'kasXkwe		Bowl-Woman (name)

M

h!	ma!		take it
hkt-chee'pak-o	maXtchi'pako (plu.)		shoepacks or overshoes
ahk'wa-tut	MaXk'watut		Little-Bear (name)
-lahk'seet	malaX'sit	malaX'sita	bean
ll-san'nuk	maLsa'nuk	maLsanu'kâ	flint arrowhead
an'gway	Men'gwe	Men'gweŭk	Iroquois (Seneca)

Form Used in Book	Correct Form	Plural	Translation
man-it′to	manit′to	manit′towŭk	unseen power, spirit
Ma-nunk′so-hkway	Manunk′so-Xkwe		Cross-Woman (name)
Ma-sha′pee-lo′-kas-hkway	Masha′pilo′-kasXkwe		Bead-Bowl-Woman (name)
ma′ta	ma′ta		no
mat-ta-ka′	mataka′		no, indeed
may-tay′oo	mete′u	mete′uwŭk	doctor
m′bee′ahk	m′bi′aXk	m′biaXk′ŭk	whale
me-ay-khas-kwee′-ga-mek	mieXaskwi′-gamek	-a	thatched cabin
meehn	min	min′a	huckleberry
meen′ah-pon	min′apon		huckleberry bread
mee′kwin	mi′kwin	mi′kwinŭk	eagle feather
mee-ha′ka-nak	miXa′kanak		ash wood (white ash)
mee-sing′	misingw′	misingw′ŭk	mask
Mee-sing-haw-lee′-kun	Misinghâli′kŭn		Mask Being
me-tay-wee-lay′on	mitewile′on	-ŭk	loon (bird)
Min′see	Mĭn′si	-ŭk	Munsey (a Lenape tribe)
moo′hool	mu′Xul	muXu′la	canoe
Moon-ha′kee	Munha′ki		Badger (a dog's name)
mu′koos	mŭ′kus	-a	awl
muh-win′gwes	mhûwin′gwes	-ŭk	blackberry
m′wa′ka-na	m′wa′kanä	m′wakanä′âk	dog
moon-ha′kee			

N

nahk-ay′sim-mus	naXe′simus	-ŭk	my younger sister
nahk-ee′sim-mus	naXi′simus	-ŭk	my younger brother
nah′num	na″num	na′num′ŭk	raccoon
n′a-lun-goo′mak	n′alungu′mak	-ĕk	my kinsman
Nan′a-push	Nan′apush		a mythic hero (name)
ne-gwees	ne gwis	-ŭk	my son
ne-hoo′ma	nehu′ma		I am Granny
nay	ne		the
nee′tees	ni′tis	-ŭk	my friend

ORM USED IN BOOK	CORRECT FORM	PLURAL	TRANSLATION
e-mah-ta-lo-ka'kan	nimaXtalo-ka'kan		I am a bad servant
e-mees'	n'mis'	-ŭk	my older sister
oh'koo-mi	NoX'kumĭ		Answer-Me (name of a fairy)
o'hoom	nu'hum		my grandmother
shin'gee	n'shin'gi		I'll do it (unwillingly)
wing'kee	n'win'gi		I'll do it (gladly)
hk'han	noX'han		my father
-ta-ma-es-hee'-kan	notamaeshi'kan	-a	fish spear

O

ho	o'ho		answer to hailing call
k'way-wee	oX'kwewi	-a	woman's ax
tay-ma'hee-kan	tema'hikan		
kay-ho'kee	Okeho'ki		Bark-Country, name of a clan
um'a-nay	olum'ane		red paint
w'tas	ao"tas	ao'tas'ŭk	medicine doll

P

hk-gam'mak	paXgam'ak		black ash (tree)
h-sah-ay-nee'kan	paXsaXeni'kan		slow-match, punk
'lee			fairy (from English word)
-sa'ha-man	pasa'haman		football game
-sa-hee'kun	pasahi'kŭn	pasahi'kŭnak	football
-wun-nee'kan	pawŭni'kan	pawŭni'kana	sieve basket
h-kan-dee'kan	pa'kandi'kan	pa'kandi'kana	hammer
hk-ha-kwo'a-kan	paXhakwo'a-kan	-a	wedge
'kon	pä'kon		a red dye or paint
y-ta-nay-hink'-hkway	Petanehink'-Xkwe		Fling-Her-This-Way (name)
y-lay'	Pele'	Pele'âk	Turkey Band of the Lenape

Form Used in Book	Correct Form	Plural	Translation
Pay-yay'wik	Peye'wik		It-Is-Approaching (name)
pee-mo-a'kun	pimoa'kun	-ak	sweat house
pee'seem	pi'sim		sweet corn
pee-lai'chech	pilai'chech	pilaichech'ŭk	boy
pee'shih	pi'shi		yes
Pet-hak'al-luns	Pethak'aluns		Thunder-Arrow (name)
Pet-ha-ko-way'yuk	Pethakowe'yuk (plu.)		Thunder Beings
pin-das-sen-a'kun	pindasena'kun	-ak	tobacco pouch
pe-sukw-pe-la-tay'kun	pesŭkwpela-te'kŭn	-a	glue
po'hem	po'hem		soft, white corn
Po-ko-un'go	Pokoun'go	-ŭk	Turtle Band of the Lenape
pop-ho'kus	popho'kus	-ŭk	red cedar

S

Form Used in Book	Correct Form	Plural	Translation
Saa!	saa!		exclamation: "shame!"
sah-kah-ka'hoon	sa-kaX-hä'hun	-hun'a	earring
sahk-koo-ta'kun	saXkuta'kun	-a	breechclout
sa'kwem	sa'kwem	sa'kwem (same as sing.)	ear of corn
sang-hee'kan	sanghi'kan	-a	fire-making set
sa'pan	sa'pan		mush made of crac corn
say'hay!	se'he!		hush!
see'meen	si'min	-a	hickory nut
see-meen'shee	simin'shi	-ŭk	hickory tree
shai	shai		immediately
sha-wa-na'mek	shawana'mek	-mek'ŭk	southfish (shad)
Sha'wa-no	Sha'wano	Shawano'wŭk	Shawnee
shee'kee	shi'ki		fine, pretty
shwon-hil'la	shwonhi'la	shwonihi'lawâk	shore bird

Form Used in Book	Correct Form	Plural	Translation
is-kay-wa'hos	siskewa'hos	siskewahos'ŭk	clay pot
is-kuh-ha'na	Siskûha'na		Muddy River (Susquehanna)
is-kuh-ha'na-wuk	Siskûha'nawuk		Muddy River people (Susquehannocks)
s-see'lee-ya	sisi'liya	sisili'ya-âk	buffalo
ɔo-tay'yo	sute'yo		cooked, hulled corn
ɔun'gweh	sun'gwe	sun'gweŭk	weasel

T

ɪ-a'ne	taane		where?
ɪhk-gohk'	taXkgoXk'	-ŭk	box turtle
ɪh'han	ta'Xan	-a	firewood
ɪhk-wa-ho'a-kan	taXkwaho'a-kan	-a	mortar for pounding corn
ɪhk-wa-ho'a-kan-ee-min'shee	taXkwaho'a-kanimin'shi	-ŭk	mortar tree (tupelo)
ɪk-ta'nee	takta'ni		I don't know
'lee	ta'Li		there
-ma'kwa	tama'kwä	tamakwä'-âk	beaver
ɪ-ma'kwa-week'it	Tama'kwä-wik'ĭt		Beaver-House (name)
-mask'was	tamask'was	-ŭk	muskrat
t'gusk	tat'gusk		game of hoop and spears
y-ma'hee-kan	tema'hikan	-a	ax
y'pee	te'pi		that is enough
ɪ'dai	tin'dai		fire
ɔk'kweem	P'tûk'win	-a	round nut (walnut)
ɔol-pay-oo-ta'nai	Tulpeuta'nai		Turtle-Town
ɔok'seet	Tûk'sit	Tûk'sitŭk	Round Foot, the Lenape Wolf band

W

ɪa'lum O'loom	Wa'lum O'lum		Red Score (Lenape history)
ɪ-nee'shih	wani'shĭ		thank you

Form Used in Book	Correct Form	Plural	Translation
way-ma-tay-gun'is	wemetegun'is	wemategun'-isŭk	fairy
wee-sa'ho-seed	wisa'hosid	-ŭk	sturgeon
Wee-sao'suh	Wisao'sû		Yellow, a dog's nam
wee-sa'mek	wisa'mek	-ŭk	fat fish (catfish)
wee-sa'ak	wisa'âk	wisa'âkâk	yellow tree (an oak)
wik'wam	wik'wam	-a	house or tent
win'gay-musk	win'gemŭskw		sweet grass
woo-la-mo'wee	wulamo'wi		truly
w'tee'heem	w'ti'him	w'ti'him (same as singular)	heart berry (strawberry)

Y

ya-hel'la-ap	yahe'Laap	-a	fishnet
ya'kwa-hay	ya'kwahe	-âk	naked bear (mythic monster)
yoo-hoo	yuhu		a hailing call
yoo'ta-lee	yu'taLi		right here
yoh!	yo!		all right!
yun	yun		here, this

CPSIA information can be obtained
at www.ICGtesting.com
Printed in the USA
LVHW112357231120
672548LV00005B/128